GINO

PATRICK
JOHNSTON
&
PETER
LEECH

GINO

THE FIGHTING SPIRIT *of* GINO ODJICK

GREYSTONE BOOKS
Vancouver/Berkeley/London

25 26 27 28 29 5 4 3 2 1

Greystone Books Ltd.
greystonebooks.com

Cataloguing data available from Library and Archives Canada
ISBN 978-1-77840-270-8 (cloth)
ISBN 978-1-77840-271-5 (epub)

Editing by Brian Lynch
Copy editing by Derek Fairbridge
Proofreading by Alison Strobel
Indexing by Stephen Ullstrom
Jacket design by Marley Grayson
Jacket photograph by Ian Lindsay/*Vancouver Sun*
Text design by Fiona Siu

Printed and bound in Canada on FSC® certified paper at Friesens. The FSC® label means that materials used for the product have been responsibly sourced.

Greystone Books thanks the Canada Council for the Arts, the British Columbia Arts Council, the Province of British Columbia through the Book Publishing Tax Credit, and the Government of Canada for supporting our publishing activities.

EU Safety Information: Easy Access System Europe, Mustamäe tee 50, 10621 Tallinn, Estonia, gpsr.requests@easproject.com.

Canada

Greystone Books gratefully acknowledges the xʷməθkʷəy̓əm (Musqueam), Sḵwx̱wú7mesh (Squamish), and səlilwətaɬ (Tsleil-Waututh) peoples on whose land our Vancouver head office is located.

CONTENTS

FOREWORD

GINO WAS OUR HERO. He was the only boy in our family. He was spoiled because of that, but he was still our everything. Gino had so much respect for his sisters and his parents. The respect that he had for his family was big.

Our family was fortunate to have him go out and represent us in the world. He got to do it, and he did it. But he never forgot his roots. He never changed. He was just so... *Gino.* That's hard to explain. But how about this: when Gino would come home, his jeans would be full of holes. He'd come home and his family would clean him up. It was like he was young again.

For Gino, Maniwaki was home, but Vancouver was *his* home. He'd come back here, see his old friends, see his family, but Vancouver was where he wanted to be. He had these different worlds.

Gino talked about writing a book all the time. He should have ended up writing a book. And I felt Peter should have been one of the people to help write it. Peter found Patrick to put this book together. Peter and Gino had talked about writing a book in the years before he died; Patrick had written a couple stories about Gino for the *Province* newspaper over the years. He seemed like a good choice. I wanted this book to be for people to get to know the real Gino. He had a big heart. He loved people. He was a famous hockey player—but he had another side too.

Peter spent the last ten years of Gino's life—twenty-four hours a day, seven days a week—with him. They had a really good friendship. How many people would put their lives on hold for a friend, like that? He was Gino's brother, but it goes beyond that. Family can be hard. These two were more than family.

I've always said, I couldn't be more grateful to Peter for being there for the last ten years. I'll forever be grateful for him. Peter gave Gino those extra years because there's no way Gino could have done it on his own.

DINA ODJICK, Maniwaki, Quebec, March 2025

INTRODUCTION

WHEN YOU GET ASKED to write a book for the first time, you're intrigued. What a prospect, you think. What a task. How does one write something that long? Then you get asked to write a book about Gino Odjick and the gears in your head start to turn.

Nature took Gino from us. He's not here to tell his story. Instead, we are left asking his family, his friends, his teammates, his coaches about what they have to say. None of us knows the whole truth, but we all know some of it. What truth did they know? Who was he to them?

Gino Odjick cared a lot about the people around him. He sought to help just about anybody he could. Most of the time, his kind nature drew him close to good, usually great, people, like his teammates. He loved to have a good time. He loved to be social. He loved to love, for better or worse. He couldn't be alone.

He was a good son, a good brother, a friend to many, an inspiration to Indigenous youth across the country.

He was a father eight times. He loved his kids. His kids loved him. But it wasn't easy. Those eight kids had six different moms. That meant six different experiences. Gino did what he could to look after them. But none were conventional situations.

Gino was a larger-than-life character—just like his dad, Joe. His dad grew up fatherless; Gino's grandfather died while fighting Nazis in a small village between Normandy and Paris, days after the French capital was liberated. Gino's dad knew to provide for his family, and the memory of his experience in residential school lingered. He became a powerful role model for many in his family.

Gino was, most famously, a thrilling hockey player, one of the National Hockey League's toughest guys. He battled hard for his teammates. He was the protector, and best friend, of the first truly great Canuck.

But there were also struggles: alcoholism, parenthood, relationships, mental illness, a huge beating heart that turned out to be doomed by genetics. Yet no one had a bigger heart, as just about anyone who spent time with him would say, be they teammates, friends, or family. He was beloved by just about everyone he met.

GINO ODJICK ARRIVED on the Vancouver hockey scene almost out of nowhere. He gave fans young and old something to cheer about, after years of few thrills. As the 1990s began, fans were ready and waiting for a hero. Gino became one, not because of his hockey talents, but because of his fists and his smile. There were times when you'd look down from the stands, see his giggling face, his awkward skating stride and think, "Gino's one of us. What is he doing out there? Maybe we can all get out there too." Of course, he was wildly more talented than any fan with a ticket. It's the NHL, of course, and you don't get there without being able to play at a pace few fans can even fathom, let alone attempt. He was at the vanguard of an incredible era of Canucks hockey.

Gino would roam the ice, bashing opponents into the boards, then dropping the gloves with the other team's tough guys. The job was to fire up his team, and to keep the opponent from playing dirty against his star teammates. Whether a fight really energizes a team is up for debate, but there's little doubt the crowd always roars for guys who play with the kind of abandon that Gino did.

That opened the door for fans to love Gino—but it was his persona that truly won them over. Gino loved playing hockey. He loved being alive. That's what glowed through whenever people saw him away from the rink. He loved meeting fans, and they always remembered their encounters with him.

At American Thanksgiving in 1992, the Canucks piled onto a commercial flight, as they did in those days, headed to Minnesota. Among the other passengers was eleven-year-old Jeff Cullis and his family, on a trip to visit relatives in the United States. Growing up in Vancouver, young Jeff was a Canucks fan, but he never expected to find himself sharing a plane with some of his heroes.

Pavel Bure and some teammates were playing cards in the row behind. Jeff had some hockey cards with him. He also drew a couple pictures. The Canucks around him signed them. And then Gino sat down in an open seat. "I couldn't believe how big he was, he seemed to tower over me just sitting there. He had a big smile on his face, and I think he had a tooth missing or something," Jeff recalls. "But he was such a friendly and warm person, just entertaining us and telling jokes. Definitely seemed larger than life to me at the time."

That was just Gino, people would say. He didn't have to be a hockey player to be like this—he was just a guy, looking to do the right thing. A guy whose memory stands tall today. When the Canucks play a game at Rogers Arena in downtown Vancouver, there's always a cascade of jerseys worn by fans, in both of the main liveries the team has worn over the years: the black-yellow-and-red "Flying Skate" jerseys, which first emerged in the 1980s and were worn through most of the 1990s; and the blue-and-green classic, whether in its original "stick in rink" incarnation or the more modern orca design. Fans tend to wear jerseys with current players on their backs, but there are always jerseys from deep in the past. An Odjick Flying Skate jersey is not an unusual sight.

"Even now, when you see a fan wearing that Odjick 29 jersey, fans our age just nod, say, 'Oh yeah.'" That's Canucks radio commentator Randip Janda. He grew up in Vancouver, a huge fan of the man who became known as the "Algonquin Assassin."

The Canucks' run to the Stanley Cup final in 1994 was the first time young Janda really took notice of the local team. He was seven. The Canucks had stumbled a little during the 1993–94 regular season: a .506 record, though they still won forty-one games. Then the playoffs came and the magic began. Randip, like so many other young fans in BC, was swept up in the excitement. Gino's role was small in those playoffs, but he still stood out to Randip and his friends: "He may not have been the most skilled guy, but he was there for his teammates."

Most fans of the era would pick Bure or Trevor Linden as their favourite players, but there was a certain type that would gravitate toward Odjick. "There was street cred in Gino," Janda explains. Whereas Linden and Bure hovered above the earth as the team's stars, you could imagine Odjick just hanging out.

That was a real thing for Gino. After retiring from the NHL in 2003, he moved back to Vancouver. Janda would spot his old hero working out at the same gym as him. There was this hockey hero, a man of the people. "He's an everyman," Janda says. "He was just a dude. He wore his emotions on his sleeve. You could see what he thought in his reactions. You'd see him try as hard as he could. Everyone has a friend who plays sports like that, who just can't help but give their all. He seemed like one of those guys. You could see one of your friends in him."

PATRICK JOHNSTON STARTED covering the Vancouver Canucks in 2018. Born and raised in Vancouver, he was nine years old when Gino made his Canucks debut. To young Patrick, Gino was what he was to many of the team's excitement-starved fans: a revelation. A wild, exciting new focus of energy.

Fast-forward to 2018: Patrick is on the Canucks beat for the *Province* newspaper in Vancouver. Inevitably, by the fall of 2019, he and Gino had spoken a couple times, but Patrick had no reason to think he'd stand out in a crowd for the retired Canuck. Little did Patrick know that one of Gino's great talents was remembering the face and the name of just about everyone he ever talked to.

One night, Patrick was on his way to the press box from the elevators. He spotted Gino and his pal Peter Leech coming the other way down the narrow hallway. Before Patrick could say anything, Gino blurted out, "Patrick! So good to see you!" As if they were old friends reuniting.

That's how Gino was with everyone. In the years Ed Willes was covering the NHL for the *Winnipeg Sun*—before Willes moved to the *Province* in 1998—Gino would greet him similarly. "I don't know if he remembered me from the Memorial Cup or what," Willes remembers. "But he would always say, 'Oh hey, Ed, how are ya?' when the Canucks would pass through Winnipeg."

WHEN GINO FIRST met Peter, he said to the powerfully built but short-in-stature Leech: "Hey, you're small." That was in the early 1990s, when the two were working at a hockey camp for young Indigenous players put on by former Canucks player turned long-time scout Ron Delorme.

Gino told Peter he'd heard that he'd had some success as a boxer. "I heard you're strong... but you're so small," Gino repeated. "Fast hands," Peter replied, with a grin. "When you're fast, you don't get hit!" Meeting Gino the first time was an exciting moment for Peter. A member of the T'it'q'et Community Village of the St'at'imc Tribal Nation near Lillooet in the BC Interior, Peter had played a little bit of minor pro hockey and had been a good soccer player, as well as a pretty good amateur boxer. Gino was interested in Peter's boxing experiences. Gino asked him about Roger Adolph, a boxer from the Fountain reserve, also near Lillooet, who had turned pro in the 1960s and won some fame. Peter had a family connection to Adolph.

In 1998, New Jersey Devils defenceman Sheldon Souray invited Peter along to a summertime meeting for the NHL

Players' Association in Whistler, BC. Souray had gotten to know Peter as well as Gino while coaching at the Delorme hockey camps. At the Whistler get-together, the players would meet to discuss NHL issues in the morning, then play golf in the afternoon. It was on the golf course that Peter and Gino truly hit it off. Peter had just started doing leadership workshops with Indigenous youth and was finding some success in it. The next summer, Peter invited Gino to help him lead a youth workshop he was organizing. They'd go on to lead workshops together for the next twenty-three years.

GINO'S SISTER DINA was the one who played the most with him while growing up in the Odjick household in Kitigan Zibi, a long-standing Indigenous community in an area of Quebec just north of Ottawa, up the Gatineau River, next to the town of Maniwaki, known for logging, hunting, and farming. Just a year younger, she spent lots of time with him. It wasn't obvious then that he'd become an NHL hockey player, but like many Canadian kids, Gino still harboured the dream. When he was eleven or twelve, the community buried a time capsule. When they unearthed the cache in the year 2000, they found a note written by Gino.

"In the time capsule it was written, he was gonna either play in the NHL or he was gonna be the next George Jones," Dina remembers. Her brother loved singing, but he was never going to be a famous country singer. He did become a famous hockey player—and many people are thankful for that.

1

"WHICH ONE IS SADDAM?"

THE FAN'S SIGN was topical and direct: "Not even Saddam Hussein would mess with Gino." Gino Odjick was just six weeks into his NHL career but he'd already made quite a name for himself. From his first NHL appearance in late November, he'd won over Canucks fans. It was now January 1991, and so with the Iraqi dictator at the centre of the news, comparisons with a far-away world leader weren't really a surprise. But if you'd been told in training camp the previous September that a Vancouver Canuck would be mentioned alongside a global figure by mid-season, you wouldn't have guessed the player would be Odjick. He was a near unknown just four months before.

Gino fought two Chicago Blackhawks on his first night in the NHL and never looked back. He'd made an impression in training camp, he'd made an impression in six weeks in the minors with the Canucks' affiliate, the Milwaukee Admirals, to open the season, and then he made the greatest impression in his NHL debut. Fans quickly learned he was ready to go toe-to-toe with all comers. They also found he could play a little too: he scored his first goal in his fourth career game.

So when that fan held up his sign with the wild, worldly comparison on that chilly January night against the Winnipeg Jets, everyone chuckled. It was January 16. The United States and its allies were set to begin bombing Iraqi targets that very day.

Sitting on the bench, Odjick, the man who would be nicknamed the "Maniwaki Mauler," saw the sign in the crowd. He tapped veteran linemate Stan Smyl on the knee. "Which one is Saddam?" Gino asked. Reporters would repeat the tale earnestly as one about an innocent small-town kid who knew little of the world. How could this guy not know who Saddam Hussein was? He was all over the news! "Let it not be said that Canucks' tough guy Gino Odjick is a genius," Scott Morrison wrote in the *Toronto Sun* a couple of weekends later. "Overheard on the Canucks' bench was Odjick asking... who this Saddam guy was. He thought he played for the Jets."[1]

Over the years, Odjick would play along. "I wasn't very well educated," he would say. But if you knew the man, you'd know he was a voracious reader of newspapers and books. Gino might have played down what he knew in public, but he knew. Smyl, the Canucks' captain through much of the 1980s and one of the most well-known and popular people in Vancouver, said his old teammate was taking everyone for a ride.

"Oh, Gino knew. He knew," Stan Smyl says, looking back. It was just more fun to play the yokel. What the likes of Morrison didn't know was what Smyl had seen, levelled right at him: the wide, wry grin his giant, young teammate was flashing. It was a whip-smart comment, not naivety. He was a tough guy, a guy from a small place, a guy who hadn't seen much of the world, but Gino Odjick was no dummy, Smyl quickly realized.

"He was such a great personality. He made people laugh." The memory of Odjick's smile still lights up Smyl. "I see his face right now looking at me—just winks at me." Was Gino so on point that that wink was about the moment—but also about him forming a plan to send a silly story off and running into the wilds of hockey reporting? Probably not, but it's not impossible.

This would be the final year of Smyl's NHL career. The torch was being passed from Smyl's era to a new one. He'd already given up the captaincy the summer before. Although it wasn't obvious at the time, in many ways Odjick's arrival in the NHL heralded a new start for the Canucks. For one, he was big: both in how he played and in character. Most point to a trade made near the end of the 1990–91 season as the beginning of an era of success that peaked in 1994, the first true winning era in Canucks history, two decades into the franchise's existence—but Odjick's arrival was actually the first broadside in this revolution.

"Spot on," Trevor Linden says, with three decades of hindsight, of the premise that Odjick was at the vanguard of this new Canucks team that would thrill the NHL in the early to mid-1990s. Linden was the first of general manager Pat Quinn's young guys, drafted second overall in 1988, the guy who would become the face of the franchise and take over from Smyl as team captain. Yet it was Odjick, drafted in the fifth round, two years after Linden, to much less acclaim, who heralded the new beginning.

When Quinn had taken over as the Canucks' "superboss" in 1987, he'd found a franchise that was somewhere between spinning its wheels and circling the drain. The team played uninspiring, losing hockey and was drawing flies to the Pacific Coliseum, just seven or eight thousand fans a night. The arena seated more than twice that number.

Quinn was hired by owner Frank Griffiths to lead the team to success. Griffiths, a successful owner of TV and radio stations, had bought the Canucks from original owner Tom Scallen in 1974, after Scallen went to prison for securities fraud. Hiring Quinn—the seventh man to hold the title of general manager in the team's seventeen years—was the end point of a process begun in 1985, when Griffiths and his son Arthur fired Harry Neale. The Griffithses spent two years looking for a superboss to take over the team, someone to run hockey operations as general manager and also serve as president, guiding the franchise's business operations.

The owners called Scotty Bowman, who coached the "Flying Frenchmen" Canadiens of the 1970s and then ran the Buffalo Sabres as general manager through much of the 1980s, and Sam Pollock, who had been Bowman's boss in Montreal and understood the NHL so well he was constantly ahead of the curve in the late 1960s, putting in work that would result in those 1970s Canadiens being among the greatest hockey squads of all time. But Bowman was happy in his job running the Sabres, and Pollock, who'd quit as Habs GM in 1978 and moved into a corporate, non-sports job in property development, also said no.

They tried Al Arbour, the four-time Stanley Cup–winning coach of the New York Islanders, and John Ferguson, the Vancouver-born GM of the Winnipeg Jets, who was the toughest player in the NHL in the 1960s. They weren't interested either.

In late 1986, Vancouver hockey builder Coley Hall, who had run the minor pro versions of the Canucks in the 1950s and 1960s and helped run the Canucks in the early 1970s while Scallen fought his legal battles, suggested to Griffiths that he try for Quinn, a defenceman on the original NHL Canucks who was then coaching the Los Angeles Kings and had previously run the Philadelphia Flyers. Hall said there should be three names on their search agenda: Pat Quinn, Pat Quinn, and Pat Quinn.

The hiring of Quinn went smoothly, then not. He was still coaching the Kings when Arthur Griffiths approached him with an offer to take over the Canucks the following summer, once his contract with LA was up. Quinn and Griffiths thought the offer was above board—the coach, who had gone to law school, arranged a clause in his contract that required the Kings to offer him a promotion or a contract extension by October 1, 1986, neither of which the Kings did. But when the Kings and the NHL found out, things got very messy. The Kings wanted to keep Quinn. "I think he is the most knowledgeable hockey person I've ever had the pleasure to meet," Kings owner Jerry Buss said in 1987.[2]

Initially, NHL president John Ziegler Jr. wanted to toss Quinn from the league altogether, but after a few weeks of consideration and investigation, he chose to fine both teams and suspended Quinn from coaching until the 1990–91 season.

The coaching ban was probably a blessing in disguise. The Canucks needed a lot of work, Quinn knew. When Jack Gordon took over as a caretaker GM after Neale was fired in June 1985, the Canucks were already a mess and were coming off the worst season in team history. And the two seasons under Gordon, directed on-ice by coach Tom Watt, were equally bad. Off-ice, Gordon didn't help himself, infamously trading away Cam Neely (and a draft pick that would become long-time NHL defenceman Glen Wesley) to the Boston Bruins. Neely would have a Hall of Fame career with the Bruins, while the player the Canucks got in return, Barry Pederson, had once been a star but after a pair of shoulder surgeries was a diminished talent. Pederson played alright, but nothing close to what Neely did for the Bruins.

The roster Quinn took over as GM had some good players, like Smyl, defenceman Doug Lidster, centreman Patrik Sundstrom, plus wingers Jim Sandlak, Tony Tanti, and Petri Skriko, but the team had little in the way of size, aside from Sandlak—and no prospects. And no first-round pick that summer—the second hard truth about the Neely trade.

Quinn moved quickly to begin reshaping his team: as 1987 training camp opened, he traded Sundstrom to the Devils for Kirk McLean, who would be the No. 1 goalie for much of the following decade, and winger Greg Adams, who brought size and scoring. An important trade, though the team still struggled to win that season.

The following summer, Quinn finally had an opportunity to draft in the first round, and because his inaugural squad had been so bad, he found himself with the second-overall pick. Quinn's selection would be vital in his efforts to turn the moribund Canucks around—and, boy, did he ever get it right: he drafted Trevor Linden, a lanky, hard-working, skilled winger from Medicine Hat with strong leadership qualities. The selection of Linden would also become a theme for Quinn and his scouts: big forwards who could skate.

GINO ODJICK WAS very raw when he made his NHL debut as a fourth-line left winger, but he was a quick study. Smyl was his first mentor. "Stan's like the old horse on the farm teaching the young one," Odjick told the *Province* in November 1990, less than a week into his career.[3] He didn't need much guidance, Smyl says, laughing more than thirty years later at his old teammate's comparison. Even as a fresh-faced NHLer, Gino clearly understood the enforcer's role. He'd been the team tough guy with the Laval Titan of the Quebec Major Junior Hockey League (QMJHL). It had got him to the NHL. "That role is so hard and he was quiet," Smyl recalls. "He came to the rink, did his preparation, but he knew what he had to do. And as linemate, you want to make sure he's doing it with the right people."

The players he would face didn't scare him. "I think he felt comfortable as he went along," Smyl says. "And not only with his teammates and with the coaching staff but with the fan base. You know, he came in and did what he had to do. And everyone respected that, everyone from teammates to the fans." Odjick was in the NHL with a purpose: to use his fists. This was an era in hockey that was dominated by the biggest and strongest pugilists.

No doubt, Odjick fit the bill: he played just forty-five games in his rookie season, but he still managed to pile up 296 penalty minutes—six-and-a-half penalty minutes per game. Odjick was so tough, maybe so crazy, that anyone who messed with him during that rookie season felt it. And that's why the fan's sign was so apropos. Saddam Hussein was considered by most to be a madman. The winter of 1990–91 saw plenty of intrigue around the Persian Gulf, as the Iraqi strongman invaded oil-rich Kuwait, thereby pushing against the United Nations' will to maintain order in the region. His forces were eventually driven out of Kuwait by the US and its allies, but his name dominated the news for months.

According to the NHL's record keepers, since the 1990–91 season, on average 125 skaters make their debut in a given season. Some might score a goal in their debut—a dream start that every player wishes for. Some might get into a fight, usually to show that they are tough enough to play in the toughest league in the world. For most, not much happens. They get a taste of the show; they see what they need to do to stay.

Gino didn't score a goal in his first game in the NHL, but he did get into two fights, and that is what he will forever be remembered for. His debut was like a rocket screaming to the moon, a blaze of glory streaking across the night sky.

November 21, 1990, was a dreary, chilly, drizzly day. Pretty typical for late November in Vancouver. It's what hockey weather looks like on the West Coast. No one knew what was about to happen that night at the Pacific Coliseum. Odjick was an unknown, a mere footnote in the lead-up to the game.

Trevor Linden didn't have a clue who Odjick was either. There was no internet in those days, obviously. No culture of prospect watchers. The only information you could get was in the paper, in the *Hockey News*, on local TV broadcasts, on *Hockey Night in Canada*, or in the printed game notes that players and reporters could pick up at the rink. A fifth-round tough guy? "You didn't know what was going on," Linden says. "We call this guy up, I have no idea who it is."

The only note about Odjick in the papers at the time was from Mike Murphy, the Canucks' minor league coach: "He arrives in a mean disposition every night," he told the *Province*.[4] On top of being ready to fight at all times, he was an aggressive forechecker, Murphy added. This was the kind of player Quinn was after.

That night, the Canucks hosted their toughest opponent of the season to date: the league-leading Chicago Blackhawks. The Mike Keenan–coached Blackhawks were anchored by the hottest goalie in the game, Ed Belfour, who allowed them to play a defensively driven style. They would wait for their opponents to make a mistake with the puck, then exploit that error by launching a counterattack. Through twenty-four games, they'd given up the fewest goals in the league and had the third-best goal differential. And on top of being able to counterstrike with goals, they could counterpunch too: to that point in the season, no team in the NHL had taken more major penalties, and they led the league in penalty minutes, averaging more than twenty-eight minutes per night. (Historically, that's an eye-popping figure. From the beginning of the 1990–91 season to the end of the 2023–24 season, if you total up all the penalties taken in that time, the Vancouver Canucks averaged the most penalty minutes of any team: a comparatively light 15:27 per game.)

The game would be memorable, right from the hop. First of all, there was Gino's jersey, No. 66. The unusual number caught your eye, Linden recalls. And then there was the way he played. He was a nobody, from nowhere as far as his new teammates knew, but he went hard. "It was really obvious he was a fierce competitor," Linden says. "He really, really came in with a bang."

Chicago had won four straight. Quinn saw that his team needed more punch in their physical play, literally, so it was time to see what Odjick could do. The game started well for Vancouver: they got an early power-play goal from Jim Sandlak.

Then gritty winger Garry Valk scored a second for Vancouver before the first period was up.

To shake his team up, Keenan pulled Belfour from the net for the second period, subbing in veteran backup Jacques Cloutier. A coach will sometimes swap goalies after the first period if he thinks a dramatic change like that will catch his team's attention—and Keenan was known throughout his career for making dramatic moves with his goaltenders. But the change made little difference: goalies don't typically score goals. The second period went no better for Chicago. They poured twenty shots on the Vancouver goal, but it was the Canucks who scored as checking forward Robert Kron put the home team up 3–0.

It's in the third period where Odjick's story truly begins. Early in the period, the Canucks scored a fourth goal, by Russian star centre Igor Larionov, which turned the game into a farce. The frustrated Blackhawks became uninterested in playing hockey for the remainder of the night. From then on, the game would be all about aggression—and, as a result, about Odjick's reputation.

Just over a minute after Larionov's goal, Odjick had his first NHL fight, taking on big, tough Chicago defenceman Dave Manson. An imposing figure at six foot two and about two hundred pounds, Manson had recorded more than three hundred penalty minutes in each of the previous two seasons, no doubt a very tough customer. Odjick, six foot three and 220 pounds, performed capably, doing what he was paid to do. It was a short scrap, with Manson knocking Odjick off-balance after each man had only thrown a punch or two. And Odjick wasn't done for the night. Round two for Gino came against no shy opponent: Stu Grimson. The "Grim Reaper" was relatively new to the league himself. He'd been a pro for just over three seasons but had appeared in only four NHL games. He'd mostly been a minor leaguer until he joined Chicago before the season. The six-foot-five Grimson had booked more than three hundred penalty minutes in the previous two seasons in the minors. He'd fought ten times in twenty-three NHL games that season. What Odjick didn't know was this game was especially important to Grimson: it was his first visit to his home province as a professional. His dad had been a Mountie and Grimson had lived all over BC, from Osoyoos and Kelowna to Kamloops and Dawson Creek.

Before any game, a team's tough guys would look at the opposing roster and figure out who would likely have to drop the gloves. The Blackhawks would have looked at the Canucks' roster and known that the big, raw rookie was there with a job to do. Odjick was already on Grimson's radar before the game started, though he didn't know much about him. Three decades later, Grimson remembers first making note of Odjick's work in the fight against Manson. "Gino was brand new," Grimson says. "You wanted to make sure that in that role, nobody caught you by surprise. You want to have a book on anybody you potentially would lock horns with." That night, Grimson and his teammates knew Vancouver had called up some young kid who'd been playing junior the season before, and who apparently was a ready and willing fighter. But that was it. "Back then, there was no YouTube, there was no Twitter, there was nothing," says Grimson. "Really there was little to know about him." So when Odjick threw a hit on him early in that same shift, Grimson figured the time had arrived and tracked down the young Canuck.

Smyl saw the hulking Blackhawks bruiser steaming his way toward the rookie and for a moment it seemed Smyl might yet intervene—and there was a time when Grimson would have engaged with the always-feisty Smyl—but it was his young linemate's time. And so, right in front of the Canucks bench, Odjick traded haymakers with Grimson.

Grimson was five years older, but he was Odjick's equal in terms of reputation: a rookie enforcer looking to establish his place in the NHL. "I got the advantage on him and the fans just went crazy and they started chanting 'Gino' and our relationship started right there, the first game," Odjick recalled of the bout.[5]

The Manson fight had revealed a few things about Odjick to Grimson. He saw that Gino was a right-hander. He saw that Gino was holding his own against the more experienced Manson. This was a fighter he'd definitely have to contend with. This was an important fight for Grimson. He'd made the NHL to that point, but at every level before, he'd carried doubt about himself, never sure if he was going to make the next step.

"I jumped from one level to the next and the next and the next, thinking, 'Well, gosh, do I have what it takes? Maybe I have what it takes?'" Grimson muses. As the newest Blackhawks tough guy, he could see that fighting the upstart Odjick would at least show he wasn't going to stop trying to prove himself.

With Grimson's help, Odjick's legend had begun, because of the fight but also because of what happened next. Since there was less than five minutes left to play, the officials sent him and Grimson straight to the dressing room. On his way past the Canucks bench, Odjick looked at Bob McCammon, his new coach, and quipped, "Don't fuck this up!" His teammates exploded with laughter.

"Gino played with inspiration," McCammon told the *Vancouver Sun*'s Elliott Pap after the game. "He played just like Mike Murphy told us he would."[6] Odjick had figured things out pretty quickly in Milwaukee, as the Canucks brass had hoped. After all, they'd drafted him as a twenty-year-old, and when you draft a kid who is two years older than most of the kids in a given draft, you're doing so because you think they're just a step away from making the NHL.

GINO'S SPECTACULAR NHL DEBUT occurred just a couple of months after he'd come up short of making the big club right out of training camp. He wasn't quite ready for the NHL, but he'd confirmed what the Canucks' scouts had believed: he was ready for pro hockey. When assistant general manager Brian Burke called Odjick to his room near the end of training camp to deliver the news to the rookie that he didn't make the NHL team, he'd asked scouting director Mike Penny to join him. Burke wasn't sure how the big man would react. But upon being told that the Canucks weren't going to send him back to his major junior team in Laval, but rather to the Canucks' minor league team, Odjick sprang out of his chair and shook Burke's hand in delight. He was so grateful to be handed a new opportunity.

By finally making the Canucks, his NHL dream realized, his career was obviously advancing. Odjick knew that much. But how long would he stay in the NHL, he asked McCammon. The veteran head coach replied that it could be either. "He said it's up to me. I really wanted to make sure that I stayed," Odjick recalled in 2021, just before he was inducted into the

BC Sports Hall of Fame. "I was just soaking it in, I was so happy to be in the NHL. I really wanted to make sure I didn't miss my chance."[7]

First, though, was a change in number. No. 66 was the number he'd worn in training camp, but it was pointed out to him that only one other player in the league wore a double-six: Mario Lemieux. Was that really the comparison he wanted to be setting up for himself? So Gino asked if he could wear something else.

Gino's choice of No. 29 was significant. It had been his dad's residential school number. His father, Joe, was a central figure in his life, a man who would become well known to his teammates. When Gino stepped onto the ice with No. 29 on his back, he was carrying his dad with him. Joe taught Gino a lot of life lessons. Look after your family, his dad told him. Look after your friends too, he said.

The brutal treatment Joe endured as a young boy at residential school taught him that the right way to act was the opposite: to look to those around you, to see what they needed. His son's role as the Canucks' tough guy was in that mould. Gino kept the other team's tough guys in check, away from his teammates.

Grimson said he knew right away that Odjick was likely to have a long future in the league. "I might be older than this guy, more seasoned than this young guy, but he's a handful, he's gonna stick around. That was my lasting impression," Grimson recalls. "He's gonna be able to hold his own with a lot of the top-end guys in this game."

THE 1990–91 SEASON would be filled with turnover for the Canucks, as Quinn looked to reshuffle the room in terms of attitude, skill set, and, yes, size. Quinn made a trio of trades in January 1991, then two more at the trade deadline in March. These moves would dramatically reshape the Canucks' roster, setting the stage for the good days that were soon to come. Small forwards Petri Skriko and Brian Bradley were shipped out. In came a pair of veteran blueliners: a skilled one in Tom Kurvers from Toronto and a hard-hitting one in Gerald Diduck from Montreal. And at the end of January, Quinn fired his friend McCammon as head coach, and put himself behind the bench, where he'd stay until 1994. But these moves were minor in nature in comparison to the trades Quinn pulled off on March 5. In the biggest move of the deadline, a pair of local heroes in skilled Burnaby-born centre Cliff Ronning and speedy goal-scoring Victoria-born winger Geoff Courtnall, plus hulking, rough-and-tumble winger Sergio Momesso and another tough blueliner in Robert Dirk, came to the Canucks—all in one trade. To get the quartet, Quinn shipped fan favourite and bruising defenceman Garth Butcher to St. Louis, along with skilled but flaky forward Dan Quinn. Butcher was the guy that Blues GM Ron Caron coveted; Pat Quinn knew this and ground Caron down until he got the return he wanted, while also disposing of Dan Quinn—no relation to the Canucks' president—a player whom everyone in Vancouver had tired of. He'd been named before the season as one of the team's "tri-captains," along with Linden and veteran defenceman Doug Lidster, but Quinn pouted often and was scratched for his poor attitude more than once. Butcher did prove to be an astute pickup for St. Louis, where he played for a few more seasons and became the Blues' captain for a time. Quinn, on the other hand, bounced around, playing for five teams in the ensuing six years, never leaving much of a positive impression anywhere he played. What the Canucks got out of Dirk and especially Courtnall, Ronning, and Momesso far exceeded what the Blues got in return.

The other deadline-day trade brought in yet another tough defenceman in Dana Murzyn, from Calgary, in exchange for hard-working but undersized winger Ronnie Stern and lanky spare-part defenceman Kevan Guy. Murzyn would become a stalwart on the Canucks' blueline for the rest of the decade. The Canucks were truly becoming the hard-rock squad that Quinn had longed for. And it was a team that Odjick now truly made sense on. Odjick was still the lead heavyweight, but he was not alone in the rough-and-tumble department. With Momesso, Diduck, Dirk, and Murzyn now in the fold behind Odjick, the Canucks wouldn't just battle their way through games anymore—they'd pound their opponents into submission through hard forechecking, aggressive work around the crease, and, yes, from time to time with their fists. "Gino was definitely the first," Linden says in retrospect. "Look at that list of guys. We're a different team at the end of that year, we're incredibly different, just from a size, physicality, hard-to-play-against standpoint."

On the surface, Odjick's job as enforcer was to take on the other teams' tough guys, to be ready for a fight every night. For years, the rhetoric across the top levels of hockey was that the tough guys policed the game, they made the game safe for skill players. But for many, this was hard to square with the reality that tough guys never fought the other team's stars, just the other team's enforcers. How could two toughs facing off possibly have an impact on the rest of the game, many pondered. But skill players such as Courtnall—and later Pavel Bure—said they felt the impact that teammates like Odjick brought to the lineup.

Without Odjick, the other team's hits felt heavier and harder. With Odjick in the lineup, the hits were fewer, and the discreet little shots here and there, away from the puck, in battles in front of the net, they just weren't quite the same. But Courtnall and his mates wouldn't notice the Odjick effect right away, as a week before the trade deadline, Gino broke his cheekbone when the Penguins' Jay Caufield clipped him with a high elbow. He would miss five weeks.

Courtnall brought speed and scoring to the table, and Ronning provided crafty centre play, while Momesso and Dirk added hard edge to the lineup, buttressing the size element that Odjick was by then on the leading edge of. They made the Canucks better. Meanwhile, the Blues stumbled down the stretch and into the playoffs. Courtnall had been the best of the Blues' secondary scoring but had seen his role diminish in the weeks leading up to the trade, while Ronning had been used by the Blues as a power-play specialist, otherwise toiling on the fourth line. Both became front-line members of the Canucks' offence.

The trade also brought on a true change in team culture, Courtnall believes. He got to know some of the team's younger players because, like them, he found himself living in the hotel that the team put new players in. "It was evident that they all felt that they were not really respected," Courtnall says. But these young players, like Odjick, saw new openings. There were fewer personality conflicts in the new dressing room. It would become as strong a team culture as could be.

NOW, THE CHANGE in the team after the trade with the Blues wasn't instant, results-wise. Team morale was better and so was the way they were playing. Still, in the eleven games after the trade, they only went 4–5–2—yes, they lost more than they won. But in the twenty-one-team NHL of the day, that was still enough to stumble into the playoffs, if only just. The Canucks only made the post-season because they snagged a win in the final game of the season, at home against the Winnipeg Jets, to put themselves into the playoffs. (A tie would have left their fate still hanging in the balance.) As if written by a Hollywood screenwriter, that final game went to overtime.

And it was Courtnall, the local boy, on his fifth team in four seasons, who scored the overtime winner and whipped the city of Vancouver into a frenzy. The fans and players were thrilled to make the playoffs. So was Gino, who had recovered from his busted cheekbone and was ready to make his return to the lineup in Game 1 of the playoffs in Southern California.

But on the road, up against the high-powered Los Angeles Kings—led by Wayne Gretzky and a clutch of old Oilers teammates—Odjick and his fourth-line linemates barely saw the ice. The Canucks finished the season thirty-seven points behind the Kings. Despite the disparity in the standings, the Canucks swore that the team they'd be in the playoffs was the one they'd been in the stretch run, the one that had found its identity after the trade deadline, rather than the one that had stumbled brutally through much of the middle of the season. They'd play hard-nosed, hard-checking hockey. And in the two games in Los Angeles to open the series, they were very much that. The Canucks won Game 1 6–5 on a wild third-period battle back, where the Canucks scored three unanswered goals on their heavily favoured hosts. Odjick showed up twice on the scoresheet, but only for minor penalties.

Game 2 saw the Canucks take a 2–0 lead early in the second period, but LA slowly clawed their way back, tying the game early in the third. And then Wayne Gretzky—who else?—scored the winner in overtime. The Canucks were massive underdogs, yet they had been *this* close to going back to Vancouver up 2–0. Both games were feisty, with a slew of roughing and slashing penalties handed out to both teams, a sign of how testy things already were between the two squads. But despite the game's fractiousness, Odjick and the fourth line didn't see much ice time.

With Game 3 in Vancouver, Odjick was raring to go. As the home team, the Canucks would get the last line change, and Gino knew Quinn would look to his fourth line to make an impact. The rookie also knew he would have to be smart. "It's going to be a long series," he told the *Province*'s Jim Jamieson. "There's a time for everything. You can't go looking for revenge and end up taking stupid penalties."[8]

A year before, playing in junior for Laval, he might have let the moment get to him. But in the NHL, even as a rookie, he knew better. Over the course of the season, Odjick had learned quickly what it meant to be in the NHL: the margins for error are very slim, mistakes will get you scratched and quickly sent back to the minors. If he was going to stick, it wouldn't just be because of his fists, it would be about his overall play. That applied to the overall direction of the team itself too. There was a sense of where the Canucks could go. They could get on the other team's nerves, they could play tough when needed, then they could find some goals. Add it all up and they would keep their fans on their feet, roaring in excitement.

Game 3 was exactly as advertised. The Vancouver fans were into it. The *Vancouver Sun*'s Lindsay Kines reported, on the day, that the Pacific Coliseum hadn't been so loud in years, not since the 1982 Stanley Cup playoff run. All night it was a game played on a knife's edge. Referee Dan Marouelli called nineteen penalties in the first period alone; ten were for roughing, three for slashing, two for unsportsmanlike conduct. At the end of the night, he'd assess thirty-six minors in all, and that added up to twelve power plays between the two teams. And Odjick found his fight, taking on Marty McSorley, one of the toughest tough guys the NHL has ever seen. Oh, and the Canucks won the game in overtime, with Cliff Ronning scoring his fourth goal in three games.

Game 3 would turn out to be the high-water mark for the Canucks, though, as LA took control in Game 4, beating the Canucks 6–1 before smashing the Canucks again in Game 5 back in LA, 7–4. The Kings were just too strong and too powerful. They sealed the series in Game 6 back at the Coliseum, winning 4–1. The series was over, the dream of an upset was dead; had the Canucks won, they would have been the second-biggest standings underdog to win a playoff series in NHL history, behind only the 1982 Kings, who had finished the regular season forty points back of the Edmonton Oilers yet would still win their first-round series. Vancouver was rejuvenated, despite the loss. It had taken Pat Quinn four years, but he finally had the foundations of a team that would be able to play the fast and skilled, big and bruising hockey he wanted. And Gino was going to be a big part of that. "He was a silent leader," Courtnall recalled of his young teammate. "He didn't say a lot, but he was the ultimate protector."

THE SUMMER OF 1991 saw another big transition: Stan Smyl retired. Early in his career, the Canucks had burned brightly, though just for a moment. He'd been the captain of that 1982 team that had surprised the league by marching confidently to the Stanley Cup final. Sure, they benefited from the Kings' upset of the Oilers, clearing a much easier path out of the Campbell Conference. And sure, they'd been utterly dominated in the final by the New York Islanders, one of the great dynasties of hockey history. But they'd shown enough to suggest that maybe, just maybe, they'd be a pretty competitive team for a few seasons to come.

Smyl was a true hometown hero: although originally from St. Paul, Alberta, he'd moved to the West Coast to play junior hockey, first with the BC Junior Hockey League's Bellingham Blazers, where he was first called "Steamer" in recognition of his hard-nosed, never-quit playing style, then with the major junior New Westminster Bruins. He helped the Bruins to four consecutive appearances in the Memorial Cup, winning twice. He's the only player to have played in four straight Memorial Cup finals.

Drafted by his hometown team in 1978, the same year the Canucks introduced their radical "Flying V" uniforms, he made the jump straight to the NHL. He became the face of the Canucks in the 1980s, leading the team to that surprising appearance in the Stanley Cup final in 1982. Smyl was named captain the following season but the team slid quickly and sadly back down with brutal on-ice results. By 1984, they were in the wilderness, winning just a third of their games. There was little to cheer for—especially playing in the same division as the high-flying Oilers and Calgary Flames—but Smyl battled on, ever the optimist.

He was still captain when Quinn arrived, but he was beginning to decline. He'd suffered knee injuries in 1985–86 and 1986–87. His skating suffered and he scored just twelve goals in 1987–88, Quinn's first season as president. It was the first time since Smyl's rookie season that he hadn't scored at least twenty goals. By the time Gino arrived, Smyl had become a part-time player, his leadership role taken on by the likes of Trevor Linden and Doug Lidster.

When Smyl retired he stepped into a new role that seemed like a good fit for a guy who'd given so much to the team and who still had strong leadership qualities: he became an assistant coach. His role was now to guide young players like Gino. Even when they were teammates, Smyl could tell the youngster was different. Most rookies come in hoping to make a difference and to simply avoid making mistakes. They are filled with equal parts talent and anxiety. But Gino didn't seem to carry those concerns around. He certainly knew his place and what his role was, but instead of being weighed down by the fear of making mistakes, he carried a wry smile around, always ready with a joke. He wanted to keep everyone loose, and he knew exactly how to do that. He was smart enough to know how he'd be able to move forward doing things his way.

"The biggest thing is the respect he showed everyone around him. That made it easier to talk to him and to get to know him quicker. And how kind he was," Smyl recalls. "He was very intelligent, a really smart guy. I believe we all have smarts. But we all handled it in different ways, that intelligence part of it. He knew everything that was going on around him. He knew everything. What he had to do. And he was smart enough to keep it to himself and get the job done. And away from the rink, like I said, he was really respectful. He wasn't loud and obnoxious."

In a game that values hustle, hard work, and a touch of community, it's no surprise that Gino, ever the man thinking of others, would present himself as a calm and considerate person. "One of the hardest things in sports and in hockey is that you meet so many people and you tend to kind of just forget certain names, but he was always really good. He knew everyone around him. He knew the people who were in the media. He knew everyone and he didn't show it," Smyl says. "He wanted to be treated the same way he would want to treat other people and that's the way he did it. He just treated everyone the same. There was no one special to him. He wanted people to feel comfortable around. And so he treated everyone the same."

Tony Gallagher, whose coverage of the Canucks over the decades for the *Province* newspaper was honoured in 2020 with the Hockey Hall of Fame's Elmer Ferguson Memorial Award, recalled Odjick being open and friendly from the start. "I loved the guy for many reasons early on," Gallagher says. "Gino was one of these guys who was incapable of lying. He couldn't lie. You'd ask him a question and he'd just tell you. It stood out: you know how hockey guys are, so guarded. No filter whatsoever."

But at a certain point, Gallagher came to feel that Odjick's willingness to just dish was problematic, so the columnist started to pull back from using all of Gino's answers. "He would let it all hang out. I came to think it would be too exploitative to use it all," he says. "I'm pretty sure he had his ears pinned back a few times about things that would get out."

Odjick's friendly nature most often worked to his advantage, though, Gallagher said. People would go the extra mile for him because he was so friendly, so good to people. Gallagher recalled a tale that Bob McCammon relayed to him about an early road trip, perhaps Odjick's first. If it was the first, the story is even better, but even if it wasn't, it still shows how at ease Gino was with everyone and how quickly everyone would feel an attachment to him in return. According to McCammon, Odjick arrived at Vancouver International Airport without his passport or any identification at all. He'd left it all back in his hotel room at the Atrium Inn across from the Pacific Coliseum. That, of course, would be a big problem. There wasn't exactly time for him to get a ride all the way back to the hotel, find his passport, then get a ride all the way back to the airport.

"So McCammon tells him to call the hotel and see if they have someone who can run up to his room to get his ID and passport," Gallagher says. As the story goes, Odjick simply greeted the front desk person in the familiar. "'Uh, it's Gino here,'" Gallagher says. "So friendly. As if they were supposed to immediately know who he was. Fortunately, they did. He'd been there just a handful of days and he's already made a name for himself. He'd befriended all the staff. They all snapped to attention, got his ID, and a guy rushed it out to him at the airport." That gregarious, friendly nature won him all kinds of friends.

This apparent lack of travel savvy on Odjick's part is understandable, Linden says. Gino was a bright guy, a guy with good street smarts, his long-time teammate says. But in the early days, there was definitely a lot of catching up to do. "I grew up in a small town," Linden says, referring to Medicine Hat,

Alberta, which in those days had about forty-five thousand people in it. Gino's hometown numbers about one-tenth of that. "But Gino grew up far more rural," Linden adds. "Some of the social things weren't that polished."

He wasn't polished, but he was a good teammate, a good friend, and tough as nails. The first two came naturally. But even with his imposing size, he had to learn the third.

2

"GET ME A TOUGH GUY"

IN 1989, when Canucks scout Ron Delorme first walked into the Colisée de Laval in Montreal's largest suburb, set to watch a pair of tough guys play for the hometown Titan, he looked up and immediately thought, "I'm in the right place." Hanging high above the ice, a huge sign, written in English, declared this was the "House of Pain." Rough-and-tumble hockey for a rough-and-tumble crowd.

It was the right place, and Delorme was the right scout to find a player who could play the rough-and-tumble style: he'd been an NHL tough guy himself. During nine seasons of NHL action with the Colorado Rockies and then the Vancouver Canucks, Delorme dropped the gloves more than fifty times. The most famous image from Delorme's playing days isn't of his own face, but rather that of an opponent named Grant Mulvey, a Chicago Black Hawks forward whose face Delorme had beaten to a pulp in a 1982 playoff tilt. Mulvey had come off the Chicago bench and whacked Delorme's teammate

Lars Lindgren in the face with his stick, leading to a brawl and Delorme pummelling the tough Black Hawk. Delorme could play the game—he had nineteen- and twenty-goal seasons for Colorado before arriving in Vancouver—but for the Canucks he was on the roster for his physical presence. Years later, he'd arrived in Laval to look for a player who could fill the same role. The two youngsters he would have his eye on: Gino Odjick and Sandy McCarthy.

President and general manager Pat Quinn's directive to his head scout, Mike Penny, for the 1989–90 hockey season had been clear: he didn't want his Canucks to be pushed around anymore. "Get me a tough guy," he told Penny and his three other scouts: Delorme, Ken Slater, and Jack McCartan.

Three seasons into his tenure as the Canucks' superboss, one thing was clear to Quinn: his team was too small. In the era of the super heavyweight enforcer, size and strength mattered as much as scoring skill. In the late 1970s Quinn had taken over a Philadelphia squad that had earned the nickname "the Broad Street Bullies" as a team that would slug you with their fists all over the ice, beating you into submission. Quinn wanted his team to be one that could also skate opponents off the ice and out of breath. But he also knew his team needed big guys who would keep the other team's players honest—at least that was the de rigueur theory that most hockey people espoused at the time. Much like the era's nuclear powers, the NHL's enforcers kept each other in check. They acted as a kind of deterrent. But while the United States and the Soviet Union never actually launched their missiles, the NHL's tough guys would occasionally use their fists on one another as a demonstration of power.

The Canucks team Quinn took over in 1987 wasn't very good. The roster did have some toughness in the likes of

Garth Butcher, Daryl Stanley, and Dave Richter, and a true super heavyweight in Craig Coxe. Coxe was one of the best fighters in the NHL and his bloody tilts with Bob Probert are still famous today for their brutality. He was only a fighter, though: in 235 career NHL games with the Canucks, Calgary Flames, St. Louis Blues, and San Jose Sharks, he scored just fourteen goals, against 713 penalty minutes. He certainly wasn't Probert, who could put the puck in the net on top of beating the pulp out of his opponents. What point was there in having tough guys who couldn't score if you weren't winning any games?

It was going to be a slow turnaround, Quinn told Canucks ownership. There was no quick fix. First, he needed to find some younger talent through the draft. Second, he knew that he could find some new players that would contribute if he was shrewd in his trading. The 1987 trade for McLean and Adams was the first example of this. But as Quinn warned, there would be growing pains. The 1987–88 Canucks won just twenty-five games. They gave up the fifth-most goals in the league that season.

But a year later there were nascent signs of a turnaround: at the end of the 1988–89 season, the Canucks, an undersized team that was big on hustle and desire, made the playoffs. They were one of the NHL's best defensive outfits, and they pushed the eventual Stanley Cup–champion Calgary Flames to seven games in their first round series. In the final game of the series, Calgary won in overtime on what's still a controversial goal—just about any Canuck player or fan will tell you that Calgary's Joel Otto kicked that puck in. The officials didn't care; there was no video review in those days. The Canucks lost but there was something inspiring about them. Between the solid regular season and the tight, albeit short, playoff run, it felt to Canucks fans like a step in the right direction after years of mostly hopeless hockey.

But 1989–90 proved to be a step backward. Their defensive play regressed—they gave up the sixth-most goals against in the league—and their offence still sputtered, scoring just 245 goals, fewer than the year before. Three years into his project, it was clear Quinn still needed to do a lot more to improve the roster's talent level, plus his team wasn't as intimidating as he wanted it to be. That's why he wanted to find toughness in the draft.

Everyone knew that, with the second overall pick, the Canucks were likely to go after skill. Most observers figured Owen Nolan would be drafted first overall by the Quebec Nordiques, and he was. But sitting second overall, it wasn't quite clear what the Canucks would do. Size, everyone knew, was also on their mind. Hulking Keith Primeau, who'd tallied 127 points for Niagara Falls in the Ontario Hockey League (OHL), certainly had size. And as shown by his scoring record, he had a streak of skill too.

There was also a likely fit with Mike Ricci, a skilled, feisty centre who had started the season as the consensus No. 1 pick, but whose buzz hadn't quite kept up with Nolan's or Primeau's or that of silky, skilled Czech centreman Petr Nedvěd. Despite his aggressive nature, Vancouver never seemed to have their eye on Ricci; the Philadelphia Flyers, set to pick two spots after the Canucks, were interested in Ricci and talked to the Canucks about swapping picks. Reports at the time suggested that to snag the Canucks' spot at second overall, the Flyers offered to part with the fourth-overall selection, plus either power forward Scott Mellanby—who would spend twenty years in the NHL, playing 1,431 games in all—or bruising defenceman Terry Carkner. But Quinn turned them down.[9] When it came time for the Flyers to pick at fourth overall, Ricci was still there and they grabbed him.

The best player in the 1990 draft, though, would be Jaromír Jágr. The lanky Czech had sublime skills but was a big unknown in the draft. It was understood he'd still have to perform his national service in the Czechoslovakian military... unless, of course, a team was willing to grease the skids through back channels to make that national service go away.

They'd worked for several years to bring in Soviet stars Igor Larionov and Vladimir Krutov, eventually paying a big transfer fee to sign the skilful duo for the 1989–90 season; the idea of making payments in order to get access to a player still on the wrong side of the Iron Curtain didn't interest the Canucks' brass in the slightest. If they had been willing to make a payout to the Czechoslovakian powers that be, they'd surely have drafted Jágr at second overall. Instead, they turned their eyes toward a different Czech: Petr Nedvěd, who'd fled his homeland the year before and then skated with the Seattle Thunderbirds for a season, tearing up the Western Hockey League (WHL). His skills were sensational, but big and tough he was not. The Canucks apparently were won over by Nedvěd's playmaking. They knew there was risk in going for the slender centre, but they believed Nedvěd would develop into a truly elite playmaking centre, the kind of talent that was rare to find. Toughness would have to be found elsewhere in the draft.

They wouldn't have to wait long: the Canucks had a second first-round pick that year, picked up in another deadline-day trade with St. Louis, but in 1990. Yes, two years in a row the

Canucks and Blues made big deals at the deadline. In this 1990 trade, Quinn had traded veteran defenceman Harold Snepsts, who was something of a cult hero in Vancouver. The rugged blueliner had won over Canucks fans with his hard-nosed style in the 1970s and early 1980s, but in 1990, he was thirty-five years old and pondering retirement after the season. St. Louis GM Ron Caron, who was unintentionally an important supporting character in the growth of the 1990s Canucks, asked for Snepsts in a trade. The Blues were headed to the playoffs, the Canucks weren't, and Caron wanted to add a little veteran grit to his lineup.

Quinn wanted everything he could get. Caron was willing to oblige: he traded his 1991 first-round pick, plus promising young defenceman Adrien Plavsic. Vancouver also shipped gritty winger Rich Sutter to St. Louis. With that bonus first-round pick, which settled in at eighteenth overall, Quinn began his add-toughness campaign: he selected a giant in Shawn Antoski, an OHL pugilist. Antoski had scored twenty-five goals in fifty-nine games for the North Bay Centennials, to go with 201 penalty minutes. But there had been every reason for Antoski to dominate in junior like he had: he was already twenty.

Nowadays, no one picks a twenty-year-old so high in the draft, let alone using a first-round pick on a player who wasn't known for offence, but in this era, when toughness was a highly prized attribute, it did make some sense. Quinn wanted big players who could skate and put the puck in the net, guys to match up against the likes of Probert and McSorley.

As the Canucks' scouts told anyone who would listen, Antoski could skate. And he was big: he stood six foot three, and while he was a little lean, the Canucks believed he would easily bulk up to a boards-rattling 240 pounds. "When we talked to people in the OHL, everybody told us Antoski was the toughest kid in the league. [Owen] Nolan even told us he had trouble with him," Canucks assistant general manager Brian Burke crowed in an exclusive column for the *Province* the day after the draft. Big and fast, Antoski was perfect for the kind of hockey the Canucks wanted to play, Burke said.[10]

Antoski was the first of four bruising players the Canucks would draft that year. Darin Bader, a power forward for the Saskatoon Blades of the WHL, was drafted in the fourth round. Odjick went in the fifth (Delorme had actually pressed Quinn in the previous rounds to select the big winger from Laval). In the ninth round, the Canucks picked another big tough guy, this time a defenceman: Mark Cipriano from the WHL's Victoria Cougars.

Quinn first laid eyes on Odjick at the 1990 Memorial Cup. He saw what his scouts had seen: a big, aggressive player who kept the other team's agitators and tough guys in line. There were fewer liberties taken on the ice because of Odjick's presence, Quinn and his scouts believed.

"He made a difference in what happened," Quinn recalled in 2014. "Gino impressed me because I didn't want just a goofball where you pushed him out on the ice and said, 'Go fight.'"[11]

In a similar vein, Antoski was a tantalizing athlete. Big and rangy, willing to drop the gloves, a powerful skater. But he never quite put it all together in the NHL. After cups of coffee in the NHL in 1990–91 and 1991–92, he made the Canucks roster out of training camp in 1992. But he barely played during the first month of the season and was sent back to the American Hockey League (AHL). A knock against him was that he'd sometimes struggle to focus, something that was especially important for a guy who wasn't playing much from night to night. Upon arrival in Hamilton, he went AWOL for a while. When he returned, he pulled himself back together, buckled down, and did his best to heed the guidance of his coaches.

The lessons apparently stuck. A year later, he was back in the NHL. For good, this time. He pushed Odjick from the lineup in the playoffs that year, during the Canucks' magical run to the Stanley Cup final, but his long-term position on the team never cemented, and it was Odjick, in the end, who remained the better player. Odjick would be a Canuck until 1998; Antoski was traded away in 1995, after playing seventy games for Vancouver across parts of five seasons. Antoski's wild style of play ended up doing him no favours: he managed just 183 NHL games, for the Canucks, Flyers, Penguins, and Anaheim Mighty Ducks. Concussions, to no one's surprise, proved to be a big problem for the winger, who never played in a full NHL season. It wasn't an on-ice injury, though, that ultimately ended his NHL career: it was a fractured skull suffered in a car accident in November 1997.

Odjick and Antoski both made it to the NHL. Neither Bader nor Cipriano amounted to much, but you would be wrong to think the Canucks' 1990 draft was a bust—it wasn't. Petr Nedvěd played nearly a thousand games, though mostly not for Vancouver. Jiři Šlégr, a defenceman picked in the second round and the son of former Canuck Jiři Bubla, played more than six hundred NHL games—also mostly not for Vancouver. A draft pick is generally deemed to have been a success if the player skates in two hundred NHL games. In the 1990 draft, the Canucks picked three guys who more than met that requirement, and Antoski would have been a fourth but for injuries. If you can find two two-hundred-gamers in the same draft, you've hit a minimum standard in modern assessment; that the Canucks hit on three, nearly four, made this a successful year for the scouts.

Nedvěd had the best overall career, but as a Canuck, it's Odjick who stands out as the best of the quartet drafted that year. Nedvěd played three seasons in Vancouver before his holdout in 1993–94, but his best years were elsewhere. Šlégr played parts of three seasons in Vancouver, then bounced around the league for more than a decade—including a brief return to Vancouver in 2003–04—but on the whole never quite delivered on the talents he possessed: he had sixty-four points in his first two NHL seasons, both with Vancouver. Odjick was tougher than the rest and ended up contributing as a player too. Odjick never had a season like Nedvěd's 1992–93—the slick centre scored seventy-one points in eighty-four games—but he also never asked an opposing superstar for a souvenir the moment his team was eliminated from the playoffs, as Nedvěd did following the team's shocking playoff ouster in 1993, when he asked Wayne Gretzky for one of the Great One's sticks. That would prove to be Nedvěd's last act as a Canuck and it drew the ire of fans. Gino played 444 games for the Canucks—exactly double the amount of games Nedvěd played for Vancouver—tallied up a team record 2,127 penalty minutes, and never asked for a single stick. And no Canucks fan ever once booed him.

WHEN THE 1990 DRAFT reached the fifth round, there were two obvious choices in the eyes of the Canucks scouts: Odjick and Sandy McCarthy, the two tough wingers on the Laval

Titan, champions of the QMJHL. The duo usually played on the same line for Laval; 1989–90 had been Odjick's second season in Laval, the second year he'd made an impact for the Titan in the Memorial Cup tournament. McCarthy had just finished his first year of major junior, but he'd followed the same path as Odjick, spending a year with Tier II Junior A Hawkesbury Hawks before making the jump to Laval. Delorme had already suggested Odjick a couple of times in the previous rounds, but his bosses had said the second round was too early for a raw tough guy, and they saw a better overall player in Bader, who had scored sixty-one goals across the previous two seasons for Saskatoon in the WHL.

"The difference to me, between him and McCarthy, was Gino could play," Mike Penny recalls of the pick, thirty-four years later. Odjick wasn't just a knuckle-dragger who would push off from the bench, then wander around the ice looking for an opponent. He could forecheck, he could take and give a pass, he could put the puck in the net. McCarthy would probably make the NHL too, but the scouts saw more of a complete player in Odjick.

"And he had a nickname: the 'Algonquin Assassin.' He lived up to that name," recalled Ron Delorme. "We had so much in common. We were both First Nations."

As fifth-round tough guys went, he was an intriguing project. Teams dreamed of finding the next Bob Probert, who for years reigned as the NHL's top heavyweight, but who also could put the puck in the net (he scored twenty-nine goals in the 1987–88 season while amassing a staggering 398 penalty minutes), or the next Marty McSorley, who regularly played huge minutes for the Los Angeles Kings. Generally a defenceman, McSorley was versatile enough that he could also play on the wing. Indeed, in 1990, he was coming off a fifteen-goal season, the second year in a row he'd scored double-digit goals for the Kings, while also recording more than three hundred penalty minutes. Not only could they fight, and fight well, but they could also play. McSorley broke into the NHL in 1983, straight out of junior, with the Pittsburgh Penguins, but he made a name for himself with the Edmonton Oilers. Oilers coach-GM Glen "Slats" Sather traded for McSorley in 1985 to be the next Dave Semenko, another fighter who could also play. Sather was a player in the 1960s, when there were tough guys, enforcers, sure, but they weren't Coke machines on skates. Montreal's John Ferguson—yes, who was Winnipeg's GM in 1985 when Frank Griffiths tried to hire him to run the Canucks—was the ultimate example: he could score and he could fight. In the 1970s, the Philadelphia Flyers' Dave Schultz, nicknamed "The Hammer," intimidated his opponents and could put the puck in the net: in 1973–74, he scored twenty goals and served 348 minutes in penalties. The next season, he set an NHL record with 472 penalty minutes—a record that still stands. Semenko didn't fight nearly as much as Schultz—he never had more than two hundred penalty minutes in a season—but he could score, and did so in double digits across three straight NHL seasons, from 1980–81 until 1982–83.

In McSorley, Sather obviously saw a player in that same mould, a player who could play tough and also contribute. "Some coaches are worried that if the guy plays, he's going to get away from being the mean, tough guy when you need him," McSorley says. "I don't think Slats was worried about that with me. He'd reward me with the second part of the power play or he'd put me out there with [Mark Messier's] line. That was awesome. That allowed me to grow as a player."

That was the kind of player the Canucks wanted to find, a guy who did more than just fight. He was still pretty raw, but there was obvious talent. "He was good at puck possession, using his size to protect the puck, at moving the puck," Brian Burke recalled years later, about what they saw of Odjick in junior.[12]

The player Odjick would become was an admirable one in McSorley's eyes. "To truly be an effective tough guy, to be a constant presence on the ice was a huge advantage," McSorley says. "For Gino to be able to go out there and be defensively accountable, to get on the forecheck, to finish his checks... that's the biggest thing. You can't go on the ice and cost your team with a) a penalty and b) poor defensive play."

And the Canucks immediately recognized Odjick was a smart guy, on and off the ice. "Our interviews with Gino before the draft came back really high," Burke added. "For leadership, for being a good teammate, for listening, for responding to coaching tips. There were stories we heard about the sacrifices he made to play, where he didn't have any money but managed to work part-time to make money to buy skates."

GINO HAD FIRST SKATED when he was about five years old. His father, Joe, a fine player as a young man, figured Gino might like the game he loved too. "He took me to this out-door skating rink and he just let me go," Odjick told long-time

Vancouver sports media personality Bob Marjanovich on a podcast in 2022.[13] But there were no teams on the reserve for kids as young as Gino, so Joe signed his son up for figure skating lessons. "And that's how I learned how to skate," Odjick said. "It was just a way to get out there and skate." He remembered that it didn't take him long to figure it all out. He started by pushing a chair around for a while, then found his balance unaided. How quickly he picked up new things would be a theme in his life: coaches and teammates at every level would say he only had to be shown something once before he began to master the skill.

Still, he had to deal with skating in an actual game. Once, he fell to the ice and caught a skate blade in the face. In those days, there were no masks, so he took a nasty gash in the forehead. "That's the first thing I remember about playing hockey," he told Marjanovich. He didn't fall like that many more times. Soon he sorted out what was required for skating in a game.

Like his dad, Gino played defence on his first team. Like his dad, the rink was where he would come to be happiest. Unlike his dad, he wasn't there to escape brutality; he was just there to experience the purest joy. And unlike his dad, he had grown into a giant, a lumbering skater who had a lot of power but lacked proper training in how to make his stride more efficient.

"We'd give anything to get ice anytime we could," Odjick told the *Vancouver Sun*'s Iain MacIntyre in 1991. "There was an outside rink. That's where we played most of our games. We'd get sheets of plywood, cut them up, put our skates on, then push the snow off. I was a goal-scorer. I'd score a few goals every game. One game we lost 6–5 and I scored five goals."[14] Gino and some of his friends played for mostly non-Indigenous teams in Maniwaki for a time, but over the long run, it was playing for reserve teams in Indigenous tournaments, where they'd travel to other reserves and face off against other Indigenous teams, that they lived for. They were industrious in how they raised the funds to make the trips. "A week ahead, we wouldn't have any money. So we'd go into the bush and cut firewood and sell it. That's how we earned our money to go," he told MacIntyre. Sometimes they'd just organize casual games on their own, facing up to whomever was interested.

The teams that were organized on the reserve would sometimes play in non-Indigenous tournaments too. Racism, he said, was never felt on the ice. "It's not on the ice a Native player has a hard time," Odjick said. "It's always off the ice." There were slurs, but he would always downplay what he'd faced from opposing players or fans; he chose to approach life positively, he'd say, so he wouldn't take note of the insults being thrown his way.

His friend Andy "Itchy" Dewache still lives in Kitigan Zibi and has been a cop in the community for years. He said that the racism was definitely always there; the two friends played on all kinds of teams together. The teams from Maniwaki, Dewache noted, were nicknamed the Braves. "Their logo was an Indian, with a tomahawk," he points out. You look at team photos from the 1970s and early 1980s and rarely do you spot a player from the reserve. The teams were filled with white kids. The Indigenous kids who did make the teams, Dewache says, were often there for political or money reasons. "How you made those teams was because your parents had businesses or political pull. Maybe some will disagree, but most will agree," he says. "Indian kids just wanted to be a part of society and to be welcomed, so making these elite teams was a big deal."

But Itchy believes that over the years the teams have done more harm than good for his community. If you weren't from Maniwaki or Kitigan Zibi, you could easily misunderstand who made up the Braves teams. The way in which these teams played would get tied to the Kitigan Zibi community, for better or worse. Mostly worse, Itchy implied. "What we didn't know was that Indian logo caused hatred toward the Algonquins," he says. "Those teams had no Indigenous players, but it's guys like this that started rivalries with outside municipalities, and the other teams believed they were playing against us Indians."

In atom division, it was Joe who first pulled eleven-year-old Gino and his teammates together for a Kitigan Zibi team. Joe coached, drove, figured out the budget, everything. The next year, as pee-wees, they were invited to the famous Quebec International Pee-Wee Tournament, where they played well despite difficult conditions: a strike by unionized workers at Quebec City's Colisée meant that there was no one to resurface the ice. Instead, volunteers shovelled snow off the ice after every sixth game. Teams playing in that sixth game—like the team from Kitigan Zibi—faced playing through several inches of snow build-up on the ice. "That was fun," recalls Gino's old friend Jan Cote, who was also on the team. "My dad kept blaming the ice, we were trying to pass the puck but it didn't work," Cote adds with a laugh. The ice was ridiculous, but the kids didn't care. Maybe it was their experience of playing outside in Kitigan Zibi, on the rivers and outdoor rinks, that kept them from complaining. Hard outdoor ice is tough, and the snow builds up wherever.

Gino played a half-season of pee-wee in the Maniwaki town league but felt out of place. Maniwaki may have had a long association with Kitigan Zibi, but the town was still mostly white in those days. Gino, the big Indigenous kid, stood out. In the end, hockey in town "just wasn't the thing to do," he told Iain MacIntyre. So, instead of playing in the more competitive week-in, week-out league in town—at the rink which now bears his name—he went back to playing with his friends on the reserve.

Gino told Roy MacGregor in his 1995 book *The Home Team: Fathers, Sons & Hockey* that those days, playing with his friends, were pretty much the definition of carefree: "We didn't really care about the hockey. We were just out to have fun."[15] And his dad was there to empower their fun. "He didn't give any speeches and he'd only get mad when we were being lazy. He kept us honest," Gino recalled. The only time winning mattered to any of them, he said, was in the tournaments against other Indigenous teams.

GINO WAS GROWING into a big boy. He knew how to play the game hard. He loved scoring goals. But he had no idea how big he could really play. He'd long dreamed of making the NHL, but didn't think that was in the cards. The big leagues were a long, long way away, and nobody scouted kids from the reserve anyway. If he couldn't become a hockey player, he also dreamed of becoming a country singer, like his hero George Jones. But like the NHL dream, he had no idea how to make that happen either.

Instead, Gino was thinking about the rest of his life. In the fall of 1987, he was still in high school. At seventeen, he and his high school girlfriend June Wawatie were already parents to Ashley-Ann, born in 1986, and June was pregnant again. (Their son Patrick would be born early in 1988.) Hockey, music—those weren't in his future, he thought. Instead, he signed up for a welding course down in Ottawa. He also talked about becoming a cop. Those were long-term plans. In the short term, he didn't even sign up to play hockey for anyone. The season before, he'd played midget hockey with some friends, like Itchy, but with the 1987–88 hockey season under way, instead of hitting the ice, Gino was out in the bush near Rapid Lake, two hours north of Kitigan Zibi, hunting moose. He'd been out there much of the summer.

His mom, Giselle, was worried about what Gino would do once he went to Ottawa. So she called up Louis Branchaud, a family friend, to see if there was a men's league hockey team her son could join. Instead, he said Gino should go try out with the Hawkesbury Hawks, a junior team that played in a town an hour and change east of Ottawa. His son Michel had just made the team. They weren't terribly good and they had just fired their coach, but they could probably use a big, strong kid like Gino. So Giselle sent a message up to Rapid Lake, which somehow landed with her son, who pondered a moment and said, "Sure, why not?"

Before Hawkesbury, Gino was not a fighter, but in Hawkesbury, that's what they needed. "I was the best player on the team. I was the leading scorer," Gino recalled to Marjanovich about the kind of player he'd been in Kitigan Zibi.[16] There was a bench-clearing brawl once in bantam. "We were playing our native team against another team, non-native... it went on and on for about 20 minutes," he told MacIntyre.[17] Gino dropped his gloves then; he ended up fighting the other team's coach. But fighting wasn't really what he was interested in. Not then, anyway.

But Hawkesbury's new coach, twenty-seven-year-old Bob Hartley, who'd been the team's goalie coach, didn't need another defenceman who couldn't skate all that well. Sure, Gino could deliver a pass and pot the odd goal, but that wasn't what Hartley needed. He had enough guys who could do that. What he needed was a big bruiser who was ready to stick up for his teammates. Who would drop his gloves if need be.

Michel Branchaud had made the team as the fourth-line centre. Gino was put on left wing next to him. When he arrived, after a summer in the bush, Gino wasn't in hockey shape. "But he had charisma and he had potential, and he was my friend, so Bob Hartley kept him," Branchaud recalls. Hartley had once planned to be a teacher, but his father died just a few weeks before he was to start at the University of Ottawa. Instead, he went to work at the paper mill in town, where his father had worked. When the paper mill closed, he got a job at the PPG car windshield factory. After work, starting in 1987, he coached the Hawks.

So Hartley had a big guy, a guy who was apparently willing to do whatever it took. But there was a catch to Gino: he had never really seen a practice before. At home, all he and his teammates had ever really done was scrimmage. "Scrimmage, that was our practice. You get to junior, these guys are skating around, flying around, doing all kinds of drills," Gino said on the Marjanovich podcast. "I was wondering what the hell is going on? So from there I figured out that I wasn't as good as the other guys were, I had to find a role to stick with the team."[18]

Gino quickly figured it all out. He figured out the drills. He got to work on his skating. And he learned how to be a tough guy. It didn't take long for him to discover he really loved getting into fights. In forty games that year, he picked up 167 penalty minutes—not quite a fight a night, but not far off. He also gained a nickname: the "Algonquin Assassin." The fights, though, aren't what you'd usually imagine a hockey fight to be, Branchaud says. "When he started, he was only wrestling really. He'd grab the guy and he'd flip him over. We wore full cages, so a fight wasn't that easy anyway."

Hartley had a lot of time for Gino. He saw how hard Gino worked, so he made him a promise. "He told me, you're not going to play much, but if you do this job for me, I'll get you drafted into major junior," Odjick told Marjanovich.[19] He'd get on the ice once or twice in a game, long enough to get in a scrap. Those moments won him plenty of affection among the Hawks faithful.

Hartley helped the Hawks rookie secure a proper outfit from a clothier in town; he was a big believer in having his youthful charges show up to games well dressed, that focusing on their attire would lead them to focus on their preparation for games as well. Gino was fond of telling a story about how, before just his fourth game for the Hawks, he had stumbled into Hartley's office, his new clothes torn and bloodied. Hartley was speechless about his newest player's ragged appearance. Then Gino flashed a big smile. "Come with me," he said, and led Hartley to the parking lot. Outside, standing next to his car, was Joe Odjick, Gino's dad, also casting a big smile. Joe popped open the car's trunk to reveal a freshly killed deer. For Gino's first few games, Joe would drive down to Ottawa, pick up his son, then drive him to Hawkesbury.

On this afternoon, they'd been driving to the game when they spotted the deer not far from the road. Presented with the chance to bag some fresh meat, Joe pulled over and shot it dead. Gino was tasked with retrieving the carcass. It wasn't far from the road, but he had to manage his way around a barbed-wire fence. "[Hartley] thought I'd killed someone," Odjick laughed.[20]

"I will never forget those two smiles, for a job well done," Hartley told *The Globe and Mail* years later. "To kill a deer and try to win a hockey game on the same day. Not many people can say they did that."[21]

Not long after that, Joe got his son a car, a little Dodge Colt, so Gino could get to and from Hawkesbury on his own. Michel also kept living in Ottawa, and the two would carpool out to Hawkesbury for practices and games. Gino jammed into the Colt, his big frame leaning on the steering wheel, was a funny sight, Michel says. Gino didn't like city driving either. "He wasn't as comfortable behind the wheel of a car in downtown Ottawa as he was dropping the gloves against a tough guy of another team, I'll tell you."

Late in the season, a number of players quit, and Hartley had no choice but to give the lanky kid from Kitigan Zibi more ice time. "I just played really hard and kept playing tough," Odjick told MacIntyre.[22] At the end of the season, Hartley kept his word, recommending Odjick to Laval. Junior coaches are asked for input by scouts from higher levels all the time. And the connection Hartley forged with Laval's brass in his rookie campaign would stand him in good stead, as the Titan hired him as coach a few seasons later, a big step forward in a coaching career that would eventually see him win the Stanley Cup in 2001 with the Colorado Avalanche.

IN LAVAL, a step up in skill and speed and profile, Odjick's path to the NHL started to accelerate, all because of Laval's skills-first coach, former NHLer Paulin Bordeleau. In his playing days, Bordeleau was a crafty, smooth-skating forward. Drafted by the Canucks in 1973, he played three seasons in the NHL, then jumped to the World Hockey Association's Quebec Nordiques, where he had the best scoring seasons of his North American professional career.

As a player, Bordeleau thought about the game a little differently than his contemporaries: the scrappy Canucks didn't know what to make of him. He got a chance to score early on but went into a slump, and Vancouver bumped him down the lineup. Asked to play a checking role, he pouted. Frustrated with his team, he could have let his time go to waste, and to a degree he did, but he also came to understand himself better. More and more, he saw how the game worked.

He scored in Quebec and a won championship there, but again learned how fickle pro hockey managers can be. When the Nordiques were one of four teams brought over to the NHL following the WHA's 1979 collapse, he was cast aside. He loved the game, but he found, as so many others have, that the game didn't love him back. He turned away from an offer to play for the Montreal Canadiens' farm team and instead took a whole year off from hockey. But in the summer of 1980, he moved to France and played in a professional league there for eight years. He even played for France at the 1988 Calgary Olympics. By the end of his career in Europe, he was a player-coach.

BORDELEAU AND ODJICK would be tied together in Laval by the Morrissette brothers, owners of highly successful construction and roofing materials businesses in Laval. They bought the Titan after a season of turmoil in 1987–88. The team featured three coaches and two GMs, plus a cumbersome ownership structure with a dozen investors. The Titan finished second in the division, and in the playoffs came a win short of making the final; it's remarkable the players found any success at all, given all the turmoil.

After a summer of talks about the future of the team, the Morrissettes were locked in as managing partners of the Titan in September 1988. They had been in the coalition of Titan owners since 1985. Over the next decade, seven Morrissette brothers would have business interests in three teams around the league. In Laval's case, five of the brothers invested in the Titan.

"They were real hockey fans," Bordeleau recalls. "They liked rough stuff. It was the 1980s! Anyway, the previous season, they had a coach, and things didn't go very well... They wanted some guys that were rough and tough."

The Morrissettes had made their money in Laval and were proud of their community. They coveted physical players because they believed that the fans of Laval wanted the team to be a reflection of their own blue-collar outlook on life. At the same time, the brothers believed the Titan could win championships and not just the hearts of the fans. But to do so, the team needed stability, as they and everyone else could see. They needed a coach they believed in.

In the off-season, the Morrissettes urged GM Richard Lafrenière to bring in Bordeleau, who had spoken with a few junior teams about returning to Canada. To the Morrissettes, Bordeleau seemed an intriguing choice, so they offered him a chance to coach an up-and-coming junior team in Quebec. He wouldn't have to head back to Europe.

ODJICK WOULD CREDIT Bordeleau for seeing that the lanky, goofy kid from Kitigan Zibi actually had some hockey talent—that he wasn't just a goon. Gino bought in and worked relentlessly on improving his overall game. He once recalled how important Bordeleau was for his own growth as a player. "All his practices were about doing the skills," Odjick said. "He'd coached in Europe, where they were more focused on developing skills."[23]

Bordeleau also understood what young players needed to hear about how to find success as they moved into professional hockey. When he made it to the NHL in the early 1970s, he hadn't been ready for the challenge the world's top hockey league presented: for all the talent he'd showed for the Toronto Marlboros, the opponents there varied greatly in ability. In the NHL, there were no stragglers. All the players in the NHL are like you: the best players on their teams in junior. The ones who make the NHL are the ones who come to understand how to maintain what talent and skills got them this far—and then what can be improved. The adjustment is a big mental challenge. And Bordeleau came to realize he didn't deal with it very well. He'd come into the NHL with dreams to be rookie of the year, to win championships. That didn't happen. "I wasn't ready mentally to play at that level. Physically and skill-wise, I was there, but it's not an easy place," he says.

"A lot of guys are ready to take your spot if things don't go well and that's what happened to me."

By the time he arrived to coach in Laval, he'd come to understand why the NHL had proven to be such a struggle. He figured he could help these young players on the Titan recognize how they had to keep working to make themselves better, even after they'd made the NHL. They needed to hear the truth. He was tough, but honest and fair.

"That's how I wanted to be treated when I played: fair," Bordeleau says. "I wanted to help the young guys, I wanted them to achieve and to get to where they wanted to go. That was my goal: to make a young man better and help him along the way to play well and also to be a good human being as well. Eventually, they'll be married, have kids, have families."

When Odjick first arrived at training camp in Laval in the late summer of 1988, Bordeleau wasn't quite sure what to make of him, other than that he was a hulking kid who fit the bill for what the team's owners were after. "He had skates that were very old. They were all soft," the coach says. But Odjick kept up. "We had a few exhibition games and he played okay," Bordeleau says. "And he was tough. He got in a few fights." The Titan were a smaller team, so Gino's toughness won his coach over quickly. Gino, once he got comfortable, showed plenty of personality—a young man who marched to the beat of his own drum.

Late in camp, with a Friday-night exhibition game on the schedule and a morning skate too, Gino was nowhere to be found. "We had no idea why. He just left," Bordeleau remembers. Gino missed the game. Missed a weekend practice too. No word, no sign of Gino. When he didn't show up for a Monday morning workout, Bordeleau and the team started to worry. Obviously, it would have been disappointing if he'd quit and gone home. The coach saw something special in him.

And then, a day or two later, Odjick appeared. He walked into Bordeleau's office and dropped a couple of moose steaks on his desk. "Gino, where did you go?" a befuddled Bordeleau asked.

"Hunting," Odjick said, flashing his now-familiar grin. Bordeleau couldn't help but laugh. The player was back, and he had a pretty good reason for being away. "I couldn't say anything," Bordeleau says, almost four decades later.

Even if Gino could have been a better communicator, the coach quickly learned Odjick was no dummy. As everyone who came across him would learn, this guy was sharp.

"He was a real student of the game," Bordeleau says. "He wanted to learn. He wanted to play. He wanted to be a hockey player. And he didn't know how to get there. And so I said, 'Listen, we'll go step-by-step and see how it goes. First of all, you're going to have to be a better skater.' So we worked a lot on that. And as time went on, he started having confidence in his demeanour on skates. And eventually he was playing a regular shift. And he was a presence on the ice and in the dressing room. All the guys liked him a lot."

Because Gino wasn't very good at skating backward, Bordeleau kept him at forward, even sometimes putting him on a line with crafty forwards like Donald Audette. He wasn't graceful skating forward either, but his aggression more than made up for that.

Audette scored 161 points in 1988–89, leading the Titan to the QMJHL championship and then to the Memorial Cup. It was such an electric season that the Buffalo Sabres used a ninth-round pick on the little winger that summer. Audette moved up to pro hockey that fall and eventually skated in 735 NHL games.

Odjick and Audette would be lifelong friends, even in the years when they weren't teammates in the NHL. Only when the Montreal Canadiens traded for Audette late in the 2001–02 season, which proved to be Gino's final season in the NHL, were the two old friends finally reunited as teammates. But that's not to say Gino didn't do his best to look out for Donald anyway. They played for different teams from 1990 until 2002, but in those intervening dozen years, Gino would take notes about what was going on in his friend's games.

"If anything would happen with Donald, a cheap shot, Gino would get even when they played that team next," Bordeleau says. That happened a few times, Audette said. Like the time Edmonton's Craig Muni smashed Audette mid-ice during Audette's rookie season with Buffalo. The collision left Audette with a serious knee injury and knocked him out of the lineup just eight games into the campaign. He missed the rest of the season and the playoffs, though he was ready to play again at the start of the 1991–92 season. Odjick made sure to rub out Muni in a game later that season.

"That was for my friend," Gino apparently told Muni after the hit. A few seasons later, Muni found himself traded to the Sabres, where Audette was still playing. "Hey, your buddy came after me," Audette remembers Muni telling him. That's what it meant to be Odjick's friend. He was as loyal as could be.

AUDETTE WAS A hometown hero for the Titan. After starring in the Quebec midget hockey league for the regional Laval squad, he moved up to the Titan in 1986–87. His first season in major junior was relatively quiet, as he made his way into this freewheeling, high-scoring, fist-swinging league. His second year—the wild three-coach, two-GM 1987–88 campaign—was a big step forward: 109 points in just sixty-three games. If he'd been taller, he probably would have been picked earlier than the ninth round of the draft. Remember how Pat Quinn was on the hunt for big, tough wingers then? He wasn't the only NHL GM looking for big players to draft.

Odjick's first season with the Titan, 1988–89, was Audette's third. After his strong season in 1987–88, Audette was expected to lead the way under Bordeleau's leadership. It wasn't long before the winger made friends with Odjick, and not just because the newcomer was there to make life easier for Audette: it was also about something much simpler. In junior hockey, players who come to the team from afar end up billeting with local families. It's a long-standing tradition, one that provides young players living away from home with a supportive, familial environment.

Unlike many of his teammates, Audette was actually from Laval, so he just lived at home. Next door, Odjick found his billet family, the Davids, and he quickly became part of the Audette household too. Gino took a shine not only to Donald, but also to Donald's father, Claude, his mother, Veronique, and his brother Rich. But as in most of his interactions in those days, he kept quiet. In hindsight, it's clear he was just taking in information, learning, waiting for his moment to start speaking up. Waiting for the right time.

"At first, he was a shy guy," Audette remembers. "Every morning, he came and had breakfast at our place and had a coffee. But he didn't talk to anybody. He grabbed the paper and read it while he ate. My mom was always feeding him. He didn't say much. He just read his paper. And when he was done, he'd just say, 'Okay, bye.' But after a time, he got more comfortable with us." A paper to read, a mom to feed him—that felt just like home. And he also met a nice girl through the Davids, a young woman named Elizabeth Poon, who went to high school with Gino's billet-brother Dominic.

The 1988–89 season was Donald's last in major junior. The following year, the Sabres sent him to the AHL for his first taste of pro hockey, with the Rochester Americans. Donald won the AHL's rookie of the year award, scoring forty-two goals and eighty-eight points in seventy games. Rochester had a fabulous season too, winning their division in the regular season, then making it to the Calder Cup final against Springfield.

Audette starred for the Americans in the playoffs, scoring nine goals in fifteen games. But it wasn't enough: Rochester fell to the Springfield Indians 4–2 in the final. But that's not Audette's lasting memory of the series. No, what he remembers most from that series was how his dad and Gino drove down to Rochester, New York to watch what would be the final game of the series.

But here's the thing: the Calder Cup final and the Memorial Cup overlapped that year. Laval went into the 1990 Memorial Cup, held in Hamilton, with high hopes. They didn't take the final, but unlike in the 1989 Memorial Cup, they won a game at the 1990 national championship. And that was enough to put them in the semifinal against Kitchener. That game was on May 12. But they lost, ending the Titan's season.

Game 5 of the Calder final, between Audette's Americans and, again, Springfield, was on May 13. The Amerks lost

Game 5, at home in Rochester, 2–1 in overtime. Down 3–2 in the series, Game 6 back in Springfield was do-or-die. Normally, a playoff schedule sees games every other night. Sometimes there's an extra day off in the middle. But in this particular series, there was a five-day break between Games 5 and 6, presumably because the Springfield Civic Center had a previous booking.

Springfield, Massachusetts, is about a five-hour drive from Laval. Donald's dad, Claude, was going to be there. The five-day break meant that Gino was back in Laval before Claude left, and so the two of them were able to drive down together to watch from the stands. "If he liked you, he could do anything for you," Donald says. Gino and Claude would watch Donald's Americans lose 4–3 in overtime.

A month later, Gino was drafted by the Canucks. Aged twenty, he could have gone back to junior, but pro hockey was calling.

3

"THE BEST TIME OF OUR LIVES"

"THIS FINGER: tendons severed. A break in the hand, break in the wrist... right here," Gino said in a 2013 recording for *Trajectoires*, a Quebec TV hockey documentary, listing off the injuries he'd suffered over the years. He pointed to his hands, fingers, knuckles, and the rest of his body. "Severed tendons, broken bone, broken bone, dislocated fingers. My jaw popped out here, broken cheekbone, fractured skull, broken ribs, had problems at the wrist, broke a leg, got stabbed..."[24]

But that was at the end of his career. In September 1991, he returned to Vancouver ready to take on the NHL in a whole new way. With a summer of strength training and nearly a full season as an NHL rookie under his belt, he was brimming with confidence coming into the new season. Also with him was his girlfriend, Elizabeth, who had come from Laval to visit him the previous season and decided to stay.

Gino was refreshed and so was the team. In addition to shifting Stan Smyl to behind the bench ahead of the

1991–92 season, Pat Quinn continued to tweak his lineup. In the off-season, he flipped skilled but unhappy defenceman Tom Kurvers to the Minnesota North Stars for another experienced defenceman, Dave Babych, who would become a stalwart for the Canucks for most of the 1990s. Quinn also signed a pair of veterans with an eye toward reinforcing the dressing room's culture of positivity: centre Ryan Walter, who had grown up in the suburbs of Vancouver and who'd skated in more than nine hundred games to that point for Washington and Montreal. Quinn also coaxed defenceman Randy Gregg out of retirement to provide veteran guidance. Gregg had trained as a physician on top of winning five Stanley Cups with the Edmonton Oilers. Trevor Linden credits both Walter and Gregg with teaching him a lot about leadership, about how to act professionally in your practice and preparation, habits that had a positive impact on the whole roster, including Gino.

But the real key to 1991 was finally bringing dynamic scorer Pavel Bure into the fold. The Canucks didn't think Bure would be able to leave the Soviet Union until 1994 at the earliest, but then history intervened and Bure found himself in North America, ready to begin his NHL career. After nearly two months of work behind the scenes, Bure made his debut with the Canucks in early November 1991. Quite quickly, he formed a friendship with Odjick.

Bure added a whole new gear to the Canucks. He was a true rocket of a player, something that Vancouver hockey fans had never seen before. Every shift, he seemed determined to score. Suddenly, the Canucks were pushing not only toward playing a more entertaining brand of hockey, but also toward the upper echelon of the NHL. Bure still stands out as the most exciting player in team history and one of a handful of Canucks to be in the Hockey Hall of Fame.

Odjick's second season in the NHL went about the same as his first: lots of fights, lots of time in the penalty box, though he "slumped" a little. In his first season in the NHL, he averaged 6.6 penalty minutes per game. In season two, that rate slid a little, down to 5.4 minutes per game.

Despite this already declining trend in penalty minutes, 1991–92 was actually the most active fighting season of Odjick's career. According to data tracked by HockeyFights.com, after fighting twenty-two times in forty-five games in his rookie season, Gino kept up his rate of getting into a fight just about every other game, dropping the gloves thirty-three times in sixty-five games. Season three, 1992–93, was the last time he fought more than twenty times in a season. Even then, with his team firmly established as one of the league's powerhouses, Odjick's per-game penalties declined again, to 4.9 minutes game—or less than a fight per game, if you like, since the penalty for fighting is a five-minute major.

As he fought a little less frequently, Gino also made an effort to become a more complete player. His second season started on a high note, even before Bure's arrival: he scored on a penalty shot in a game against the Flames on *Hockey Night in Canada* on October 20, 1991. It was the first penalty shot of his life. "Heck, it's the first time I've ever had two breakaways in a game," Gino quipped to the *Province*'s Tony Gallagher.[25] He'd had a breakaway in the first period but hadn't scored. This second chance had come about because he'd been fouled from behind by the Flames' Al MacInnis as he was trying to shoot. Gino still got a shot off on Flames goalie Mike Vernon and nearly scored. Referee Dan Marouelli surprised many by pointing to centre ice, indicating a penalty shot rather than a hooking penalty. The left-shot Odjick looked left at first and then moved to his right, but still flipped the puck to his left, over the leg pad of Vernon.

Odjick said he'd taken the counsel of Canucks goalie Troy Gamble and team captain Trevor Linden, who advised him to go for a full deke only if Vernon came flying out of his crease to challenge him. Otherwise, look to take a proper shot, Linden said. "The puck started rolling at the blueline. I just looked to his left and shot the other way. It probably went in because it was rolling," Odjick said.

The goal sent the crowd into a frenzy. They loved their big, affable tough guy. Scoring goals wasn't new to him—he had scored seven in his rookie season—but to see him getting breakaways and penalty shots suggested his game was moving up to a new level. "I think he could run for election right now in BC," exclaimed *Hockey Night in Canada* commentator Chris Cuthbert, as Odjick pumped his fists in the air, threw high-fives to his teammates, and spun around and around and around on his skates in jubilation. Scored at 8:33 of the third period, the goal put the Canucks up 4–2 against their archrivals. Linden would score another to secure a 5–2 win for the Canucks.

Back home, there was a raucous group of Gino's friends and family watching the game. They'd gotten together in a bar in Maniwaki, and the place went nuts even before Gino scored, Gino's younger sister Dina Odjick recalls. Their hero had gone national.

After Gino got back to the bench and took a seat, Quinn went over to him and told him to get ready for the next shift. The crowd was going wild. He wanted him to feel the energy.

He deserved the reward of another shift. "I can't," Gino replied. "What do you mean?" Quinn said back to him. "I just can't!" Gino repeated himself. And so his coach asked him why. Gino admitted he was feeling very aroused because, right before he got back to the bench, a well-endowed woman had flashed him from the stands.

Taking down the Flames was also a big emotional moment, according to Linden. For years, the Flames had dogged them. They'd been a perpetual target for the Canucks, ever since that hard-fought first-round series in 1989. Now, two years later, with their lineup bigger and badder than it had been before, with the likes of Odjick, Sergio Momesso, Dana Murzyn, Gerald Diduck, and Robert Dirk, they were ready to give it back to the Flames, properly.

"Calgary, for lack of a better word, beat the hell out of us non-stop in prior years, not only on the scoreboard, but you know, they were big: Peplinski, Otto, Hunter, you go down the list. McCrimmon. Suter," Linden recalls. It meant a lot to beat the Flames. They would absolutely stomp the Flames at home again in March, an 11–0 drubbing of Calgary that announced a new order at the top of the Smythe Division.

How big was beating the Flames for Pat Quinn? Before the October game, Quinn had made a remarkable speech. "Not only you could smell Pat coming, because you could smell the cigar smoke before he came in the room, but once he entered... he was a big man," Linden recalls. "And he wore these cowboy boots. He would walk in the room and you could hear a pin drop. Whatever guys were doing, they stopped. Stopped taping their pads, stopped taping their sticks. He didn't have to say a word. Everybody just stopped. He walked in before that game and he talked to us about what it meant to be a Canuck. And I'll never forget: during the talk, he took his fist and he banged the top of the Gatorade jug. He had massive hands. And the top flew off! And then he finished the speech by taking his big cowboy boot in the middle of the locker room and stamping it down and twisting it in the ground as if saying, 'I want to crush these guys, like this.'"

IN JUNIOR, Gino had taken the directions of his coaches on new skills to learn, and he saw results pretty quickly. But he found developing his skills was a lot harder in the NHL. There was lots of practice time, but when your shifts were sometimes rare, finding opportunities for applied learning could be a challenge. He'd been drafted to be more than just a tough guy. To become this more complete player, he worked diligently in practice. His teammates all noticed him working on his game. But even with that effort, he didn't always deliver. By mid-season, he was a healthy scratch. Pat Quinn wanted more focus from Odjick, more attention to detail. Bure's addition, along with the roster moves Quinn made over the rest of 1991, had created a team that was contending to win the division. There was competition for spots now. Odjick had to be a dutiful all-around player. He would prove to be a work in progress for the next few seasons.

After he'd played all six games of the Canucks' 1991 playoff run, Gino was a bit player in the 1992 playoffs, appearing just four times. And then, in 1993, when the Canucks should have gone deeper than the second round, he skated in just a single playoff game. For all the security he might have offered in a regular season game, Quinn and his coaching staff looked elsewhere during playoffs when more was on the line. Odjick just didn't bring enough hockey to the table.

"It has been my biggest motivation," he told the *Sun*'s Archie McDonald the following November. He had work to do, he knew. "If I had played, I might have been satisfied, but if you don't play in the playoffs you haven't accomplished anything."[26] He'd spent that summer working on his conditioning. If he were fitter, maybe he'd concentrate longer, he thought.

"After six or seven minutes I used to lose the game plan," he told McDonald. "After four years maybe subconsciously things have begun to sink in." Obviously, head coach Quinn agreed, as Odjick spent much of the 1993–94 season on a line with Bure. What a season that would prove to be for Gino. Playing with his best friend, he'd score sixteen goals, a career high. Bure played the game at a pace that few could even dream of keeping up with. Odjick was like most: he didn't keep up. He didn't even *try* to keep up. But he did forecheck hard when he had to—a rare thing, since Bure usually in possession of the puck—and Gino otherwise kept his stick on the ice, in case a rebound popped out to him after one of Bure's audacious shots was stopped by the opposing goalie. If the rebound was there, Odjick would try to bury it.

Odjick's redeployment came with the arrival of more players who could fight, like Shawn Antoski, drafted the same year as Gino but who took a few seasons longer to make the show. Also veteran tough guy Tim Hunter was picked up off waivers from the Quebec Nordiques midway through the 1992–93 season.

Even if he was fighting less often, it was still hard to argue against the notion that, by the mid-1990s, Odjick was among the top five fighters in the NHL. He was a guy other teams feared; other teams made sure they had an enforcer in their lineup, lest he take a run at their skill players. He was so feared, in fact, it impelled another team to make a trade.

In a January 31, 1994, game against the Los Angeles Kings, Odjick had a field day. Every chance he got, he laid into Wayne Gretzky. Remember the notion that having your own tough guy would act as a safety valve, giving the other team's tough guy a target that wasn't your skilled teammates? Here was a genuine example of that principle playing out. The Kings had traded away Gretzky's long-time teammate and protector Marty McSorley the summer before. The Kings deemed the enforcer's big contract more than they could afford and flipped him to the Pittsburgh Penguins. Without a big guy to counter him, Odjick went hard at the Great One, catching Gretzky with a hit, or at least a glancing blow, whenever he could. He wanted Gretzky to feel his physical game. At the end of regulation, Odjick and Gretzky were spotted chirping at each other. Gretzky told Odjick that the next time he played, if Odjick took a run at him, Gretzky would use his stick to defend himself. Odjick told Gretzky that whatever the Great One did with his stick, Odjick would take the blow and then certainly wouldn't miss when he hit back. Odjick didn't think Gretzky would be able to hurt him much, but Odjick knew he'd hurt Gretzky.

After the game, and in the weeks to follow, reporters would ask Odjick why he had run after "Mr. Gretzky" so much. "Well, if Gretzky had taken $6 million instead of $8 million, there'd be money to have McSorley here," Gino would reply, with a grin. Years later, in the documentary *Ice Guardians*, Odjick revealed the origins of that line: it came from his pal Pavel, who had worked out the summer before with

McSorley in Los Angeles. According to Odjick, his friend told him during the season that he'd heard McSorley was unhappy in Pittsburgh, that he missed being in Los Angeles.

So Odjick figured he'd do his friend's friend a solid: he'd do what he could to get Kings management to see the light and bring back McSorley. Between the verbal potshot and the physical battering Gretzky had taken, the message obviously landed, because two weeks later, the Kings brought their former tough guy back in a trade with the Penguins. "I guess Gretzky will stop whining now," Odjick quipped to the *Province*'s Jim Jamieson. "Or he'll be whining to Marty instead of the referee."[27]

The next time the Canucks and Kings met, in Los Angeles on March 23, the two pugilists kept their hands to themselves. That night had another item on the menu: Gretzky's pursuit of Gordie Howe's all-time goals record. Fisticuffs would have spoiled the occasion. Gretzky got the record (with an assist from McSorley), but the Canucks won the game. The two squads were to meet again back in Vancouver four days later—and everyone knew how that would go. That night, McSorley went right for Odjick. The two scrapped, and afterward Odjick said he made a point of saying to his long-time opponent: "You're welcome, Marty."[28] Years later, a humbled McSorley acknowledged Gino's claim that his efforts brought McSorley back to the Kings. "I took it as a compliment," he says.

Odjick and McSorley had been pugilistic rivals for three-plus years at that point, but the veteran McSorley didn't really know the much younger Odjick that well. He was just a guy to greet at a faceoff, have a chuckle with and then maybe a fight. "It was a tough guy looking out for a tough guy," McSorley said. He was very grateful that Odjick had gone out of his way to try to help a guy he didn't know that well.

The 1993–94 regular season may have been a fun one for Odjick personally, but the playoffs didn't yield the experience he'd hoped for—again. The Canucks had started the season hot but cooled off as Bure's scoring dipped a bit because of a groin issue. In fact, the team as a whole struggled to stay healthy. They'd win a game or two, then swing back the other way into the loss column. It was a up-and-down season.

Quinn continued to tweak the roster. First he grabbed Martin Gélinas off waivers from the Quebec Nordiques, the second year in a row Quinn scooped a useful depth piece away from Quebec. Gélinas filled a valuable role that season as a hard-working checking-line winger, and in subsequent years he became a very good second-line scorer. The other move was another team-defining trade with the St. Louis Blues.

After a strong 1992–93 season when he scored thirty-eight goals for the Canucks, Petr Nedvěd was looking for a big raise. But Pat Quinn was known for playing hardball in negotiations. Nedvěd held out. After a while, it became clear that Nedvěd's NHL future lay elsewhere. Quinn kept telling reporters he was exploring trade options, but it wasn't until March 1994 that anything happened. In the interim, Nedvěd played for Canada at the Winter Olympics (he'd claimed refugee status in Canada after defecting from Czechoslovakia at a youth hockey tournament in Calgary in 1989). After the Olympics, Nedvěd, now technically a free agent, signed a deal with the St. Louis Blues. But the rules at the time said the Canucks were owed compensation, and an arbitrator sent centre Craig Janney from St. Louis to Vancouver.

Janney, though, refused to report, and after two weeks of drama, Quinn traded Janney back to St. Louis for three players: speedy defenceman Bret Hedican, rookie checking centre

Nathan LaFayette, and Jeff Brown, a veteran defenceman with a booming point shot.

The two defencemen changed the mix on the blueline. Brown immediately stepped into top minutes, buttressing a defence corps that already featured quality veterans in Jyrki Lumme, Dana Murzyn, Dave Babych, and Gerald Diduck. LaFayette was an unknown, but he quickly showed himself to be so useful that he changed how Quinn proceeded with his forwards. Even so, the Canucks limped into the playoffs. After back-to-back seasons as division champions, they finished as divisional runners-up—and in the new conference-first playoff format, they finished seventh in the West, which lined them up with the Calgary Flames, who were seeded second in the conference by virtue of winning the division.

The Canucks came into the series as underdogs: Calgary had scored twenty-three more goals on the season and given up twenty fewer. They'd rightly finished twelve points ahead of Vancouver on the season. Yet the Canucks won the first playoff game 5–0, in Calgary. The form card was out the window in the playoff opener, but then everything snapped back to form. The Flames blew away the Canucks 7–5 in Game 2, then won Games 3 and 4 in Vancouver, in both cases taking close victories on the backs of strong third-period performances. The Canucks looked set for a third-straight year of playoff disappointment.

The team wasn't playing well and neither was Gino. Odjick played in the first three games of the series but made little impact. He was a scratch for Game 4, which the Canucks also lost, putting them down 3–1 in the series. With his team facing elimination, Quinn turned away from his veteran tough guy and toward the more skilled José Charbonneau, who'd scored seven goals in thirty games as a depth winger for the Canucks in the regular season. On top of keeping Shawn Antoski in the lineup, bringing Charbonneau in and keeping Odjick as a scratch were telling choices.

Veteran centre Murray Craven was knocked out of the Canucks lineup for Game 5. Again, Quinn avoided bringing Odjick back in; instead he went like for like and called on LaFayette. Conceivably, Quinn could have moved Greg Adams to centre, who had played there occasionally before, but he had already shifted Trevor Linden from the wing to centre, so picking the young LaFayette made sense. But like the choice of Antoski, going with the inexperienced LaFayette was a reminder that Odjick may have come a long way, but when the chips were down, he still was found lacking.

Gino gritted his teeth and accepted his role. If the demotion bothered him, after working hard to become the player he thought could be useful in the playoffs, he didn't let on. And while Gino watched in street clothes from above, the Canucks roared back in their first-round series to defeat the Flames. They won Game 5 in overtime on a thrilling slapshot off the rush by Geoff Courtnall. They won Game 6 in overtime as well, this time with Linden banging in a rebound on a power play. And in Game 7, it was Odjick's buddy Bure who scored a glorious breakaway goal in overtime to win the series, the stuff of dreams. Bure had been sprung on his breakaway by Brown, who delivered a pinpoint pass through the neutral zone, hitting Bure in stride as the sniper accelerated into the Calgary zone. Bure deked out Calgary goalie Mike Vernon and pandemonium ensued.

It was an upset, but given the pedigree of these Canucks, it wasn't your usual upset. In those three series-clinching wins, the Canucks really looked like they were starting to click again, the promise of the previous two seasons had returned. Quinn's big, strong, skilful Canucks were ascendant.

One might think facing the hard-nosed Dallas Stars in the second round would be an opportunity for Odjick to return to the fray, but it wasn't. Quinn stuck with what had worked, making only one change, bringing the now-healthy Craven in for Charbonneau. From the beginning of the series, the Stars went after Bure, pounding him hard every chance they got. Bure infamously took his protection into his own hands in Game 2, elbowing Stars tough Shane Churla in the head away from the play, knocking Churla out cold. The replays made it clear Bure had pulled off a vicious act, but the referee had missed it live, so Bure escaped without a penalty. But neither the abuse of his star player, nor the star having to stand up for himself, prompted Quinn to bring Odjick back into the lineup. Not, at least, until Game 4, when Gino was swapped in for his pal Antoski. The Canucks won that game and Game 5, taking a rather easy 4–1 series victory in the end. Gino stayed in the lineup in the Western Conference final series against the Toronto Maple Leafs. The Canucks won that series pretty easily too, again needing only five games.

The Stanley Cup final presented the toughest test of them all: the New York Rangers, a skilled, deep, veteran, take-no-prisoners team led by Mark Messier. Despite the ease with which the Canucks had disposed of Dallas and Toronto, Quinn wasn't afraid to make a switch, and for Game 1 at Madison Square Garden, the veteran coach swapped his enforcers.

Antoski was back in, Odjick was out. The switch surprised many, but discipline was clearly the reason. Quinn saw Antoski as a better fit on the fourth line, as a penalty killer. Tim

Hunter was on the right wing on the fourth line, and he was also viewed as a good penalty killer. Odjick didn't kill penalties, but in theory he'd rounded out his game enough to be considered an option on one of the top three lines. It had been a while since he'd lined up with Bure, so a first-line role was out of the question. Gino might have been a third-line option, but with Quinn's team playing well and other players offering just a little more, the now more versatile Odjick still had no obvious spot to fill in the lineup.

All of Odjick's rivals for a depth-forward spot had a better case than he did. With LaFayette in the lineup as the third-line centre, Murray Craven moved to the wing. Sergio Momesso wasn't as good a fighter as Odjick, but he had always been a more complete player, so he wasn't coming out. Nor were high-paced scoring wingers Courtnall and Greg Adams. Martin Gélinas wasn't a fighter either, but his two-way play—smart defensively and with a nose for the net—kept him firmly in the lineup. Gino would never get onto the ice against the Rangers. He would be but an observer of one of the all-time great Stanley Cup finals, with New York winning in seven games. "I think when you get a chance to play on the first three lines, you really have to be focused," Odjick told the *Province*'s Frank Luba between Games 3 and 4 of the final. "Some days when you don't feel that good you have to try and find a way to work through it. The first 50–60 games [of the regular season] I was focused. Somewhere along the way, I lost my focus."[29]

The plane ride home after losing Game 7 in New York City was one of quiet devastation, Odjick recalled in his 2022 conversation with Bob Marjanovich. "But I was young and naive," he said. "I thought we're going to be back next year and we're going to win it! I thought we'd be back to the finals every second year or something like that."[30] It was not to be. The 1994 squad was the high-water mark for the Vancouver Canucks until a similar heartbreak in 2011, when they again lost the Stanley Cup final in seven games, that time blowing a 3–2 series lead.

THE 1994 CANUCKS are beloved to this day in Vancouver, but most of the big moments weren't Gino's. Not getting the chance to play was hard for him, but he never let on to that in public. The team mattered more. It always did for Gino. Ronning says the 1994 team was the tightest team he played with in his career, and Odjick was a big part of it.

"I never saw that," Ronning says of the possibility that Odjick was disappointed by his lack of playing time in the 1994 playoffs. "He was definitely there, just being the unselfish teammate once again. Never moping around. Just wanting us to win, wanting to win. I've been there, I mean, I've had to sit and watch, and I learned to be just happy for everyone and your time will come. And I think that's what Gino did. That gave guys even more respect. They knew how much he cared about everyone. He just wanted to win."

So Gino helped in other ways. He was a willing target for Courtnall's practical jokes. Sometimes he'd pull off a prank himself, but mostly he was just ready to laugh, and to laugh at his own misfortune at the hands of Courtnall. Example: the case of the mysterious sweet roll.

"Oh my god," Courtnall recalls, laughing. "So, we're in Edmonton having pre-game meal, and I cut open his bun, and I put a package of sugar in it with the paper, and he ate the whole bun. And so from then on, the guys kept asking Gino, 'Hey, how are the sweet rolls?'"

Often, when the Canucks had a practice on the same day that they were heading out on a road trip, they would get changed into their travel outfits in the small weight room next to the team's main dressing room at the Pacific Coliseum. "So I put a five-pound plate in the outside of Gino's bag, and he carried it for the whole road trip, and didn't know it was in there," Courtnall says, grinning. Then there was the time Courtnall cut the crotch out of Odjick's suit pants, Ronning adds with a laugh.

Courtnall had no fear of his much bigger teammate. He wasn't afraid to trick Gino into eating spicy food, like an entire dollop of wasabi. "Or the time we're in San Francisco. Gino's never had sushi before," Courtnall says. "They come out with this big tray of sushi. And I go, 'Chief, try the green stuff. It's unreal.' So he grabbed the whole thing, and he put it in his mouth, and all of a sudden he runs over to the serving counter and he grabs a jug of water, and he's drinking the water, and he goes, 'Courts! I'm gonna kill you tomorrow at practice!'"

Odjick's ability to cut the tension kept everyone loose. "We joked around, and he never got mad," Ronning says. "He never lost it. He just thought it was funny. There's all kinds of stupid stuff we did, but that speaks to his character too, and that's why our team was so good—because we were so close, we could have fun."

"It was awesome," Gino told Marjanovich in 2022. "The best time of our lives where we're getting paid to get in shape and to be the best that we can be. Like, where else do you get that? They're paying us to play a game. We used to get together on Sundays, go down to the No5 and watch football.

Great bonding with the guys."[31] (The No5 Orange is an infamous Vancouver strip bar.)

Other times, he'd get the guitar out and belt out a song or two. Remember: in his youth he'd dreamed of becoming a country singer. His love of music was something he got from his mother. "In my mom's side of the family, they all sang," Gino's sister Dina says. "My grandfather played violin. Every time there was a party, there was always music. Gino was a pretty good singer."

4

"MIKE, YOU CAN CALL ME STUPID . . ."

DESPITE ODJICK'S LACK of ice time during the 1993–94 playoffs, the Canucks still valued him highly and signed him to a three-year, $1.6 million contract in early September 1994. It was a statement of trust in a player who had grown so much in Vancouver. But his personal life was in turmoil. And it would spill out onto the ice.

The 1994–95 season was cut nearly in half after NHL owners decided to play hardball with the players, locking them out. It was a tough season for Gino: between suspensions and injury, he played just twenty-three games that season. On the ice, there were a few incidents that make more sense when you learn that things were starting to go wrong for Gino off the ice.

For starters, his home life was in disarray. After three years living in Vancouver, Elizabeth decided she couldn't handle life with Gino anymore. The couple had a child together, Joey, born in early 1992. Gino had tried to be a good father, but most of the child-rearing had fallen on Elizabeth. (Joey was Gino's fourth kid, after Ashley-Ann and Patrick, born to Gino's first girlfriend June Wawatie, and another son named Russell, born to a young woman Gino knew from back home, Doreen Decourcie.)

For Elizabeth, her family was a long way away, which was especially tough while dealing with a boisterous toddler. It was hard for her to get to know many people on the West Coast. There were so many lonely nights at home while Gino was out on the road. Plus she'd also hear about how hockey players were always swarmed by women. "I was young. I missed my family. And I heard some stories, so I wasn't sure. I never had proof, but I decided to leave him," she recalls. Her decision to stay in Montreal at the end of the summer of 1994 rocked Gino.

On-ice, his problems started in training camp, not long after he signed that contract extension. Before the lockout came in October, NHL teams went through their usual pre-season training camp routines. Players showed up, got in shape, and played exhibition games. Gino lost his head in a pre-season game against Los Angeles. Gino was just coming off the ice on a line change, to be replaced by Sergio Momesso. But rather than stepping off the ice, he spun around and committed just about the biggest NHL no-no in the book: he was an extra player on the ice and he got in a fight.

Up until 1987–88, it was not unusual to see whole teams on the ice in a bench-clearing brawl, after an on-ice altercation escalated past the boiling point. In the 1986–87 season, there were at least seven instances of massive multi-player melees in NHL games.

Fighting free-for-alls were even taking place at the World Juniors. This was also the winter of the notorious "Punch-up in Piestany," where the final game of the 1987 World Junior

Championship between the Soviet Union and Canada was called off after a relentless battle royale between the two teams couldn't be stopped by the officials, who gave up trying to restrain the players and instead turned the lights off in the building.

Bench-clearing brawls were a black eye on hockey, so the NHL brought in a new rule for the 1987–88 season that handed an automatic ten-game suspension to any player who left the bench to engage in a fight. And in September 1994, the NHL decided Gino had done just that.

Even though he actually hadn't yet left the ice, the NHL ruled that he was supposed to be on the bench following his line change. Gino, therefore, broke the spirit of the rule when he first speared and then fought Warren Rychel. The NHL suspended Odjick for ten games.

It was a raucous start for the Canucks' new head coach Rick Ley, who was promoted from assistant coach before training camp, taking over for Pat Quinn. Quinn said his hips were making it very difficult for him to stand behind the bench for those long periods required of a coach. Ley wasn't unknown to the team: he had been Quinn's bench lieutenant for the previous two seasons. And now he would have to serve the five-game coach's suspension as result of Odjick's infraction.

"I'm not mad at Gino," Ley told the *Vancouver Sun*'s Elliott Pap.[32] "Gino's role on this club is to be a policeman and he does a remarkable job of standing by his teammates, which is exactly what he was doing in this case. He has a tough job and he does it well and I'm sticking by him."

OCTOBER CAME, and after months of negotiations with the NHL Players' Association over a new collective bargaining agreement, the owners decided to lock out the players, insisting they wanted a salary cap to keep costs under control. The players said no. It took months to resolve the situation and get back to playing games on the ice. Meanwhile, Gino, newly single, partied. A lot. What else was there to do? A few of his teammates, like Jyrki Lumme, Sergio Momesso, and his buddy Pavel played some games in Europe while they waited for the powers that be to come to an agreement. A few NHL stars joined Wayne Gretzky on a barnstorming tour of Europe; others played in a special four-on-four tournament organized by the NHLPA in Hamilton, Ontario. But most stayed home, skating and practising as they could. The only playing Gino did during this period took place in nightclubs.

When the regular season returned in early January, Gino still had a suspension to serve. But with the interrupted season schedule reduced to forty-eight games from eighty-four, the NHL agreed to shorten Odjick's suspension too, down to six games. (Ley's ban was reduced as well.) Upon his return, he vowed that he'd learned his lesson. "I've got to be more disciplined. When you're suspended, you're not helping the team," he told the *Province*'s Jack Keating. "Sure, I'm going to fight. That's my job. But I'll pick my spots more... I'm just going to go out there and play my style and not take stupid penalties. I ain't going to change anything. I'll put pressure on the [defence] and hit them all every time I can."[33]

It was a pretty familiar take from Odjick, now in the third season of his efforts to be seen as an all-around player. Things had changed in the second half of the previous season, 1993–94. After he'd burst from the gate, taking up his opportunity to play with Bure, his scoring had fallen off in the new year. He scored fourteen goals in the first half of the season, most of them alongside Bure, but then, pushed down to third- and fourth-line duty, he scored just two down the stretch. These struggles, plus his minimized role in the 1994 playoffs, were front of mind among the Canucks' brass the following season. At the same time, Quinn and Ley clearly valued Odjick's character, even after they once again displayed uncertainty about Gino's playoff utility. They held on to Gino in the spring of 1995 and traded Antoski to the Flyers.

Gino got back in the lineup after his suspension, played for about a month, then suffered a groin strain. He missed six games, returned to the lineup, but then, two weeks later, he was out again with an abdominal problem. The issue would keep him out until Game 5 of the first round of the playoffs against St. Louis.

Game 6 of that series included the incident Gino is most remembered for that season: when he ended up stripped of his helmet, gloves, jersey, shoulder pads, elbow pads, and undershirt, chasing the Blues' Glenn Anderson around the ice. With St. Louis leading 8–2 and Vancouver backup goalie Kay Whitmore in net, Odjick and his teammates took great exception to Anderson aggressively poking at the puck under Whitmore late in the third period. Anderson was already on the Canucks' radar: in the second period of the game, he'd caught young Canucks defenceman Mark Wotton in the eye with his stick. Wotton, a rookie, had played well in the series, but the eye injury would end his playoffs. And in Game 3 of the series, Anderson had high-sticked Bure in the face, drawing blood. Anderson was tossed from that game for his high stick, but after he injured Wotton, the Canucks were incensed, especially because Anderson had a reputation. He had been suspended twice in the past for vicious use of his stick: four games in 1991–92, eight games in 1985–86. He had also been fined in the 1988 playoffs for a stick-swinging incident. So when Anderson made his dig for the puck under Whitmore in Game 6, the Canucks' hair-trigger reaction wasn't a surprise. Odjick leaped across the crease to land a punch on Anderson. Captain Trevor Linden leaped on Anderson too, feeding the winger more than a few punches.

Odjick was peeled off Anderson, got himself loose, and went to whale on Anderson's teammate Bill Houlder, despite Houlder being down on all fours on the ice. A crazed-looking Odjick then skated around in circles, landing random punches on random Blues, who by this point had all paired off with Odjick's teammates.

Burly Blues centre Adam Creighton got himself loose and confronted Odjick, and after a brief standoff, the two big men started to fight. It was in this altercation that Odjick lost all the gear from his torso and arms. Initially, he looked to be in trouble against the towering Creighton, but once his equipment was gone, the tables turned and Odjick fired punches into Creighton, who dropped to the ice and covered himself up, now unwilling to fight back.

And then Odjick found Anderson, who had finally gotten back to his feet in the melee. Anderson had never been known as a fighter, but Odjick chased him. Rather than dropping his stick and gloves, Anderson simply kept backing up, waving his hands, dismissing Odjick. So the officials escorted Odjick off the ice.

"With seven minutes to go in the game, Anderson goes out and blasts Whitmore in the ribs. Sooner or later you've got to do something about it before he kills somebody," Odjick said after the game. "If you wanna live by the sword you've gotta die by the sword. And that's what happened."[34]

The damage to Wotton's eye was so concerning that he spent the night in the hospital. He was eventually diagnosed with a detached retina. "The main guy I wanted to get was Anderson," Odjick added. "The other guys on the ice play honest hockey, not trying to slash in the face like Anderson. I got him a couple of good shots when he was on the ice at the beginning there. I felt it would be kind of a shame to go after him when he was all cut up and beat up at the end, so I just skated off the ice. There's always next year."[35]

Odjick also wasn't impressed that the league hadn't done anything about Anderson's slash of Bure in Game 3. "They go out there slashing guys, trying to hurt 'em. The league has done nothing about it," he said. "Anderson slashed Pavel in Game 3 and he pretty near took Wotton's eye out. If he's going to try and hurt people, well, that's what I'm here for."

Anderson finally did draw a suspension from the league for his whack of Wotton. Former Canucks assistant general manager Brian Burke was now the NHL's disciplinarian, and he suspended Anderson for Game 7 of the series, calling Anderson's use of his stick "reckless." Burke had even stronger words for Odjick, whom he had helped guide into the NHL. Gino had been assessed two game misconducts on the play where he went after Anderson, so a one-game ban was in the offing. And Burke went further, suspending Odjick for a second game. "The manner in which he physically challenged virtually every St. Louis player on the ice clearly crosses the boundary of what is acceptable in the NHL," Burke said in his ruling.

The Canucks won Game 7 pretty handily, racing out to a 3–1 first period lead on two power-play goals and one shorthanded goal, taking the game 5–3 in the end. They weren't as coherent in their play as they'd been the year before, but they were through to the second round to play the Chicago Blackhawks. Gino had to sit out Game 1 because of his suspension.

He was back in the lineup for Game 2, but the Canucks, dealing with injuries to key players like Jeff Brown and Martin Gélinas, struggled to put up much of a fight against the Blackhawks and ended up losing the series in four straight games. It was a difficult follow-up to the sensational ride of the 1994 playoffs.

Odjick's wild, shirtless skate around the ice against the Blues remains one of two lasting memories from that post-season, the other being Trevor Linden's spectacular body-check of Blues defenceman Jeff Norton through the glass. Odjick's scene may have sent the fans into a frenzy, but things were not going well for him. That summer, he revealed he'd been struggling, badly, with alcohol abuse.

The Canucks' season had ended May 27. The next day, Gino went on a seven-day drinking binge. At the end of it, he said, he had a vision. He left his body and went to the Spirit World, he said. "He saw a black tunnel and a light, and then two native riders appeared, garbed in eagle feather," the *Province*'s Roberta Staley wrote in a July 28, 1995, article. "'Both horses were reddish—blood red,'" Gino told Staley. The riders told him his drinking was self-destructive. "They asked me if I wanted to continue living," he said. "They said if I died here, I'd die embarrassed. I'd die drunk... They said: 'It's not right. You're a role model for the First Nations people. You're destroying that.'"[36]

The vision shocked him back to his senses. He had to quit drinking, he realized. And he needed to take on an adventure to feed his spirit. So he began organizing what he came to call his "Journey of Healing." Over twenty days in August 1995, he'd venture nearly a thousand kilometres, trekking along a meandering route from Calgary to Musqueam, an Indigenous reserve on the southwest corner of Vancouver. It was a journey from the mountains to the ocean, by foot and vehicle, meeting with First Nations groups along the way, raising awareness about the devastating effects of substance abuse, hoping to meet with young people to encourage them in their education and showing them a way forward. "I'm just a little boy from the rez, look how far I got," he'd say.

On the journey, he'd be joined by friends, teammates, and on-ice foes, including Calgary Flames tough guys Sandy McCarthy and Rocky Thompson, best friend Pavel Bure, as well as Stan Jonathan, Gino's childhood hero, an Indigenous NHLer who had been one of the toughest guys on the 1970s Boston Bruins.

Gino had worked at hockey schools almost from the day he'd made the NHL, so working with Indigenous youth was nothing new to him. He knew that young Indigenous people were now looking up to him, just as he'd looked up to Jonathan in his own youth. Drugs and alcohol, he knew, were a huge problem. "Kids are killing themselves with it. On my reserve, all over BC they give up on life because they're drunk or stoned," he told the *Province*'s Jim Jamieson a few weeks after completing the trek.[37]

Maybe, out of his moment of crisis, he could connect with young people more broadly, go beyond the young athletes he'd encounter at hockey camp. His Journey of Healing would be the beginning of a major personal mission in the second half of his life: speaking with Indigenous youth, helping them find inspiration in his story and in themselves. He came out of his trek feeling reborn.

THE CANUCKS AS a whole thought they were set to be reborn, but it was not to be. Quinn traded for Alexander Mogilny, a supremely gifted winger, in the summer of 1995, thinking that what his core from the 1994 run needed was another potent scorer. Mogilny, a former junior teammate of Bure's back in the Soviet Union, had a marvellous season, but Bure blew out his knee early in the season and the rest of the team stumbled through much of the campaign. Instead of finding themselves set up at a high-altitude camp, close to the summit of the NHL, the Canucks went into decline. The struggles of the 1995 playoffs would prove a warning sign.

Going all-in trying to build a team that focused on scoring, Quinn had misread where the NHL was heading: instead of high-skill, high-speed hockey leading the charge, the league was being taken over by what became known as the "clutch-and-grab" style, a defence-first approach that figured referees couldn't possibly call every infraction. So why not hook and hold as much as you could? Big, strong defencemen became essential players on NHL rosters. It didn't matter if they could skate, they just had to be strong so they could keep opposing forwards from getting to the net.

The Canucks weren't built like that. They were built to play fast, with skill, looking to outscore the opposition. This new style of play didn't faze Odjick, but the Canucks stumbled through the season. Odjick fought way less than he ever had, partly because the Canucks had added a new young tough guy named Alek Stojanov, and partly because this new Gino wanted to be closer to the player he'd been in the first half of the 1993–94 season, when he was skating with Bure and bagging goals, and less the wild man who'd finished the 1994–95 season without a shirt.

Bure was lost for the season with a torn ACL, but the offence that Quinn had built was pretty resilient. Even without the "Russian Rocket," the Canucks proved pretty adept at scoring goals. But the defence just wasn't good enough. The Canucks slumped to a first-round exit at the hands of the Colorado Avalanche, who would go on to win the Stanley Cup. For Gino, the series wasn't a total writeoff: after playing twenty-seven playoff games without a goal, in game twenty-eight—Game 2 versus Colorado—he scored twice. He added a third later in the series. Gino, though, wouldn't play another playoff game for six years, for the Montreal Canadiens. And the Canucks wouldn't play another playoff game for five years, well after Gino's time in Vancouver had come to an end.

The summer of 1996 would prove to be a real turning point in the fortunes of the Canucks. Behind the scenes, a gap had emerged between Quinn and new owner John McCaw, who'd bought out Arthur Griffiths over the previous year. McCaw was keen for Vancouver to sign the biggest fish in the sea: free agent Wayne Gretzky. The Great One had lost a step at age thirty-five but McCaw and his key lieutenant Stan McCammon figured putting No. 99 on a Canucks jersey would put bums in seats—and bums in seats are, well, the aim of the business. Quinn, though, wasn't convinced it was a good hockey decision. Nevertheless, he went along with it because the owner wanted to and he was the one who paid the bills.

As is well known now, Gretzky very nearly did sign with the Canucks. A late-night meeting in McCaw's Seattle offices between the Canucks and Gretzky's camp ended in a verbal agreement that the Great One would land in Vancouver. Gretzky said he'd sign the proposed contract in the morning. But McCammon insisted that Gretzky sign the contract then and there, before everyone went to bed. The Canucks, it's become clear, figured that if Gretzky didn't sign right away, he might take the Canucks offer and use it as leverage to work out an even better deal with the New York Rangers. Although he did end up signing with New York a day later, Gretzky has always insisted that he genuinely considered the Canucks offer, that he and his family wanted to live in Vancouver. Whatever the case, Gretzky refused the late-night demand, and the Canucks announced the next morning that the deal was off.

The Gretzky debacle occurred a couple weeks after the Canucks let Ronning walk as an unrestricted free agent. They couldn't justify the salary he was due, the team told reporters. Maybe they'd hoped that Ronning, who'd proven to be fiercely loyal to his hometown team, would accept a lower salary. Ronning signed with the Phoenix Coyotes, and when Vancouver didn't land Gretzky, the Canucks were suddenly badly undermanned at centre. Yet even without Ronning, without Gretzky, with a less confident Bure struggling to score, the Canucks as a team could still score. The big problem was they couldn't defend, so they missed the 1996–97 playoffs.

Everything would turn loopy in 1997–98, both for the Canucks and for Gino. The Canucks started the season with plenty of excitement. In the off-season, a year after missing out on Gretzky, ownership turned their sights toward Mark

Messier, former captain of the Rangers, who had beaten the Canucks in 1994. But Quinn, again, was somewhat skeptical of the whole enterprise: Messier was already thirty-six. Even in the 1990s, managers knew that a player that age was soon going to be squeezing the last juice out of his career. Still, Messier had scored eighty-four points the previous season for the Rangers, so he seemed to have something left in the tank.

But the signing didn't work. Messier played well enough, but the problems on the blueline remained. Quinn had signed super prospect Mattias Öhlund to a deal, but the rest of the blueline corps looked far too similar to seasons past, and when you don't renew your defencemen, the group can get old, fast. The Canucks just weren't good enough on defence anymore.

A crisis in goal had developed too. Kirk McLean, who'd been the Canucks' No. 1 goalie for much of the previous decade, didn't have quite the same puck-stopping magic that he once did. McLean had shared the net for the previous two seasons with Corey Hirsch, a former junior star who'd been a standout for Team Canada during the 1994 Olympics. Quinn thought Hirsch might become the Canucks' main netminder—the venerable McLean couldn't be the No. 1 forever.

Hirsch had played pretty well in the 1995–96 season, supplanting McLean as the team's lead goalie at times. But 1996–97 was a disaster for Hirsch as he struggled with serious mental health issues. His 2022 memoir *The Save of My Life: My Journey Out of the Dark* goes into great detail about his battles with obsessive-compulsive disorder. Quinn was forced to look for alternatives. Little Latvian goalie Artūrs Irbe was brought in, took Hirsch's job, and proved to be a steady alternative to McLean.

After a horrendous start to the season, Quinn told ownership it was time for him to fire coach Tom Renney, whom Quinn had hired before the previous season as a replacement for Rick Ley. Instead, ownership chose to fire Quinn on November 4, 1997, while the team was on the road in Washington, DC. It was the beginning of the end of that era of Canucks hockey. The team Quinn had assembled couldn't win, even with the addition of Messier and Öhlund.

Quinn's dismissal rocked the dressing room. The players who had been with him for much of the previous decade remained fiercely loyal to him. They had let him down in the worst way and were devastated. "It's hard to take. He was a man's man," Gino lamented to the *Province*'s Terry Bell after the boss was let go. "He wasn't too friendly with [the media], but he sure was with us. I think I speak for every player when I say we really respect him a lot. He's one of those few people who are always in your mind. He had an Indian way of thinking. He never said or did anything without first really thinking about it."[38]

Renney held on for a little while longer, but the team kept losing, so Renney too, was let go and replaced as coach by Mike Keenan. "Iron Mike" was Messier's idea. The coach's abrasive, confrontational style clashed with just about every roster he'd worked with, and it clashed very badly with the Canucks, who were used to a much more player-friendly approach under Quinn. Head scout Mike Penny was familiar with Keenan. In the 1970s Penny ran the OHL's Kitchener Rangers and Keenan was just starting out as a coach in junior B. Two decades later, Penny was one of Quinn's lieutenants with the Canucks and stayed on after the boss was fired. Keenan was originally hired as coach but he'd been coach and GM in his previous job with St. Louis and was angling to get a similar title with the Canucks. Instead ownership declared that Keenan, Penny, and director of player personnel Steve Tambellini would run the team in an unwieldy triumvirate. Working with Keenan didn't change Penny's opinion. "One of the worst people I ever worked with in hockey," he says. "I just went around and did my own thing. He was hard on players he didn't like, like Trevor [Linden]. It was chaotic."

Keenan had berated Linden in front of his teammates during a game in St. Louis. "'You shut up! You don't have a word to say. You're not a leader on this team,'" Odjick recalled Keenan saying to Linden. Gino also criticized Messier for not speaking up in defence of his new teammate. "It was just awful," he said.[39]

Keenan had no viable solutions for the floundering Canucks. He pushed to trade much of the team. The squad did need rejuvenation, but Keenan did it in such an aggressive and, at times, spiteful way that it caught everyone off guard.

He began by trading Kirk McLean and Martin Gélinas to Carolina. He would later trade away Dave Babych to the Flyers. And on the eve of the Olympic break—when NHLers were set to play in the Olympics for the first time—Keenan traded fan favourite Linden to the New York Islanders for a pair of young players, Bryan McCabe and Todd Bertuzzi, and a draft pick. A decade after Linden had been drafted and become the face of the franchise, it was clear that era was truly over.

At the trade deadline, it was Odjick's turn. He was traded to the Islanders, rejoining his old captain. Odjick claimed to the *Province*'s Tony Gallagher a few weeks later that Messier was the real problem, not Keenan. He didn't like the coach but knew that he wanted to win. But Messier had coasted early in the season, Gino insisted. That was the main reason that Quinn and Renney lost their jobs.

In Odjick's eyes, this was not a leader who was helping bring his team together. This was not what he expected from a player hailed as the greatest leader in hockey. "I'm nobody. I'm not the kind of player who can carry a team or make a big difference," he told Tony Gallagher in 1998. "I haven't won six Stanley Cups, but I've always been able to look everyone I've ever played with in the eye. I've been honest and I've got to be honest. [Messier] just wants to destroy everything so he gets the power. Everyone is brought in to play for Mark."[40]

When asked at the time by Iain MacIntyre about Odjick's comments, Messier shot back. "Gino is one of the most giving, kindest men in the game," the captain said. "But I think this is a lot more than Gino Odjick coming forward. I think there's a lot of people who don't have the courage or guts to say it to my face and they used Gino as a vehicle to do it. It shows you the kind of people who were here and why we needed the changes. There was a real comfortable group of players here that weren't doing the things to be successful."[41]

Linden was deeply touched by the way his old friend Gino stood up for him against Keenan. "He was a loyal person," he says. "For him to do that for me, it's very meaningful." Years later, Odjick would say that Messier was immediately critical of his new teammates, accusing them of being too relaxed, too much like a country club. For Odjick, it was a stunning take from a leader with his reputation. "Right from the bat, he didn't believe in our group," Odjick told Bob Marjanovich.[42] It has been suggested that Odjick's defence of Linden landed him on the coach's bad side, though it's obvious Gino chose to take the high road.

In his 2024 autobiography *Iron Mike: My Life Behind the Bench*, Keenan acknowledged that Odjick had stood up for Linden, but didn't connect it to Gino's subsequent trade. Still, the fiery coach was critical of the culture he found when he arrived, echoing Messier's criticisms. The large group in the dressing room who were holdovers from the 1994 cup run was too comfortable, he believed, concurring with the guy who'd captained Keenan's Rangers to victory over the Canucks in 1994. "They were not in good shape compared to elite NHLers and in terms of the levels I demanded for my teams," he wrote. "And the atmosphere was far too relaxed, like they were still living off the accomplishment of losing in Game 7 of the Stanley Cup final a few years earlier."[43]

It's worth noting that criticizing the fitness level of your new players is something many coaches say when they take over: it's an convenient thing to scapegoat if your team is continues to struggle after a coaching change. It's an easy delaying tactic—of course, what you're risking as a coach is that the changes you think need to be made may not matter, whether the players are fit enough or not. At the end of the day, if your team isn't talented enough—or they simply don't believe in their coach—no amount of effort is going to make a difference. (Keenan's changes didn't turn the Canucks' fortunes around, and he would in fact be fired halfway through the next season by new general manager, Brian Burke.)

Keenan also criticized Pat Quinn in his book. He acknowledged that Quinn was a "terrific coach and manager," but Keenan felt his predecessor had kept certain players for too long. "I thought he overextended their time as Vancouver Canucks. You can't hang on to players forever."[44]

Keenan had tried to make similar comments about Quinn in front of the players, but Odjick wasn't having it. He confronted Keenan, warning him that insulting Quinn was a line he shouldn't cross. Over the years, Gino recounted the story a few times. According to him, this is what he said: "Mike, you can call me stupid. You can call me a stupid Indian. But don't ever talk like that about people I respect."

If Keenan couldn't respect that line, he would have an issue with Odjick. In Gino's version of the incident, Keenan shut up quick. Gino's sister Dina laughs about the tale, which she certainly heard more than once. There was little doubt in her mind that her brother had no time for Keenan. "Gino would have told Mike Keenan that there was only two of them in the office, and you knew which one was going to walk out," she says.

Linden wasn't surprised Gino stood up for Quinn. "Pat had his back," Linden says. It was a common thing for Quinn. He cared about all his players, but he had an especially strong bond with Odjick. Players who hadn't been given a chance elsewhere, like Ronning or Momesso or Dirk—he gave them a chance. "He afforded them so much confidence that they recognized how much they owed to them. I'm the same way. I think Gino was the same way," Linden says.

GINO'S CAREER WOULD carry on, first with the Islanders, then with brief stops in Philadelphia and Montreal. Gino's arrival on Long Island was a relief to Linden, the former Canucks captain says. He'd been living at the Long Island Marriott since the trade, which is across from a massive parking lot near the Nassau Coliseum, home rink for the Islanders at the time. Gino was more than a familiar face, he was a fellow traveller. He understood what had come to an end in Vancouver. And, of course, he had his remarkable spirit, one that lifted up everyone in his company. "We're in this place that neither one of us really knew how we got there," Linden says with a laugh. "We have this bond. We're both going through the same thing, we're both mourning the loss of the team we played on. And we're both pissed off at what happened and how it happened."

Gino also found comfort of a different kind in that Marriott: Jolene Commanda, his girlfriend from Kitigan Zibi and mother to his sixth child, Bure, named for Gino's best hockey friend, born the fall before. At first Gino, Jolene, and baby Bure lived in the Marriott, but they soon realized more space and comfort was required for family life. After a little while, Gino announced he'd found a place to rent—the home of Gerald Diduck, his former Canucks teammate. Diduck had played for the Islanders a decade before, at the beginning of his career, and had held on to the home even as he meandered through the league, first to Montreal, then Vancouver, Chicago, Hartford, Phoenix, Toronto, and finally Dallas. The young family would live there until early 2000, when Gino was traded to Philadelphia.

On the road with the Islanders, Odjick and Linden ended up being roommates. They became closer friends than they'd ever been with the Canucks. They played a full season together in New York in 1998–99, with Linden as the team's captain. Odjick was looked to for veteran leadership by the team's coach-GM Mike Milbury. Despite the big opportunity, the 1998–99 season was a dud for Gino. In early December he suffered a trio of abdominal tears, an injury that required surgery, putting Gino out for the rest of season. As for Milbury, he was a bit of a madcap manager who was constantly making trades, constantly flipping his roster in surprising ways. Halfway through the season, with his team stumbling along, Milbury resigned as coach, a day after he'd accused his players of quitting. It was the second time he'd stepped down as coach: he'd done the same thing two years before. Then he'd put himself back behind the bench, just six games into Linden's time as an Islander.

Gino's life as an Islander was comfortable, but the public profile was definitely different. In Vancouver, he'd been king of the castle. On Long Island, he was just another guy. Die-hard Islanders fans might have recognized him out in public, but it was still a far cry from his celebrity status in hockey-mad Vancouver, where he'd regularly get asked for photos and autographs on the street. And while he was a valued veteran in the Islanders' dressing room, he was wearing a different number: he wore No. 24, because defenceman Kenny Jönsson was already wearing 29 when Gino joined the team.

Behind the scenes, the Islanders were as chaotic as Milbury's roster management. The summer before Linden and Odjick became Islanders, the team's new owner, John Spano, was revealed as a fraudster. Long-time owner John Pickett, who thought he had sold the team to Spano the previous fall, was forced to retake the helm and provide some temporary stability. With the NHL's help he managed to sell the team quickly to new ownership: a trio of colourful businessmen in Steven Gluckstern and the Milstein brothers, Howard and Edward. They initially suggested they were ready to invest in the team, by trading for players like Linden, for example. But with the

Islanders struggling to attract fans to their dilapidated arena, and burdened with a bad lease, the owners quickly switched to austerity. At one point, there was noise the Islanders might move to Hartford, which lost the Whalers to Raleigh, North Carolina, in 1997. The Islanders didn't move, but they did trade Linden to the Montreal Canadiens. Gino, meanwhile, remained an Islander for another year.

Again, he got a regular shift in 1999–2000. And he felt especially responsible for protecting the team's young players. In a game on December 30, he sucker-punched Pittsburgh defenceman Darius Kasparaitis after the burly Penguins defenceman put a dangerously low hit on young Islanders centre Tim Connolly. Kasparaitis suffered a concussion, and Gino was suspended by the NHL for eight games. "I thought I gave him what he deserved," Odjick commented to the *Hockey News*. "And I got what I deserved. I thought he went out of his way to hit Tim. It was one of those things that to me was crossing the line."[45]

Gino was soon on the move again. He was flipped to the Flyers at the 2000 trade deadline. The Islanders were dragging at the bottom of the league, while the Flyers had Stanley Cup ambitions. The chance to play for a contender again excited Gino, and Flyers GM Bobby Clarke was delighted to add another tough guy. "If you're going to go to war, you have to have the weapons. Our preference is for all these guys not to take penalties but to play clean and hard. By having this muscle in our lineup, there will be less reason for other teams to want to mix it up with us," Clarke told the Associated Press after picking up Odjick.[46] Jolene and young Bure moved with him.

Despite the hopeful words from Clarke, Gino proved to be just a bit player with the Flyers and didn't dress for a playoff game. "I'm a plane crash away from starting tonight," Gino quipped to reporters at one point during the playoffs, about how far he'd fallen down the Flyers' depth chart.[47]

He was back with the Flyers the following season. But the pre-season didn't go as planned: Gino suffered a bad facial injury and concussion during an on-ice workout. The team was doing some skating drills when Gino stumbled and fell, hitting the opening for the bench door and then rolling over and smashing his face on the ice. He cut up his mouth, tongue, and jaw. His face was all stitched up and his concussion was so bad that he spent a week in bed. He survived on milkshakes and Popsicles. And he was spitting up blood clots all the time.

In 2014, at a head-injury symposium in Vancouver, Gino told the audience how he struggled just getting around town after the concussion. "People just looked like Martians. They looked like they were from another planet. I couldn't remember how to get to the rink," he said. "I was totally forgetful. I couldn't remember what time it was, what I was supposed to be doing. It was just one turn to the right, one turn to the left to get to the rink, but I got lost just going there. Everybody wanted to play me in the simplest of card games because they knew they could beat me."[48]

Once the season began, Gino told his coaches he was ready to play. But he still didn't have a big role and played only seventeen more games for Philly before he was traded to Montreal in December 2000. As if things couldn't get more complicated—the day after the trade, Jolene gave birth to their second child, a boy they would name Tobias.

Playing for the Canadiens was something of a thrill, of course. After growing up in Quebec watching the fabled Habs, playing for them was a childhood dream come true, even if he'd been a fan of the Bruins' Stan Jonathan. On many nights in Montreal, he got to play in front of his parents and his kids. "I remember it was the best I ever played," Odjick told Marjanovich. He was asked to play on the third line by Canadiens head coach Michel Therrien, a role he'd relished under Quinn, but which Keenan hadn't given him. He'd gotten lots of ice time in Long Island, but in Philadelphia he had been a bit performer. "I went seven games one time without taking a penalty," he said of the smart game the Canadiens looked to him to play.[49]

Playing for Therrien was a great fit for Gino, says his pal from junior hockey days, Donald Audette, who would become Gino's teammate again, joining the Canadiens via trade early the 2001–02 season. Gino and his coach had something in common beyond hockey, Audette says with a laugh. Like Gino, Therrien was a well-known smoker. They'd smoke together in Therrien's office. The abrasive coach and the lovable tough guy got along great. Gino would offer himself up as a coach's target, because he thought it would help the team's culture. "He used to go in the office, tell the coach, you know, 'You come into the room and give me shit because I took a penalty. Don't be afraid: it's gonna wake up the players,'" Audette says.

Off the ice, Jolene and Gino's relationship was running into trouble. They moved into a home in Kahnawake, an Indigenous reserve just across the river from Montreal. But Gino had already been in Montreal on his own for a month or so by the time Jolene moved north with her two young boys, and Gino had settled back into a party lifestyle. All his friends were coming to visit him. Also, as a French-speaking player in Montreal, he was instantly popular with the French-language media. His gregarious personality was a natural fit for a hockey-mad market that always cherishes players who hail from La Belle Province.

He was back to being king of the castle. The mostly quiet life he'd led for the previous two-plus years in New York and Philadelphia was over. But then, in early January, Gino suffered a wrist injury in a game against his former team, the Islanders. Again, he needed surgery. Again, his season ended early.

Next year, his first full season in Montreal, wasn't easy on the ice either. Before the season, he signed a two-year deal, ready to do the job he'd always done. But a bad back slowed his start to the season, and in early November he was sent down to the minors for the first time since his first pro season, when he played in those seventeen games for Milwaukee, got called up by the Canucks, fought Dave Manson and Stu Grimson, and never looked back. Publicly, he maintained up his upbeat persona. But he was very, very frustrated. He was angry at Therrien, at Canadiens' management. He also wasn't handling home life with Jolene and the boys very well either. Those who knew him at the time say in hindsight his behaviours may have been early signs of the mental distress that would plague him in retirement. It's around this time that Jolene moved back to Kitigan Zibi, their relationship at an apparent end.

JUST BEFORE CHRISTMAS, Gino was called back up to the NHL. He may have been a mess off the ice, but on the ice he became a regular player again—until early February, at least. That month, after a poor game in Ottawa, he didn't head to the airport with his teammates: he went AWOL instead. The team suspended him and said they didn't know where he was.

As his relationship with Jolene was ending, he'd started seeing a new girlfriend, Caroline Forester. She knew where he was when the team declared him missing: at her place. She was there when he decided to walk out on the team. Originally from Maniwaki herself but a decade younger, she was a university student in Montreal, and she'd come to Ottawa to catch the game. When he left the Canadiens' dressing room post-game, she immediately saw he was upset.

"He walked out, and I could see it in his face," Caroline recalls. "I said, 'Are you all right?' And he's like, 'I'm done.' And I'm like, 'What do you mean?' He just said, 'Let's go.' Because obviously he was supposed to go in the bus. And I just said 'What?' again. And he's like, 'Let's go.' He says, just, 'Let's go.' So we're walking away, and he's obviously coming with me in the car. And then he just left, and then everybody's looking at him drive away. And I said, 'What are you doing?' He's like, 'I'm not getting humiliated like that. Being sat on the bench.'"

It was especially hard for Gino, because here was his good friend, Therrien, the head coach, benching him. So for the next few days he stayed with Caroline at her tiny apartment in Hochelaga-Maisonneuve, a very rough area in the east end of Montreal. "All this time he was in this dinky little apartment and on the TV they're like, 'Where is Gino? Where is he?' And we're watching it," she said. "And so I said, 'Gino, you have to report back. You can't be caught here!'"

There were sex workers standing on the street corner outside her apartment. It was a less-than-ideal living situation for a university student, let alone a well-paid hockey player. "He didn't care," Caroline says. "He would very often go out for a cigarette, and when he did he gave like twenty dollars to the prostitutes, just to help, because that was him."

After a few days, Gino finally went back to the Canadiens. Caroline remembered that when the reporters asked him where he'd been, he grinned. "Oh I went to a funeral home," he joked. "I needed some new dentures."

More seriously, he and Therrien had a frank chat about where things were at. Both coach and player emerged singing from the same songbook: Gino was a valued veteran and he played an important role, the coach said. Gino said he understood and was ready to be a part of the team again. But Odjick's frustrations were long-simmering: he felt he deserved more ice time. He'd been playing just seven minutes a night; two seasons before, with the Islanders, he'd averaged more than twelve minutes per game. He re-signed in Montreal the summer before on the expectation he'd have more ice time with the Canadiens. When the playoffs came, he did play a bigger role, especially after star winger Richard Zedník was knocked from the lineup by a dirty hit from the Bruins' Kyle McLaren. In Zedník's absence, Odjick was promoted to the Habs' first line, skating alongside Doug Gilmour and Oleg Petrov. Therrien commended Gino for his forechecking talents and defensive play. The Habs were eliminated in the second round, but for the first time in five seasons Gino had played playoff games, and most importantly, he'd proven that he could be a useful, trustworthy player in the post-season. But he would never play another game in the NHL.

IN THE SUMMER OF 2002, to get ready for his second season in Montreal, Odjick skated with a bunch of NHLers at a suburban rink. It's a pretty standard thing for pros to do. In one of their scrimmages, though, Gino took a puck to the back of the head. It was a freak accident: the puck had been fired on net with a slapshot, caromed off the post, and bonked him. At first, he felt fine, but when he got home, he puked. The next day, he woke up with a headache that lingered for days. It was obvious he had a concussion. At that point in his career, he figured he'd been concussed six or seven times in the NHL and on a couple of occasions in junior. This one he wouldn't shake.

When Canadiens training camp began in Colorado in September 2002, he was feeling better. He passed the camp-opening medical tests. But it took just one day of intense activity—skating on ice and then working out in the gym—for the headaches to come roaring back. He was tired but struggled to sleep, so he was prescribed sleeping pills. "He was absolutely distraught," Caroline says. "He just was sleeping, sleeping, sleeping, sleeping, and they said that was a concussion, and it was because of the change in oxygen [between Montreal and Colorado]." That was a lot for heavily pregnant Caroline to deal with.

Every doctor told him he had to stay off the ice and out of the gym. The hope was that rest would help him recover. "I just don't have the same energy," he told legendary *Montreal Gazette* reporter Red Fisher in November, two months after his brief appearance in training camp. "I'm sensitive to light, sensitive to noise. And I don't seem to have the same appetite. It's not bad, but it's not good... know what I mean?"[50]

He had Caroline's company and their newborn girl, Rose, but he still missed hockey. And the headaches, he said, made him feel like he was hungover when he woke up in the morning. "The headaches are the worst part of it, not being able to train, not being able to play, not to be around the game... be around the guys. I try to go for walks, try to keep busy, see my friends once in a while, do a little banking. But I can't seem to get away from the headaches," he went on. "Do I ever feel they won't go away? I try not to say that to myself. I just have to tell myself they're going to go away."

In February the team's doctors told him he was well enough to start working out in the gym again. Initially, Gino felt excited to get back. But the symptoms returned. Not long after, Canadiens general manager André Savard wanted to send him to the minors, to see if he could handle the rigours of play again. Odjick refused to go. "It was too soon," Odjick explained to the Canadian Press' Bill Beacon. "I still had symptoms. They ran out of patience, I guess."[51] A few weeks later, the team and Odjick agreed to terminate his contract. If it had been up to him, he'd have kept playing forever. He loved playing hockey, and he did later find ways to keep playing—for a senior AAA team, for Indigenous teams, for teams organized by friends, but never again in the NHL.

Gino got a good payout from the Canadiens as part of his termination, but he acknowledged he wasn't happy about what had gone down. At one point, the Habs had tried to argue he shouldn't get paid because the injury happened on his own time. The issue would be resolved, but the bad taste in his mouth lingered, right through to the end, when he insisted he wasn't ready to return to action. "It's been very frustrating for me," he told Beacon. "Sometimes I wish I didn't have the responsibility of having children and a family to support or I'd have told them to take their money and shove it."[52]

The abrupt arrival of Gino's post-career life was a bit of a shock. "That's why I say you've got to appreciate every minute that you get to play in the NHL... you never know when it's over," he told Bob Marjanovich in 2022. "Once it's over they give you a 'thank you very much for playing and we appreciate what you've done for us,' but you're on your own after. You don't have your teammates every day to be around."[53]

In January 2014, years after his playing career ended, Gino admitted to a crowd that he realized in hindsight he'd become addicted to getting punched in the head. "When you're designated as an enforcer, on a regular basis, there comes a time when you're addicted to hitting," he told the audience at a concussion symposium at the Chan Centre for Family Health Education at BC Children's Hospital. "When you don't get hit in the face for a while, it kind of bothers you. It made me feel alive, to get hit. It showed that I was involved, sticking up for my teammates. It was something I could never understand, myself. I felt the need to get hit."[54]

"What's the difference between depression and concussions?" Gino asked the *Province*'s Ed Willes later that same year. He knew he was facing the consequences of his playing days, but he wasn't going to quit on what he was doing. "It is what it is but I'm not going to lie down and die. I'm going to make a difference. They're telling me one thing but I'm going to fight with what I have. I believe I'll live until I'm 150."[55]

"DID HOCKEY DO THIS TO ME?" Gino once asked Peter Leech, after he'd moved into Peter and Charlene's home in Burnaby in 2014. He was up in the middle of the night, sitting at a table, something he often did. He had a hard time sleeping. Many nights, he wouldn't even sleep in his bed, he'd just doze on a comfy couch, watching TV. But on some nights Peter would sit with his friend and listen to him. He knew that his brain wasn't firing like it should. There was the mental illness. Then there was the literal physical damage he'd suffered. Many other former enforcers in hockey, plus tough tacklers in football and rugby, were also dealing with many of the same issues, like depression and challenges to their cognitive functions. Many of these players were being diagnosed posthumously with chronic traumatic encephalopathy (CTE), a degenerative brain condition that was more and more suspected to be caused by repeated blows to the head. Gino would sit at the table, listen to music, and think about his life.

The deaths of NHL enforcers Derek Boogaard, Wade Belak, and Rick Rypien in the summer of 2011 had shaken Gino immensely. So did the ongoing struggles of his old friend Chris Simon, another fellow enforcer, whom Gino would ask Peter about when they'd get word of Simon's latest struggles, whether with money or family or otherwise. "How can we help him?" Gino would lament to his friend. Hearing about the struggles of any of his peers was tough to take. Simon would take his own life in 2024 and an examination of his brain revealed he had suffered from CTE.

Boogaard, a giant of a man who was considered the NHL's top enforcer in the late oughts, died of an accidental overdose of alcohol and oxycodone. He had been trying to cope with his failing mental health for years. He became hooked on pain-killers and sleeping pills, many prescribed to him by team physicians. Research by Boogaard's father, reported by *The New York Times*, found that over the final three years of his career, Boogaard had met with at least a dozen doctors connected to the Minnesota Wild and New York Rangers and had been given more than a hundred prescriptions, many of which were for narcotic painkillers and sleeping pills. He went to rehab several times in an effort to treat his addictions to those pills. A posthumous examination of Boogaard's brain found he suffered from CTE.

Both Belak and Rypien took their own lives. Belak was known as one of the most happy-go-lucky figures during his decade as an NHL tough guy, but after his death, word slowly trickled out that he had confided in more than a few associates that he suffered from depression. Rypien had suffered from clinical depression for years as well. In both cases, it was never clear that fighting played a role in their mental illness.

But whether the trio died because of hockey-related causes or not, Gino was scared by their stories, just as he'd been scared by the death of former rival Bob Probert in 2010. Probert had lived with drug and alcohol addiction for most of his adult life—even as he managed to play sixteen years in the NHL—and died of a heart attack. After his death, his brain was examined by experts at Boston University; they found evidence of CTE. Those experts have examined the brains of other former hockey players in the years since and have found CTE in many, though not all, of their brains.

"What drives a person to that point, to take their own life?" Gino said to Peter. It's about pain and turmoil, his friend told him. "You fear what might happen if you tell people about what you're enduring," Peter added.

AT THE TIME of his comments at BC Children's in 2014, Gino had only just found mental stability. The previous year had been a hellacious conclusion to a very difficult ten years. After the end of his NHL career, Gino and Caroline moved back to Vancouver in 2003. Gino's post-concussion symptoms did eventually clear up, but other mental issues began to emerge. He wasn't yet diagnosed with bipolar disorder—that wouldn't happen until 2009—but his moods were unpredictable, regularly running between manic periods and periods of borderline psychosis. Living with him was hard.

On the many good days, he'd have all the energy in the world, fully engaged in his work with youth, in his business interests. But when he'd descend into psychosis, it was a terrible scene. He'd accuse those who were closest to him of plotting against him, of seeking to do him harm. He was deeply paranoid. The fact he was also self-medicating with Sudafed, the nasal decongestant popular with hockey players for its stimulant properties, as well as Percocet, an opioid painkiller, and more, didn't help either.

After his diagnosis, he was given prescription drugs, including Clonazepam, but that dimmed his personality, Caroline said. He became less vibrant, "a little bit robotic," she noted. "And then you kind of lose that charisma of who you are." He and Caroline broke up that same year, though they remained business partners. Gino would move in with his cousin Stéphane for a time. They were joined by Gino's oldest son, Patrick, who moved west to try Vancouver life in 2010.

After his outburst, Gino would seek to make amends with those around him. "After calming his brain down, he'd say, 'You know, I gotta go make some apologies,'" said Kumi Kimura, who began working for Gino in 2008. "He came to say sorry to me, and I said, 'You don't owe me an apology.' And he said to me, 'When you do wrong and you know you did it, then you apologize. It doesn't really matter, you know, in what capacity, but if you know you did wrong, you apologize. And if they accept your apology, that's fine, but you got to do it.'"

Gino's mental health took a serious turn for the worse late in 2012, after a doctor prescribed him the anti-inflammatory prednisone, not knowing Gino's history with head injuries. Research has found that treating people who have a history of head trauma with corticosteroids—the class of drug that prednisone belongs to—can cause sometimes serious cognitive side effects. It was prednisone that unleashed chaos in 2013.

His bipolar episodes became more pronounced as the year progressed. After an outburst in June 2013, he was deemed a threat to himself and others and was committed to the provincial psychiatric hospital in Coquitlam, BC, which has changed official names over the years but is still known colloquially as Riverview. Here he was prescribed a series of drugs, including the antipsychotic perphenazine, plus the common antidepressant Prozac. He spent the summer at Riverview and was released in September.

5

"HE TAUGHT US TO STICK TOGETHER"

THE AREA AROUND Maniwaki, Quebec, where Gino Odjick was born on September 7, 1970, to Joe and Giselle Odjick, was first settled in the early nineteenth century by a group of Algonquin people led by Chief Pakinawatik, who moved north from the Oka area, near where the Ottawa River meets the St. Lawrence. The people named their settlement Kitigan Zibi and called themselves Kitigan Zibi Anishinabeg. For generations, before they moved to the area permanently, they would travel up the Ottawa River, up the Gatineau to the Désert River, to hunt and trap. They knew the land well.

It's rugged but beautiful country, the essence of the Canadian Shield: heavily wooded with lush trees, mostly maple, birch, beech, and ash, and speckled with trout-bearing lakes. The rich soil is good for farming, there's plenty of wildlife for hunting, and the fishing is abundant. Summers are fine, but winters are cold.

As you drive north from Ottawa toward Kitigan Zibi and Maniwaki along Quebec Route 105, dipping through small villages and farms, the houses nestled among the trees, rocky cliffs jut up here and there next to the path that had been cut for the road; you can imagine that Gino, with his wide shoulders, his prominent cheeks and his big hands, had been cut from that ancient rock.

Not long after the Kitigan Zibi Anishinabeg became established here, Europeans arrived and set up a Hudson's Bay Company trading post, then a Catholic mission—both signs that the settlers weren't going to be leaving anytime soon. The settlement grew into a townsite, which came to be known as Maniwaki, Algonquin for "land of Mary," a reference to the Catholic missionaries who'd colonized the spot.

A strong, close-knit community had developed in Kitigan Zibi, but the European settlers threatened the Kitigan Zibi Anishinabeg way of life. Chief Pakinawatik made a trio of canoe trips to meet with the colonial authorities in Toronto, asking that land be set aside for his people. By 1853, a proper reserve was demarcated. (In 2019, the band council and the federal government agreed on a land claim settlement for the Kitigan Zibi area. Other claims, farther south in the Ottawa area, remain unresolved.) A century and a half later, the Kitigan Zibi Anishinabeg counts about 3,700 members, roughly forty percent of whom live on the reserve itself.

JOE ODJICK WAS born in 1939 in Rapid Lake, a small Algonquin community a few hours north of Kitigan Zibi. His mother was Marie-Antoinette Marchand, part French; his father, Basil, was Algonquin, a trapper and fishing guide. Life was harsh in Rapid Lake. The living conditions were poor. There was little work. People abused alcohol.

Within a year or two, the family left Rapid Lake and moved back down to Kitigan Zibi, to be closer to Basil's family. The community was a little bigger than Rapid Lake and there was a little more work, in logging, for instance. Maniwaki was the northern end of a rail line that ran up from Ottawa, but life was still hard. The Depression was over, but the Second World War raged in Europe. The economy had become geared toward defeating Nazism.

By the winter of 1944, Basil, by then working as a logger, decided it was time to volunteer. The army would be a big adventure, and it would also pay him a steady wage and feed him well. There was no doubt, too, his family could use the money. He made out his will, leaving everything to his wife. There was a family history in the army: Basil's grandfather Patrick had signed up in August 1914 and fought on the Western Front until he was killed in Flanders in January 1916, just two months shy of his fortieth birthday.

Basil's older brother Robert had signed up in August 1943. The two were close—they went to residential school together. Basil was sent when he was seven and stayed there until he was sixteen. He dreamed of catching up to his brother. In February of 1944, he hopped the train to Ottawa and transferred to another to Kingston, where he enlisted, like his brother, in the Royal Regiment of Canada. He was then sent off to Farnham, Quebec, for basic training.

The months passed by. June 6, D-Day, came and went. The Allies had secured a foothold in Normandy. The Canadian Army was moving its forces over to Europe as fast as it could.

By late June, Robert and his unit were back in Kingston, getting ready to sail to Britain. Basil, still in Farnham, requested a transfer to the Kingston depot so he could be shipped overseas along with his brother. Maybe they could even be posted to the same unit. But army policy sought to keep brothers separated from each other because of what had happened in the First World War, when brothers were allowed to sign up and stay together, only to be killed side-by-side in the trenches of northern France, wiping out whole family lines. So Basil's request was denied: the Odjick boys would go overseas separately. They would never see each other again.

When Basil shipped out from Halifax on July 12, he was two weeks behind his brother. The voyage across the Atlantic took about a week. Upon arriving in England, Basil and his unit were sent to a transfer encampment in the south of England to await further deployment. The Allies had secured their beachhead in France and were consolidating their position; around the time Basil arrived in England, the Allies were pushing into the next planned phase of the war.

Basil received his orders to sail for France on August 12. Three days later, fighting to the east of the town of Falaise, his unit found itself in the big push by the 1st Canadian Army to cut off the retreat of the German 7th Army. This would become known as the "Falaise Pocket," where tens of thousands of German soldiers looked set to be encircled. In the end, the Allies moved too slowly and couldn't seal off the pocket: the Germans were able to escape. Still, the operation was deemed a success for the Allies and a decisive defeat for the Germans because most of the German troops were either killed or captured. Thousands of Germans did escape, but they left all their heavy equipment behind. Further, the operation concluded the Normandy campaign: the Allies had secured a broad area of French coastline and inland areas from which to push on to Paris and the rest of France, while the Germans had lost around 450,000 men, more than double the official casualty figures for the Allies.

On August 25, the Allies liberated Paris, but the fighting around the City of Light continued. Three days after the liberation, Basil's unit found itself pursuing members of the German SS, the elite guard of the Nazi regime, into the town of Saint-Ouen-de-Tilleul, on the road from Normandy to Paris, just south of the city of Rouen, within sight of a long, slow, lazy bend in the Seine. The Germans were armed with rocket launchers and anti-tank guns. As the Germans yielded position after position, they still fired their heavy weapons with abandon, smashing walls, knocking all kinds of bricks and debris about. One of those flying bricks caught Basil in the head, killing him. He was twenty-four years old.

Basil was one of thirteen Canadians killed in Saint-Ouen-de-Tilleul. Robert fought on with the Royal Regiment, but would be killed the next spring, during the liberation of Holland. The Odjick boys were among three thousand Indigenous Canadians who fought in the war, and among about two hundred who lost their lives.

There's a small memorial to all of Kitigan Zibi's veterans, including Basil and Robert, inside the Kitigan Zibi Anishinabeg Pimadjiwowinogamig, the community's cultural centre.

The story of Basil's sacrifice would be passed along to Joe's kids and grandchildren. Where the family came from, who they'd been, was a point of pride for the Odjicks. Joe grew up without a father, but he made sure his kids knew his father's story.

"I was always proud of that," Basil's great-grandson Joey Odjick, one of Gino's eight children, says. Now in his early thirties and a father himself, he recognizes the importance of his family's story. "As a kid, I was able to say 'My great-grandfather fought in World War II and he died in the war. He died serving the country. He died a hero.'"

Despite their bravery, Indigenous soldiers were not treated like other Canadian soldiers. Benefits flowed to the widows of veterans—but not to the widows of Indigenous soldiers. The *Indian Act* prohibited it. So Basil's widow, Marie-Antoinette, was left to struggle on, on her own, with Joe and his siblings.

CANADA'S RESIDENTIAL SCHOOL policy said that if children were in a family situation that was judged at all untenable by the authorities, those kids could be sent away with little notice or review. For more than a century, the Canadian government, working in many cases with religious authorities, removed Indigenous children from their communities and sent those children away to residential schools far from home. Joe, nine years old and fatherless, was ripped away from his family home and put on a train, bound for the residential school in Spanish, Ontario, a tiny village near the northern shore of Lake Huron that served as a stop on the Canadian Pacific Railway and where electricity didn't come until 1951.

"The priest would just round us up like cattle," Joe told Roy MacGregor years later for his book *The Home Team*. "They'd come into Rapid Lake and half would be sent off to the orphanage at Amos and half would go to Spanish."[56]

It took two days to get there. Young Joe had no idea where he was going; he just knew he wasn't with his family anymore. In Spanish, there were two school buildings: St. Peter Claver School for Boys, run by the Jesuits, and St. Joseph's School for Girls, run by the nuns of the Daughters of the Heart of Mary. At the Spanish school, young Joe was piled in with Indigenous boys from all over, some from as far west as Manitoba.

The government's plan was to assimilate Indigenous children into the dominant European settler culture, driven by historically British and to a lesser extent French and American values, by isolating them from their own cultures and traditions. Like students at every residential school in Canada, young Joe was forbidden by the Jesuits in charge to speak his own language. Many former students have spoken out about the abuse suffered by students at the school—mental, physical, sometimes sexual. Students were often referred to only by their assigned numbers as the system sought to strip away the last vestiges of their culture and their individuality. In 2015 the Truth and Reconciliation Commission of Canada called the system "cultural genocide" and in 2022, the House of Commons and the pope recognized that system engaged in genocide.

"The day I got off the train," Joe told MacGregor, "they took us in there and pulled our pants down and gave us such a licking. Then, when we were all crying, they told us, 'Don't let us ever catch you speaking Indian again.'"[57] The priests knew how to hit, anyway. One once boxed him about the ear so hard it burst his eardrum, and he never fully regained his hearing because of it.

Thousands of children died over the century-plus that Canada ran its residential schools. In 2021, when news came out that evidence of burial sites had been found on the grounds of the former residential school in Kamloops, BC, Gino said he felt it in his heart.

"I don't get emotional often, but I was thinking of what my dad went through," he said at the time. "My dad was a thousand miles away from home."[58]

Gino had been working with Indigenous youth for more than two decades by that point; he'd seen all kinds of poverty in his travels across the country. He'd worked with Indigenous leaders, like Phil Fontaine, National Chief of the Assembly of First Nations. He'd supported Wendy Grant-John and Jody Wilson-Raybould in their efforts to become leaders of the British Columbia Assembly of First Nations. And yet the news of the potential graves caught him in his tracks. "How did [the government] get away with it?" Odjick said. "How did you end up with 215 kids buried in the ground?" The National Centre for Truth and Reconciliation at the University of Manitoba has identified twenty-one boys as having died at the school in Spanish, which was in operation from 1878 to 1958.

His father lived through it. Odjick and his sisters lived through the generational trauma of it. Though Joe would contend that he got through it all right because, at nine years old, he'd been a bit older than many of his fellow students at the time of arrival: many were just aged five or six, with no understanding of why they'd been ripped away from their homes. This shattering of his family left a lasting mark on Joe, and when he had a family of his own, he did his best to do exactly the opposite.

"He taught us to stick together," Gino would often say of his father.[59] Papa Joe showed his only son the importance of looking after your family, of being honest in your labour, of treating others with respect. Most importantly, the home Joe and Giselle built for their kids was filled with love. Joe told his kids that they should always be on the lookout for others.

You do what is necessary to have a good life, Gino's parents taught him. Whatever challenges you face in life, you find a way to get it done. You look out for your family, you look out for your friends. Friends staying over were a regular feature of the Odjick household, as were foster kids, thirty-two of whom were taken in by the Odjicks over the years. "My dad, he always said kids should never have a hard time," Gino's sister Dina remembers. "And he said, 'If we have money to feed one, we have money to feed all.'" This philosophy grew out of the horrors of his youth as a residential school survivor.

Joey spent a lot of time with his grandfather, in Laval, and also in Maniwaki and Kitigan Zibi. So impactful, it would seem, that as an adult Joey settled in Maniwaki. "He was a very big influence," Joey says of his Papa Joe. "At a young age, he taught us about hard work. It was always important to work and provide for your family and be there for your family. And family was always first. I think a lot of my dad's character comes from that as well." Joey's too, as you can imagine.

Even if Joe was philosophical to a degree with MacGregor about his time in residential school, the experience wasn't something he was ready to talk much about, Dina says. It clearly scarred him. "I'll only tell you about it once," he told his kids. And what he did say wasn't much, but it was telling. "He had scars on his feet," Dina remembers. He told his children the scars were from having scalding water poured on his feet as punishment for speaking Algonquin. (Joe, though, held on to his language: Gino was a proud speaker of Algonquin, along with English and French.)

Joe also told his kids about his cousin Victor. "He had one leg shorter than the other," Dina says. "He had it rough. He'd be scared, he wouldn't want to get up because of the way he walked. He'd get beaten. So my dad was like his protector, because he would pee in bed, and then, I guess, the priest would beat Victor."

Joe told MacGregor that in the years after he left Spanish, every time he would sit down to eat, he would think of what he'd experienced under the Jesuits. In adulthood, he said, groceries became the most important thing in his life. When he was at Spanish, he and his friends would steal food from the kitchen, then trade it around. But in adulthood, with kids to feed, he always made sure there was more than enough food in the house. "When I cook, I overcook," he said. "If there's no potatoes in the house, I'm not well."[60]

GINO TOLD ANYONE who would listen about how hard his dad worked to support him, his mom, his five sisters, and all the kids who came to stay in their home. "My dad looked after all of us," Odjick said. "His whole life, he worked to take care of us—he went to work in Detroit, New York, working on building the high-rises and bridges, wherever the work was. It didn't matter what the economy was doing, he always found work. There was never a time when any of us were hungry or cold or didn't have good clothes to wear."[61]

Joey says his grandfather's instincts to provide extended to his grandchildren as well. With his dad off making a living in the NHL, Joey and his seven siblings mostly grew up away from their father. But they weren't without a father figure:

Papa Joe would step in. When Joey had a hockey tournament, it was his grandfather who would drive down to Laval, a three-hour trip, to pick him up and take him to his games. "My grandfather was the glue to our family," Joey said.

It was the same for Joey's older brother Patrick, Gino's second child. He played hockey all through his youth; he was born when his dad was still in high school, so most of his growing up occurred while his dad was in the NHL. "Papa Joe was the one that was taking me to my games," he said, the pride swelling in his voice. "He was big on family. He meant a lot to us kids."

That caring spirit is present in all of Papa Joe's kids. Dina, for instance, now works as a family support worker. As an adult, with kids of her own, she's cared for foster children as well. So has her sister Janique, who now lives on the US side of the Akwesasne reserve.

Once, Dina encountered a pair of brothers who had lived in ten different foster homes. She was asked if she would take one of them on. "How about both?" Dina replied. "My father would never let two kids get separated, two brothers," she says. "That's all they have, is each other. So I said, 'I'll take them both in.' It was just normal to do it, because, I mean, we've seen my dad do it right all our lives. So it was kind of like 'No, we'll do it.' You don't want to see kids suffer."

OVER THE SEVEN-PLUS YEARS Gino played for the Canucks, Joe would often fly to Vancouver and stay with his son. He was around the rink all the time. Gino's teammates got to know him well. Stan Smyl recalled a truly caring father. The first time Joe came out west, Gino invited Smyl, his respected veteran linemate, to come out for lunch and meet his dad, play some pool. To this day, it's a fond memory for Smyl, a quiet, humble moment for a guy who was Mr. Hockey in Vancouver for a decade. If you were Gino's friend, you were Joe's friend, he quickly came to realize. "His dad treated people with a kind manner. You could see where Gino got it from," Smyl says. Gino's instinct to bring people in, to make them feel included, came from his parents.

"His dad was a great man, and I think that's really why Gino had the work ethic and the drive to become who he became," Geoff Courtnall said. "I would talk to [Joe] a lot, especially when we'd be on an East Coast swing. His stories of working in New York, building those towers. A lot of those guys came from Gino's band. Stories of how they grew up, where they came from, the hunting stories. Grassroots guys that came off the reserve and how hard they had to work to be successful."

Treating others with respect, especially if they respected you, was a value Joe passed down to his son and grandchildren. Being there to support those around you, struggling in a common cause, was inherent to everything he did.

Mike Murphy, who was coaching the Canucks' minor league team in Milwaukee in 1990, where Odjick played his first pro games before that fateful November call-up, remembers a young player filled with respect. "He wasn't boisterous," Murphy recalls of the lanky twenty-year-old, in an interview before Gino's induction into the BC Sports Hall of Fame in 2021. "He was a good teammate, an accepted teammate. The guys on the team really liked him."

Gino's agent and former NHLer Gilles Lupien learned about Gino's deeply respectful demeanor during their very first meeting, when Gino was making his way as a young player in junior hockey with the Laval Titan. Speaking in French on the television documentary *Trajectoires* a decade ago, Lupien, who died in 2021, recounts hearing about this big kid who'd arrived from Hawkesbury, who seemed to have some talent, but whose skating wasn't very good.

"Hello, Gino, how are you?" Lupien asked. Young Odjick replied, but kept his eyes fixed on the ground. Lupien was taken aback and told him he could look up at him, in the eyes. "He said, 'I can't look you in the eyes.' So I asked why. 'I have too much respect for you,'" Lupien said. The response threw him off, but Lupien soon realized Gino was a player full of heart, full of desire. He would discover Gino to be a reflection of his father. "I don't think this arena is big enough to hold his heart," Lupien said, pointing to the walls of the old rink where he was being interviewed. "I saw that Gino wanted to help everyone. He fought for his teammates."[62]

For the first year of their relationship, Gino addressed his agent not as "Gilles," but always with a deeply respectful "Monsieur Lupien." Lupien's influence was vital for Gino—a deeply motivational one. "He said, 'If you keep working hard, and keep at it, you have a chance to be drafted into the NHL,'" Odjick told Bob Marjanovich in 2022. Keep working on your skills, but also get stronger, get fitter, Lupien told the young Odjick. You'll make the NHL as an enforcer, but the guys in the NHL are the strongest in the hockey world. You need to be ready, he told him. "From that time on, I went to the gym every day and really got strong," Gino said. "Every team asked me, 'Do you work out, do you lift weights?' I told them, 'Yeah, I do.' That was important to them, that you worked out and lifted weights. Even back then in 1990. They wanted you to be fit in the gym, fit in your cardio."

Gino's hesitation to look Lupien in the eye doesn't surprise his sister Dina. That was a cultural thing, she said. And it was exactly as her brother had told his future agent: it was a sign of the respect Gino had for Lupien. "To us, it's hard to look somebody in the eye," Dina explained. "Gino was young, he was intimidated, I guess. And for us, you look at somebody in the eye for respect. Back in our days here, we all didn't really do eye contact."

JOE WAS DELIGHTED that his son became a professional hockey player. Joe had been a pretty good player himself. For him, athletics provided a kind of liberation. The boys at the residential school in Spanish felt they had at least some control over their situation when they played sports. The rest of their lives was outside their control. Hovering above everything was the onerous *Indian Act*, which required them to attend school until they were sixteen and restricted contact with their families. And then there were the daily, often abusive whims of the Jesuits running the school.

But hockey was a release from all that. The Spanish boys took to hockey. Their team was very good; according to Roy MacGregor, their local opponents would often sign up ringers to make sure they weren't embarrassed by the poor boys from the residential school. On Saturday nights, if the older boys had been well behaved, they'd get to listen to *Hockey Night in Canada* on the radio, with Foster Hewitt on the call.

On the ice, no opposing ringers could hide the fact that Joe was a special player. A smooth-skating defenceman, he played a smart game on the blueline. And when he turned sixteen and was able to leave the residential school, hockey was a way forward, almost literally skating him away from the brutal life in Spanish. Freed from residential school, he chased a hockey dream, working and playing for teams across northern Ontario, and eventually making his way from the shores of Lake Huron to Winnipeg. He found himself in the system of the Winnipeg Maroons, then a perennial Allan Cup favourite as the best senior (read: semi-pro) team in Canada.

But making the Maroons was tough, especially for an Indigenous kid in a world dominated by white Canadian culture. After a few seasons in Winnipeg, here he was, at the age of twenty-seven, unsure what his playing career really held for him. He was lonely. So one Christmas, with his teammates all scattered for the holidays, a letter and a train ticket arrived from his mother. He leaped at the chance to go home. He got a job at a paper mill in Maniwaki and married Giselle. Joe had previously fathered two daughters, Debbie in 1963 and Shelly in 1964, with two other women. The couple was already parents to Judy by the time he moved back home. They took in a foster son named Steve.

The mill job was good, but Joe was laid off every winter. A growing family needed more than this seasonal work could provide. So it was off to Edmonton. Boom town. In the Alberta capital, he found work with a steel company building skyscrapers, work that would become familiar to him in the years to come.

After four months of working the night shift, though, Joe looked at Giselle and said, "Let's go home." Life in Edmonton wasn't for the Odjicks. As they wound their way back across the country, Joe considered ways he could support his family. There wasn't much work back home. And now Giselle was eight months pregnant—another mouth to feed was on the way. A stopover in Thunder Bay revealed an opportunity: the giant Abitibi pulp mill. Joe inquired about a job and was hired practically on the spot. Giselle carried on with the kids, taking them back to Maniwaki while Joe stayed on, now on the shores of Lake Superior.

Not long after, Gino was born. Joe was still away from home, but when the news arrived in Thunder Bay he was elated. Boy or girl, it didn't matter, Joe would insist. The baby was healthy and so was his mother—that's all that mattered. But now that Joe had a son, it meant that he could teach some of his culture's more male-focused traditions, like hunting and fishing. And Gino came to love heading out into the bush to do both.

After Gino came two more sisters: Dina and Janique. They also took in another foster girl, Gina, who joined the family permanently. At home, family roles were largely traditional. In the old days, the women served the men. The modern version of this saw a man bang his coffee cup on the table when it became empty and hold it in the air. Joe would do that, and eventually so would Gino, and Giselle would come over and fill it. "That's just how it was," Dina says. When they were young, some of the girls would fill the cup too. "But I always said I would never serve a man like my mom did, like we did with Gino and my dad."

With no brothers in the family, Gino usually found himself playing with Dina, who was just a year younger. None of his other sisters were especially interested in hockey. But Dina was. So she'd skate with him. She played on a boys' team and got to play in a tournament in Montreal once. She met Montreal Canadiens legend Jean Béliveau there, and even got her picture taken with him. Give her the credit for teaching Gino how to skate properly, or how to fight, she says with a laugh.

It was also Dina who drove Gino to Laval for his first training camp. Of course, she did, she says, they were just that close. Brother and sister stuck together. “But then I locked my keys in the car,” she says. Before she could go find someone to help them get the door open by more conventional means, Gino took matters into his own hands: he used his elbow to shatter the window. They got the keys. They fixed the window later.

On top of their own kids, and on top of the thirty-two foster kids over the years, Joe and Giselle took in kids who came to the community to attend school. Many of these kids were from families who lived far out in the bush, like up in Rapid Lake two hours away. Kids in Joe’s era had been dragged off to residential school, but in the modern era, these kids encountered something completely opposite: the warm Odjick home.

And what a home it became. Joe built a huge place just off the reserve, on a twenty-hectare spread. The roof, he told Roy MacGregor, came together because of a deal he’d secured on steel trusses—just $160, he said. “I had to build the house to fit the roof,” he said.[63] To pay for all this, and all the things his kids needed, he continued to work all the time. He moved on from the mill job in Thunder Bay. He’d acquired some land near the reserve that he farmed along with 120 hectares of on-reserve land. On top of helping build skyscrapers in places like New York, also hauled pulp for the mills in Maniwaki, cut firewood, tended bar, and got a job plowing the Rideau Canal through the winter. That job was the one that made him the most money. Life took him where the money was, and if that meant going away for long stretches, so be it. It’s not a coincidence that when Gino had kids of his own to feed and clothe, he also went away. "As a man, you're the one to provide for your kids," Dina said. Joe went away to provide; Gino saw that, knew that, did that too.

As much as Joe wanted Gino to see that there was a big world out there, full of opportunity, he did his best not to tell his son what to do with his life. He thought Gino should go away, but he wasn't going to tell him to go away. He hoped Gino wouldn't just stay in Kitigan Zibi, that he'd explore the possibilities beyond, but he kept it to himself.

"He never interfered when school was not good. There was never any pressure on me," Gino told MacGregor in 1994, describing how his dad handled him.[64] All these years later, MacGregor recalls Joe as a man of great emotional strength, who was carrying a mountain of trauma with him. "He had a presence and carried himself so well, for a guy who had the shit beat out of him in residential schools," MacGregor says, looking back at the conversations he had with Joe in putting together his book. "Of course, we now know the damage is generational." Somehow, Gino's dad had been able to minimize passing on the pain and suffering that he'd experienced. He flipped that suffering into providing for his family and keeping the fridge full.

Whenever the Canucks played in Montreal, Papa Joe would organize the buses and tickets to haul dozens of family members and friends to the Forum to see Gino play. Dina laughs about the first time Gino came to Montreal with the Canucks, in March 1991. Gino didn't play that night—he was out with his broken cheekbone, suffered a week or so before from Jay Caufield's flying elbow—but the Kitigan Zibi crew travelled down anyway, and they made their presence known. "A fight broke out in the stands," she says.

After the Ottawa Senators joined the NHL in 1992, Joe organized more buses, this time to make the ninety-minute trip down when the Canucks visited the nation's capital. In 1994, about two thousand people, something like forty percent of the combined population of Kitigan Zibi and Maniwaki, went down to Ottawa to take in the game. "They booked a ballroom at the hotel," Dina says. A ballroom just to host them all, so they could eat together with their hero, with their friend, with their dad. "Going to Montreal, that was fun," Gino's son Patrick recalls. "We'd get to go behind the scenes. We got to go in the back and meet the players. That's pretty cool for a kid."

But those moments were fleeting. For all the joy Gino's appearances would bring his kids, his visits would always come to an end. He knew the kids were being looked after—by their mothers and by his grandparents. In the logic of his universe, things were lined up; he'd seen his father Joe always going away to provide for the family, leaving a lot of the child rearing was to Giselle. That surely left a subconscious imprint on Gino. Hockey took Gino away from his own young family, and in his mind, that was just how things were. He was providing for them, and things advanced pretty quickly. He made the team in Hawkesbury, got better there, then made the team in Laval and got better there. He was good enough for pro hockey in general, then the NHL. He got better there too.

6

"I HAD SO MUCH FUN AND I NEVER NEEDED MONEY"

IF YOU GREW UP with Gino, you had a nickname. In fact, you probably had a few. Thunder. Ugly. Itchy.

These three are all one guy: Andy Dewache, a friend of Gino's since they were kids. Gino had called Dewache "Itchy" since high school. "It's a funny name," the jovial Dewache explains forty-some years after landing the moniker. "If you ever watch that show *Itchy & Scratchy* [from *The Simpsons*], I'm like Itchy the mouse that's picking on the cat all the time. That's how I could describe our relationship. I was that guy. I could influence him to do things: 'C'mon, Gino, let's go do something, let's go do this.'" Simple as that. Just a good name to laugh about. "It always keeps spirits up: 'Hey, Itchy!'"

Itchy, who has been a constable in the Kitigan Zibi police department for years, had nicknames for Gino too. Joe sometimes called his son Archie—Itchy would do the same.

Other times, it was a name with a pretty obvious connection: André—as in André the Giant. "We were big wrestling fans," Itchy says. Obviously.

The two boys went to school together and played on the same sports teams. "We had the right chemistry for friends," Itchy says. "We loved sports. Give Gino any kind of racquet: tennis racquet, table tennis racquet. He was really good. His agility was really amazing and his athleticism was really amazing. He was good at everything."

He excelled at softball. And hockey, of course. He wasn't a keen student, but he ate up books, and he proved an adept language student. The language on the reserve in those days was English, but, being in Quebec, everyone studied French. And Gino was good at French, Itchy says. He spoke Algonquin well too.

"You never bothered him when he was reading his paper," Itchy notes. Gino's habit of reading the Audettes' paper in Laval? That was nothing new. It went back years. At home in Kitigan Zibi, even when he was hanging out with his friends, if there was a paper about, he would grab that paper and read it—before breakfast was even on the table. He wanted to know what was going on.

FIGHTING MAY NOT have been a big part of Gino's life until he went away to play junior hockey, but Mike "Michen" Cote does remember Gino getting into scraps as a kid. Mike and Jan "Boy Boy" Cote are cousins. Mike's father died when he was young, so he grew up with Jan's family. Gino was a year older than Michen and went to a different school, but they grew up near each other, and they were good friends. Like most of the kids from the reserve, Gino went to the English school in Maniwaki. Michen went to the French school, because his dad, who worked for Canada Post, wanted Michen to know both official languages. The two schools shared the same yard. Today, kids have a school on the reserve to attend, but in the 1970s, there were only the town schools.

"Back then, there was racism and you had to defend yourself," Michen recalls, almost a half-century later. "We would fight anybody who was racist against us... I remember Gino scrapping it out in the schoolyard, bloody nose and just tough as hell." There's still racism today, of course, but the response now tends to be more verbal, he suggests. In those days, the defence was just raw physicality.

GINO LOVED THE PLACE where he grew up. "I had so much fun and I never needed money," he told the *Vancouver Sun*'s Iain MacIntyre in 1991. "I went hunting and rode four-wheelers and drove skidoos. When I arrived in the city, I couldn't get out the door without spending twenty bucks. It was tough; I always tried to get back to the reserve.

"Everybody played hockey in winter and softball in summer," he continued. "In the fall, we'd go hunting for moose and deer. After hunting, a lot of people would go trapping until December. When there was too much snow and you couldn't trap anymore it was hockey season."[65]

If there was a hockey game being played by some kids, at the rink or on the street, Gino would get involved. On the streets of Maniwaki, it was mostly white families. But Gino didn't care. He'd show up underdressed, maybe wearing a toque, maybe wearing gloves, but that was never a certainty, Michen says. What was certain was Gino's desire to get in the game.

"And some of them were, saying racist stuff… 'Get that little Indian kid out of here,' whatever." But some of the older kids, they pushed back. "'He wants to play. Let him play,' they'd say. And so Gino, at a young age, wherever there's hockey, he was playing, he was on board," says Michen. "You know those bothersome kids today, when you go into an arena and they're shooting pucks on the board, on the walls? They're running around with hockey sticks? Gino, he was that. He just didn't care. He just wanted to play."

EVEN AS AN ADULT, Gino just wanted to play. In the summers, he'd join his friends and play fastpitch softball. They'd travel around, playing in tournaments. In the summer of 1993, Gino joined the team to play in a tournament in the community of Oujé-Bougoumou, north of Val-d'Or, about six hours from Kitigan Zibi. On the field, they had a great time, as the always did. Off the field, though, Gino and his friends got into some trouble. One of the guys on their team had been fooling around with a woman from Oujé-Bougoumou. A man from the community whom she'd been seeing found out. "He ended up beating up our friend, our teammate, really good," Itchy recalls. "Almost severed his ear." The one guy had a beef, but otherwise the team was a popular group with the locals, Itchy says. They added fun to the atmosphere of the event, which, sure, had a small cash prize, but was really about having a good time.

During the tournament, Richard "Ding" Whiteduck, one of Gino's oldest friends, got back at the assailant and beat him up, Itchy says. The situation escalated from there. Because Oujé-Bougoumou is so far from Kitigan Zibi, they stayed over that night. The plan was to drive home the next morning. But as they slept in the home they were staying in, the guy whom Ding had beaten up slashed a bunch of the tires on their vehicles. The violent sound of air escaping the tires woke a few of the friends up. Gino quickly realized what was going on and woke everyone up, pulled his pants on, and took off after the culprit. Having his pants on properly proved to be a potentially life-saving choice.

"Instincts just kicked in," Itchy recalls. It's a scene that happens all the time among guys in their twenties: one guy gets in a bit of trouble and things escalate, but the group sticks together. In this case, things escalated far beyond what they expected. Gino started getting rough with the guy and the guy pulled a knife, which he jabbed toward Gino's midsection. The result could have been a lot worse: the knife hit his belt first. It pierced his skin, but not as badly as it might have. They chased off the assailant and tended to Gino. He didn't need to go to hospital, but he was wounded and the group was spooked. They gathered their things, fixed their tires as best they could, with the help of their hosts and other locals, and then drove back home to Kitigan Zibi in the wee hours of the morning.

When they got home, Papa Joe was furious, especially with Itchy. Gino's best friend should have known better, they should have just come home, Joe said, rather than looking to do a little more post-tournament carousing. As for Gino, the incident taught him not only about the risks of certain confrontations, but also about how one mistake could quickly end his ability to play hockey.

"I think he learned a lesson," Itchy says. "To be more cautious. I think he wasn't cautious at that time." In fairness, many guys in their early twenties aren't.

ONCE HE TURNED PRO, Gino really came to like working out, getting ready for hockey season. Michen recalls the difference just one season in junior made for Gino. In the summers, Gino would play fastpitch with his buddies; the summer of 1988, after his season in Hawkesbury was over and the weather was nice, Gino showed up at the Kitigan Zibi ballpark. He was socking home runs when Michen showed up. He hadn't seen his friend in months and was stunned. "His arms were so thick. Like, within a year, give or take, Gino grew so big," he recalled.

For Gino, working out also provided another opportunity to socialize. He'd invite friends in to pump iron along with him, even if it was often a struggle for them to keep up with him. Either way, it all came down to the music.

"He loved country music," Itchy says. He'd play country music wherever he went—in the car, at home, and in the gym. "This guy was skipping rope. And you don't have, like, techno going on, or anything to keep your heart rate elevated. Instead, this guy's listening to 'There's a Tear in My Beer.'" Itchy sings that last part, which is the name of a Hank Williams Jr. song, with a twang. His friends had no problem with the tunes—Itchy himself is an accomplished country musician—but it was impossible music to work out to. Jan "Boy Boy" Cote laughed at the scene his buddy Itchy presents, then exclaims, "You'd rather work out with no music!"

Michen remembers another time when Gino made a dramatic return home. Gino showed up at the gym where Michen was working out on a lunch break, in the basement of an older building. He was bench-pressing, pushing his strength to the limit. "I get up, and I'm starting to pull the weights off, and Gino was walking down the stairs," Michen recalls. Gino told his old friend he'd arrived back in town the night before. Michen was surprised to see his friend already set to pump iron. "Gotta stay in shape," he told Michen. Gino started stretching, using a nearby pillar. He'd already warmed up at home with push-ups, he told a baffled Michen. Then he laid back and fired off twenty-two reps. "I slowed down," Gino told his friend. Michen was incredulous. "Twenty-two! I said, 'I'm shitting in my pants to lift that thing six times earlier, just before you walked in.' So I said, like, 'Fuck you, dude!'" Michen recalls, a wide grin on his face. Gino started laughing, then revealed that during the hockey season, he'd do thirty-three, thirty-four reps a set. "And that's why he was in the NHL," declares Michen.

When he was done working out, Gino liked to socialize even more. He'd phone up everyone and have them over. He'd invite girls too. Gino loved women. Gino never liked to be alone. When he was home in Kitigan Zibi, he'd surround himself with friends. He'd have them over to his place, they'd sing and drink into the night. In the daytime, they'd play golf—another activity Gino loved. Most summers, he and Michen organized a charity golf tournament at one of the local courses.

He'd get dozens of friends and associates out. His dad and his dad's friends would cook the food. In many of those summers, Gino's Canucks teammates came along. Pavel Bure came one year, to great acclaim.

The event, which became officially known as the Gino Odjick Golf Tournament, was designed to be a social gathering, an annual summer party. It started in the 1980s to honour Kitigan Zibi's previous NHLer, John Chabot. Chabot's roots were on the reserve, but he hadn't grown up there, so he didn't attend every year. By 1991, two things had changed. First of all, of course, Gino had made his NHL debut and established himself in the league. Second, Michen was put in charge of organizing to the tournament. He'd started working for the band council, and one day, a director looked at him and said, "Can you take care of this event?" "Yeah," Michen replied. "But I'm adding Gino."

Michen ran with it. He would organize the event for a decade. (He would eventually pass the organizing torch to Boy Boy.) "I wanted it to be a social event," Michen says. "It wasn't there for any fundraising purposes, because I didn't want to get into, like, managing those funds or whatever. So I put all the money back into the tournament. Each year I was forecasting how much we were going to make and this and that. So what happens? A few occasions it rained and like sixty people didn't show up and didn't pay. We end up paying for the tournament and the gifts and everything."

The tournament became a little bit legendary and a little bit infamous. Between the adults carousing on the course, consuming beverages, having a good time out in the sun, and the kids running all over, climbing—and sometimes driving—the golf carts, pulling out clubs and swinging them about, you can't help but think it was a miracle anyone finished a round. One year, they put paddleboats in the golf course ponds, but all the kids, who were meant to be volunteer caddies, piled onto the boats instead. Fun was the name of the game.

WHEN GINO WAS out on the road, he'd bring friends along. "He used to call me and say, 'Come watch my game. I got some tickets. I have no one to come and see me,'" Michen recalls. "He was lonesome for his friends, wherever he was. When he was playing in Montreal, or we went down to Philly several times, we saw him play in New York. He'd give me a call and say bring someone, come down."

One Thursday, Gino called up Michen, who was out for a beer with Itchy at a local strip joint. "Hey, what are you doing this weekend?" Gino asked his friend. Michen told him he had no plans. "How about you come down to Philly? I just bought a vehicle," Gino added. It was an SUV, a big Ford Expedition. Turns out he'd bought it from a dealer in Maniwaki. "So he asked us if we wanted to drive it down. He'd take care of all our expenses," Michen says. "So I asked Itchy."

"Fuck yeah!" he recalled Itchy exclaiming with delight.

Wherever he went, Gino made connections of all kinds. Itchy, for instance, credits many of his own far-flung music gigs to connections Gino helped him make. "I travelled because of who I met through Gino," Itchy says. "Like I went to Great Bear Lake. Danny Gaudet, the chief there, I met him through Gino. I got to play music in these areas."

Not wanting to be alone meant that Gino was constantly introducing himself to strangers. "This guy would pick up a hitchhiker on the side of the road," says Boy Boy. He'd do it just for the conversation. Gino was never shy to say hello to anyone.

"If someone at the side of the road needs help, he'd stop every time. It's not always like that in the city. On the reserve, even if you didn't know someone, you'd stop and have a big conversation. I guess there, in the city, if you did that, people would think you're crazy," Itchy explained. Where are you from? Gino would ask. You hungry? "He was always surrounded by people. Friends, family—people."

When his friends came to join him in Vancouver or Long Island or Philadelphia, he made sure they had somewhere to stay, that they had things to do, that they had a vehicle to borrow—often it was his. He'd take them out for meals, for drinks. And he made sure there were always women to chat up.

Always having friends and girlfriends around also meant there were usually people around who ended up cooking and cleaning for him. "Man-child," they used to call him, Charlene Leech, Peter's wife, said. He always had people around to help him with life. Peter, whom Gino had met years before, became Gino's closest confidant in the final two decades of his life. Peter also became Gino's main helper, especially as Gino's health declined in his later years.

"We knew that he needed to be babied," Michen said. "Not babied it in the sense that, 'You're a big baby,' but he just needed to be taken care of. Stuff like that. I think his family life was very important to him, and I think he needed to find a family life outside of his family."

In a 2002 interview with Mathias Brunet of the Montreal newspaper *La Presse*, Gino connected his instinct for family bonds back to his upbringing. "We were always 10, 15, 20 in the house in Maniwaki," he said in French. "I have six sisters and there were always many kids from different communities that we put up because they went to the school in our parts. I've always lived with families from the start of my career."[66]

After he and Jolene Commanda broke off their relationship, he moved into a basement suite with the Lahache family on the Kahnawake reserve. "When you're used to living in a certain way, it's easier to live with a family," he went on. "We have the same traditions. When you live with a group, you are never lacking for support. When things aren't going so well, I have people to talk to. And anyway, I've always liked living in basements. It's cool, it's relaxing." In Kahnawake, he had also made friends with Danny Montour, who would often drive him into Montreal. Montour had first met Papa Joe years before, and he and Gino became friends over the years. Gino would also live with him for a time when he played for the Canadiens.

His easy-going, trusting nature got him near trouble too. "Pat Quinn once asked me to try to keep him away from certain guys who were a bad influence on him," Geoff Courtnall recalls. One of these guys Gino did hang around with was the aforementioned Richard "Ding" Whiteduck. Ding was about Gino's age and they'd been friends since they were young; he grew up in Rapid Lake, the small community two hours north of Kitigan Zibi where Gino's dad was born. Ding came to be something like a personal assistant to Gino. "Gino's butler, we used to call him," Michen says with a laugh. If something needed to get done, Ding would run off and sort it out. He'd fetch his mail. He'd take his clothes to the cleaners. "It was a win-win," Boy Boy says. "Gino needed someone like that, and Ding got to live the life of a celebrity."

"Ding was crazy," Gino's former girlfriend Caroline Forester says, with a hint of a smile. "Ding was there to cook, to clean, to drive us around. To get them in trouble, to party, to get them women. That was a fun time because I was, I mean, imagine this: I'm in uni. Sounds wrong. These guys, I'm nineteen, and you meet somebody like Gino and, yeah, it was just crazy time. We were out and about all the time. And then when Pavel would come into town, oh my god, we'd have crazy nights. Lots of drinks."

To Itchy, though, spending too much time with Ding put Gino at risk. "He was so close to that guy. But that guy was a bad influence. He was a terrible influence," he says. More than once, Ding got into legal trouble in the United States. He served time in Pennsylvania and in Florida. But he was a friend from way back. Gino just couldn't give him up. "He bailed him out," Itchy said.

Ding was Michen's cousin and died many years ago. "I miss him, but only certain parts of him," Michen says with a chuckle. Ding may have run the errands that needed running, but he was also running schemes on the side. And more than once, Michen had to tell him to stay away from them, to take his bad business elsewhere.

In BC, too, the good-hearted Gino pulled some shady characters into his life. For a time, Gino made friends with a Vancouver biker named Bob Green, who was a well-known member of the Hells Angels. Both Peter and Itchy confronted Gino about his friendly relations with Green. They were baffled that he would spend time with such a notorious guy—that he would even visit him and his associates at local Hells Angels clubhouses.

"Gino, man, you shouldn't be fucking hanging out with people like that, like you're gonna fuck yourself up," Itchy told him at one point in the early 1990s, before he himself became a cop. Years later, Gino would tell Peter, "Oh, these are good guys." Peter would say the same as Itchy, but in less colourful language.

GINO'S FEAR OF being alone overlapped with his lifelong love of women too. He craved the companionship of women. Obviously, he craved intimacy, as well. But he was never able to keep himself connected to a girlfriend in the long term, for better or worse. Charlene Leech saw him as a man who just wanted a "snuggle buddy" but who did at times also find himself in more serious relationships. "He'd say he just wanted to be like us, like me and Peter. To have our kind of relationship," Charlene says. But he was never able to make it stick. "He just had a charm to him," she says of his many relationships. "They just couldn't say no to him, and he just loved every single one of them as well."

Deep down, though, especially once his health started to fail in the last decade of his life, that anxiety about being alone morphed into something more final, more core to his being. "He'd always say to me, 'I don't want to die alone,'" Charlene continues. "And I'd say, 'You're not going to be alone. One of us is going to be with you. You're never going to die alone.' And he goes, 'I'm terrified.' And I went, 'Yes, I know, I know you're terrified. I feel it every day.' And he goes, 'What if I'm alone?' And I said, 'Dude, you're never alone in this house, you either have me or my sister or Peter—like, really, you're never gonna die alone.'"

KITIGAN ZIBI IS a tight-knit community. It always has been, Itchy says. "We're proud, we're a proud people," he said. "We're deep-rooted." And people work hard. They take care of their homes. It's a clean, tidy place. But poverty is always around the corner. Many people have lovely homes. But many don't.

It's a story that plays out on reserves across the country: the consequences of a century and a half of destructive government policy still make life a struggle for many. The spectre of residential schools remains everywhere too. The generational trauma is real, Itchy is quick to remind. He sees it all the time in his police work.

"Education is power," Dewache says. Gino would add to that and say "Education is freedom." That's what Gino and Peter told young people in the youth leadership workshops they hosted in Indigenous communities, beginning in about 1999. In Kitigan Zibi, they have a strong tradition of education. "We're a well-administered community, especially compared to some communities that lack education, that lack resources," Dewache said. And they've always had the arena in Maniwaki. It gave them something to do. Today, they've got a beautiful school on the reserve, called Kitigan Zibi Kikanamadinan. And there are sports fields on the reserve too.

Boy Boy has coached and organized hockey teams on the reserve since his youth and taught at the high school for twenty-five years. There's a big poster of Gino in the gym, forever encouraging the students to focus on their education, to make something of themselves. As always, the message Gino liked to tell young people: "Look, I made it, so can you, if you work hard." Boy Boy's friend, he came to realize, had a special power to unite people. Gino's hockey career opened the door to connect with fans, then his personality solidified the relationship.

"He was glue for the community," Boy Boy said. "I've seen him be glue for other communities too. One time, we were helping with a hockey school in Winnipeg. Gino goes, 'Hey, you're gonna come with me. I gotta meet a couple of chiefs.' So we go sit at a table and those two guys, you could see they're in love with Gino. And these guys are chiefs of their community! And you could just see the love in their eyes: 'We're in the presence of Gino!'"

Boy Boy once travelled to the Seabird reserve outside Agassiz, BC, on the Fraser River. His sister-in-law married a Stó:lō man who asked if Gino would be interested in driving out to meet with people from the reserve. "The community made such a big thing about it. Gino was there to do an unofficial visit, come and see and talk to some people." They put a "Welcome, Gino" banner up at the community hall and hosted his meetings there. When Gino arrived, he saw what a big deal they were making, and he was taken aback. But he pressed on, even if this wasn't quite what he wanted to do or was expecting.

"We walk into the hall and everyone's ready for pictures and autographs," Boy Boy recalls. "Everybody's there to welcome him to their community. And what does he do? The first thing he does—this is how he never thought of himself as a celebrity, really—he sees this old man sitting on a bench on the outside wall. He's leaning on his cane. And with everyone greeting him—Gino would say, 'Hey, how're you doing?'—and him signing autographs as he walked and taking pictures with him too, he sees the old man and Gino goes and sits with him." The man hadn't even really been watching for the former NHLer. But Gino knew this was the man to talk to in the moment. "He's the guy to get the information from."

He'd do this wherever he went. He'd strike up conversations with people who didn't quite seem to fit in the moment—people who were just there, and weren't there to see him. It was something he learned from Pavel Bure, he said. Bure would speak to the people who seemed less interested in the moment, because Bure was always anxious about the people who were really there to see him. He didn't like that they were going to take his signature and turn around and try to sell it. He was looking for the people who weren't going to do that. And Gino took that lesson to heart.

IN THE EARLY YEARS in Vancouver, Gino lived at the Atrium Inn, at the corner of Hastings and Renfrew streets, just minutes from the Pacific Coliseum. Then, when he became a father for the fourth time, living with his then-girlfriend Elizabeth Poon, he lived in Port Moody, a suburb of Vancouver. After Elizabeth left in 1994, he lived downtown for a while. But the place where he lived the longest was on the Musqueam reserve.

In the Musqueam people, he found another tight-knit community. The reserve sits at the southwestern corner of the city of Vancouver, on ancestral lands at the mouth of the Fraser River that the Musqueam people have lived on for generations. There, Gino found a home away from home. He'd regularly crash at the homes of Rick and Judy Sparrow and of Wayne Sparrow, years before Wayne became Musqueam chief. Gino ended up sleeping on Rick and Judy's couch so much that in about 1996 they eventually just suggested he move in downstairs. Eventually, Gino built a small home next door. Rick Sparrow was well known in the community as one of the best salmon fishermen going. Gino liked fishing but he never liked eating fish much—unless it was Rick who was serving it. He found so much comfort there that he'd eat something he usually didn't.

"I really missed the reserve, and First Nations people, when I first got here," Odjick told Vancouver news and lifestyle website *Vancouver Is Awesome* in 2011. "So I was really happy meeting people like Wayne Sparrow. After that, I started hanging around Musqueam, and it didn't take too long before I moved here, because it felt like home."[67]

When he returned to Vancouver after retiring as a player, he was with Caroline. They first moved into the townhouse he'd built on the reserve, and later moved to a home farther north, on the western boundary of Kitsilano. He lived there with Caroline and their child, Rose, until their relationship ended in 2009.

Later, he'd live with son Patrick, who moved west in 2010, and his cousin Stéphane. Gino also lived for a time with his niece Roxane, who worked at the Musqueam golf course he would later own.

His final years were spent living at Peter and Charlene Leech's home in Burnaby. BC had become his home. Kitigan Zibi was too cold, he would say. But he also grew to prefer the more laid-back sensibility of the people he'd found out west.

"We always made it happy for him," Charlene Leech said of having Gino live with them. "I didn't want him to be stressed out. I didn't want him to be uncomfortable. I just wanted his last few years, as long as we could have him, to not to be sad.

Other people were not so nice at times, and we always sheltered him when he needed it, when things got stressful for him. We'd always take the punches."

GINO'S MESSAGE OF hope and empowerment didn't always land with everyone back home in Kitigan Zibi. For all the good things Odjick did for his community, there were still skeptics. "Some people were very jealous of him because he's successful. They'd say, 'What did Gino Odjick ever do for us?'" Boy Boy says, with a tone of disdain. He takes exception to people who would say that. "He doesn't owe you everything. He did everything on his own... and then he did everything for the kids," he says. It was pure jealousy, he felt. "Jealousy is the most powerful force in the universe. The things you could make happen with that energy..."

7

"IF ANYONE WENT INTO PAVEL'S AIRSPACE . . ."

ONE OF THE defining relationships of Gino's adult life was his surprising friendship with Pavel Bure, the Canucks' first-ever superstar and the main reason why a team that was already pretty decent became a true Stanley Cup contender. Both Odjick and Bure were outsiders, so they identified with each other. Once they had settled in Vancouver, their friendship grew. And even after their time together in Vancouver was up, they remained close.

In the winter of 2013, the Vancouver Canucks did something remarkable, something that a few years before seemed unimaginable. They coaxed Bure, who had once been the golden boy in Vancouver, home for a jersey retirement ceremony. Despite Bure's status as the most exciting player in team history, the first Canuck to score fifty goals in a season, a ceremony seemed unimaginable because he had left

Vancouver on such bad terms. Frustrated by the way he'd been treated by the Canucks' front office, he told GM Brian Burke in the summer of 1998 that he would never play for Vancouver again. It took Burke months, but in January 1999, Bure was traded to the Florida Panthers—about as far away from Vancouver as you can get while still remaining in the NHL. Bure's departure was the final nail in the coffin for the 1994 Canucks, the team that had won so many hearts in Vancouver, a team that is venerated to this day. That team's engine was now gone.

No one, at least no one in living memory, had dazzled Vancouver hockey crowds quite like Bure. But much of Bure's time in Vancouver was difficult. For all the adulation, for all the millions he was paid, he was often unhappy. He had rarely been treated fairly, he believed. His beef was never with the fans, he said, just with the people who ran the team. The fans, they'd been great. His teammates too. But he'd encountered too much contract-related nonsense over his years in Vancouver, he felt. So he did the thing that usually severs the relationship between player and fan: he asked for a trade and insisted he'd never play for the home team again.

A vast swath of the Vancouver fan base swore off him, even if he was the best player they'd ever seen. Or maybe that's why they swore off him: he was the greatest and he was walking out on their dreams. Regardless, it was far from a sure thing that he'd receive a warm reception were he ever to set foot in Vancouver again.

And yet he did. Perhaps this can be attributed to that old cliché about time—that it heals all wounds. But really, the rapprochement should be credited to Gino Odjick.

Gino had been retired for a decade by the time his old friend was finally enticed back for his jersey retirement ceremony. Gino had moved back to Vancouver after playing his final game in the NHL for the Montreal Canadiens in 2002.

The last time the two pals lived in the same city was 1998, the year Gino was traded to the New York Islanders. That they remained close over the ensuing two-plus decades is testament to how special their friendship was.

How they became friends is a remarkable story—but first, an anecdote from later in life to show the maturity of their friendship: The night before Bure's name and number were hoisted to the rafters in Rogers Arena, Odjick helped organize a special event on the Musqueam reserve. Igor Larionov was there. Pat Quinn was there. Ron Toigo, owner of the WHL Vancouver Giants and White Spot restaurants, among many other things, was there too. So was Geoff Courtnall. So was Gino's dad Joe.

"In 1993–94, when I scored sixteen goals, I had a lot of Russian in me," Odjick said at the event that night. "But in the playoffs, when Pavel knocked out Shane Churla cold, there was a lot of Indian in him!" The assembled group roared in approval of Odjick landing the perfect line. Their adopted son was bringing to his friends another person for them to take into their circle.

It was no surprise to Bure that he was immediately in Odjick's company when he returned to the city that had launched his career. But the reception by the Musqueam people: that did catch him off guard.

"I was surprised it was such a big deal for them," Bure recalls, a decade later. "I was surprised it was so many people, important people for the community. I thought it was just [because] we were there, because we're hanging around there with Gino."

Musqueam chief Wayne Sparrow was there too, of course. He presented Bure with a special paddle, crafted by a local artist, bearing Bure's name and painted in the old Canucks colours of black, red, and yellow.

"You guys make me feel at home, you make me feel comfortable," Bure told the crowd. Bure, who had so often made opponents feel humble, skating past them, his feet cutting across the ice as if he were a breeze slipping across a meadow, was humbled by the moment. Returning to Vancouver had filled him with anxiety. He wasn't sure how fans would react. The spring before, when he had visited the city and the arena as a guest of Canucks ownership in a litmus test of fan enthusiasm, he had been blown away by the raucous, all-in reception he received. The fans didn't care that he'd quit on the team. He needn't have worried about that. If the fans had once been upset about his departure, all they remembered now was his thrilling play. The Canucks ran a short video on the big screen and then introduced him to the crowd. The eighteen thousand or so fans in attendance rose to their feet, and Bure, visibly touched, waved and saluted.

The Musqueam reception hit him similarly: it was a more intimate event than his spring appearance at Rogers Arena, but the energy was similar. Everyone in attendance was thrilled to see him. And it was all because his friend Gino was doing the only thing he knew: showing immense loyalty to someone who had only ever shown him the same. Gino wanted his friend to feel the warm welcome of a close-knit community, one he'd come to know well. Kumi Kimura, whom Gino had hired to take over the Musqueam golf course in 2008, said the event was a classic Odjick gesture.

"It was quite spectacular for him to get all those people to come to Musqueam," she says. "He was always working in some other way to make sure that he doesn't get accolades but everybody else does. And always bringing First Nations people up in that way. Pavel didn't quite know what to expect. He looked in and was kind of like a deer in the headlights, like 'Holy, all these people came out here?' But that was all Gino. That's him. He did that in a span of like twenty-four hours. 'Get some food out here. Get some chow mein. Can we get this? Get that! We're doing this.'"

Bure may have been surprised at first by the reception, but once the event started, how it unfolded made total sense to him. His old friend was all about doing the right thing for people. And holding a big celebration with all his friends, for his greatest friend, was the right thing to do. "Gino truly cared about people," Bure says. "He was helping lots of people, in different ways. For kids, he would do one thing. For the adults, other things. Gino was just a great man."

"When he brings people like that to the reserve, that lifts the community up as well," Kimura adds. "It would say, 'We are equal, no one's better, when Pavel goes to the Hall [of Fame], we all go to the Hall.'"

GINO'S FRIENDS WERE on edge for the event, though. Gino had been back in psychiatric care in the weeks leading up to Bure's return. After Gino left Riverview in September, he'd moved in with his old Musqueam friends Rick and Judy Sparrow. But Judy could tell Gino was still not himself. "There's something wrong with him," she told Peter. "I don't know." He was ranting, saying all kinds of wild things. He was paranoid, hurling accusations at those close to him. He showed manic tendencies too. "All these little things. He'd call me at eleven o'clock at night and say, 'Let's go! Let's do this or that!'" Kimura recalls. And then one night he locked Kumi in his truck.

"The police had to come. It was kind of crazy," Kumi recalls. The police ended up taking him to Vancouver General Hospital. He was later transferred to UBC Hospital's psychiatric ward, where he came under the care of Dr. Edwin Tam of the UBC Mood Disorders Centre. It was Dr. Tam who eventually helped Gino find peace with his mental issues, but it would take time. And it would be far from a straight line to get there.

"We wanted him in the hospital until two or three days before Pavel's event so he would be calm, be rested and get on the regular meds that control his brain," Kumi revealed to the *Vancouver Sun* a few weeks after the Bure ceremony.[68] That was a common sentiment among his friends: Gino needed rest. He had argued the point for months, but his friends saw how much he needed help.

At the same time, a whole other health issue was starting to show itself. About a week before Bure's return, Gino went out on a day pass for lunch with Peter. After eating a little Mexican meal, on their way back to the car, he suddenly got short of breath and fell down to one knee. He was struggling to breathe, his face all scrunched up, almost like a fish, Peter remembers. Peter could tell his friend wasn't feeling right, but Gino insisted he was fine. When they arrived back at UBC Hospital, the nurses saw he wasn't fine: his blood pressure had shot up and his heart rate was irregular.

Gino spent the next week under the care of the cardiology department, which eventually diagnosed him with a heart murmur, a condition in which the heart isn't pumping at a consistent, regular rate. This would be a warning sign of bigger things to come. But Gino was focused on the upcoming jersey retirement ceremony for Bure. He was excited for his friend, for his triumphant return to the city, a return in which Gino had played a big role in making happen.

When Bure arrived in Vancouver a few days before the event, it was Peter, not Gino, who picked him up at the airport. "Gino didn't sleep well," Peter told him. The next day, Pavel was booked for a card-signing show. Gino and Peter joined him. Pavel could see that his old friend was struggling; he was having a hard time getting up and down stairs. Peter and Pavel suggested to Gino they take him to hospital, but he waved them off. "I'm fine, I'm fine," he insisted.

The next day was the Musqueam reception. His time at UBC had stabilized his mental state somewhat, but it was still frantic. And with so many people around, his friends worried about how stressed he'd get, and whether all this might trigger another psychotic episode. At one point during the celebration, Gino and Pavel went outside for a smoke. Peter came out to join his friends, but Gino got defensive, showing a hint of his still-extant paranoia: "Are you just following me?" Peter and Pavel told him to cool off. That would prove to be a hiccup: overall, Gino sailed through the three days, though his head was still in a mess and he was starting to experience problems with his heart.

In the ceremony at Rogers Arena, he was one of two friends from the past whom Bure invited to join him at centre ice. Pat Quinn was there as well. Despite all the frustrations Bure had felt toward the Canucks organization, some of them involving Quinn, Bure wanted him there. And he wanted his best friend there too.

BURE AND ODJICK had been friends almost from the day the Russian arrived in Vancouver in November 1991. To begin to understand this unique friendship, we need to dial back to the closing stages of the Cold War, to the very collapse of the Soviet Union.

Beneath all the other geopolitical machinations going on in the late 1980s were efforts by the Canucks to build sporting ties behind the Iron Curtain, taking advantage of Mikhail Gorbachev's policy of glasnost, bringing openness and transparency to the Soviet Union. In this environment, Canucks ownership saw an opportunity. They were desperate to change the narrative of the team, so they thought, "Why not the Soviets?" So Arthur Griffiths embarked on an attempt at soft power: get the Soviets on friendly terms with his team, and maybe, just maybe, it would bear on-ice fruit. They engaged in personnel exchanges: assistant coach Jack McIlhargey went to Russia—the Russians mostly him showed a good time, not much about coaching—while goalie Troy Gamble was put through a punishing training regimen. Venerable coach Anatoly Tarasov—the godfather of Russian hockey—visited Vancouver several times and the Canucks secured him medical treatment during his stay, while goalie Vladislav Tretiak, considered the finest in the game in the 1970s, was invited to lead goalie camps in Vancouver.

The Canucks' selection of Pavel Bure in the sixth round of the 1989 draft was a surprise—not because no one else was interested in him, but because almost no one outside of Vancouver thought he was eligible. He was considered by many the most exciting prospect in hockey and could have been picked in the first three rounds of the draft, but no one thought he'd move to North America for years to come.

The Detroit Red Wings did ask the league about his eligibility in the fifth round, but were told he hadn't played the required two professional seasons to be eligible to be drafted after the third round. So why did Vancouver pick him? Because chief scout Mike Penny and his staff, with the help of a Soviet source, found proof that Bure had played in eleven games for Central Red Army's senior team in 1987–88, which they claimed counted as a professional season for Bure, thus making him eligible. The Canucks believed they could pull a fast one on the rest of the league. The Red Wings, it turned out, were ready to select Bure a few picks after the Canucks, so Penny's work proved prescient.

There were immediate—and loud—protests from other teams against the Canucks' selection. The league wouldn't rule in Vancouver's favour until the eve of the 1990 draft. The *Province*'s Tony Gallagher would later allege the settlement was a quid pro quo for Quinn dropping a lawsuit against the league over his suspension for being hired by the Canucks in 1986 while still a member of the Kings organization.

By the time they selected Odjick at the 1990 draft, it was just a question of when Bure would land in Vancouver. The Canucks played coy all season. At the end of the 1990–91 season, Pat Quinn's right-hand man, the always quotable Brian Burke, cautiously told the *Province*'s Jim Jamieson they didn't expect Bure to make the jump for at least another year. Bure was the fourth Soviet player drafted in five years by Vancouver; they knew well how much of a role politics played in getting the players out of the closed Soviet system. In 1989, the Canucks had been allowed to sign two Russian stars: Igor Larionov (drafted in the eleventh round in 1985) and Vladimir

Krutov (drafted in the twelfth round in 1986) after protracted negotiations.

But with Bure, Soviet officials showed no sign of bending, even after a pair of young stars defected to the NHL: Alexander Mogilny in 1989 and Sergei Fedorov in 1990. Bure was under contract and would have no say in his future, the Soviets said. "Don't expect Bure till 1994" was the word as Bure starred for the Soviet junior team at the 1991 world juniors in Saskatchewan.

While the Detroit Red Wings, with Fedorov, and the Buffalo Sabres, with Mogilny, had worked to assist the young players in coordinating their defections, the Canucks were adamant that everything between them and the Soviets, and Bure, would be above board. "You come in the front door or you don't come at all," Burke told the *Province*'s Frank Luba during the tournament, describing the Canucks' strategy in dealing with Bure and his overlords. It was an approach that team owner Frank Griffiths had insisted upon since before Quinn and Burke took over. The policy had landed the Canucks Larionov and Krutov in 1989. Larionov worked out and would prove to be Bure's first centreman with the Canucks. Krutov, though, was a disaster. He arrived in Vancouver last and out of shape and never caught up. The Canucks cut Krutov after he showed up to 1990 training camp still out of shape. Krutov's lawyers eventually won him a settlement in front of an international tribunal.

Just as Krutov's time was coming to an end in Vancouver, the Soviet empire crumbled in earnest in the late summer of 1991. Bure and his father Vladimir and younger brother Valeri quietly slipped out the Soviet front door and flew from

Moscow to Los Angeles in early September. Bure arriving well before expected threw Quinn and Burke for a loop, and getting Bure legally into Canada became an ordeal in itself, one that Bure would never quite get over.

Even before the larger political upheavals began to roil the USSR that summer, Bure had resisted signing a contract extension with his Soviet League team, Central Red Army, for beyond the 1991–92 season. Bure's resistance drew the ire of the Soviet hockey federation, who declined to include him on the Soviet national team for the 1991 Canada Cup, which featured the best players in hockey playing for their countries, even though he had finished the previous season as the second-leading scorer in the Soviet league. Vancouver reporters caught wind of Bure's situation, that the Soviets might be altering their position, but the Canucks' response remained the same: they would only talk about Bure coming if there was an official transfer to be had.

As August closed, the Soviet economic and political system was in tatters. So Vladimir Bure and his sons arrived in Los Angeles, landing on the doorstep of Ron Salcer, a prominent agent for hockey players. Pavel Bure's American visa only allowed a one-time entry: if he went north to Vancouver, there was no guarantee he'd be able to secure a new one for re-entry into the US, which would obviously not be ideal for a team that played many of its road games south of the border. Furthermore, the NHL said they respected Bure's Soviet contract, which still had a year to run. The Canucks would have to find a way past that obstacle. The team had felt frustrated grinding out transfer fees for Larionov and Krutov, and now here was a new one. The Canucks and the NHL and Bure all thought the only way out of all this would be through the courts.

But on Halloween 1991, the courts stepped aside. The Michigan judge who had been assigned the case told the Canucks and the Soviets to settle their differences and come to a financial agreement. After some back and forth, the two sides were about $50,000 apart. Bure himself would bridge the difference by kicking in money from his soon-to-be-signed contract. The Canucks would pay him back, but, yes, this was another early entry on Bure's list of frustrations with the Canucks.

AFTER MORE THAN two years of "When will he come?" and "Will he ever come?" the Canucks now had on their roster the best player in team history—until the arrival of the Sedin twins. The roster already included the man who would become Bure's greatest North American friend, in a relationship that seemed to defy logic: a quiet Russian who played hockey with grace and beauty, raised in one of the world's great cities, and an outgoing Algonquin man who had punched his way into the NHL, who was raised in a small, rural, but tight-knit community in Quebec, for whom moving to Vancouver had spurred a dramatic leap forward in his world view. Even their approaches with the public and the media were like chalk and cheese: Odjick made an effort to leave an impression on every fan he met, whether outside the Canucks' home arena or on one of Vancouver's many bustling shopping streets, while Bure was inclined to merely smile and nod for a few supporters as he made his way to his car outside the Pacific Coliseum. It was the same with reporters. "Gino was very, very open and Pavel, you know, was very circumspect of the media," *Vancouver Sun* reporter Mike Beamish recalls.

During the first couple of practices, Bure found himself skating with some of the lesser lights on the Canucks roster, first with Jay Mazur and Andrew McBain, two little-used grinders who would fall further down the depth chart after Bure's arrival; in fact, neither would play another game for the Canucks. Next, Bure practised on the fourth line with Odjick and veteran centre Ryan Walter. The Canucks knew they had a star on their hands but weren't quite sure how to integrate him into the lineup.

In those first practices, Odjick, as friendly as could be, made the first moves toward what would become a lifelong friendship. Odjick, who probably never met a hockey drill he didn't understand right away, would mime to Bure what the coaches were looking for. And, of course, he'd slowly teach Bure the words too. In a 1993 profile of Bure by the *Sun*'s Lisa Fitterman, Odjick joked that the first things he taught his friend to say were "Oh, you commies" and "I love you, I need you, I want you."

"It was a joke right? Stuff like that. Regular guy stuff, that's all. I taught him stuff that I can't repeat to you right now," Gino added. "It's like, he gained my trust and I gained his trust and that's it."[69] Obviously, Odjick's quirky sense of humour needed no translation. Beyond the jokes and Odjick's kind nature, there are a few other obvious points of kinship between Gino Odjick and Pavel Bure, even if their origins were literally a world apart.

Both were the sons of strong, influential fathers. Both were outsiders to the dominant culture in the team's dressing room: middle-class, English-speaking Canadians. "We both were in culture shock. He left Moscow, which was a huge city," Odjick said. Of course, Odjick was moving in the opposite direction: compared with Kitigan Zibi, Vancouver was huge. For both, though, it was a wholly new city and experience. And perhaps more crucially, while most of their teammates had families, Odjick and Bure both were young (twenty-one and twenty, respectively), single guys. Their teammates would head home after the game. But Pavel and Gino, they had time to fill and money to burn. "So we have to do something," Bure recalls. Then he laughs. Gino's love of visiting bars and clubs, like the Roxy or the Biltmore, was well known. But, no, rarely did Bure go with his friend to those nightclubs.

"We'd just go for dinner. We had so many games. You had to eat every day," he says, chuckling again. "I didn't have a car. I didn't know where to go." So Gino led the way. "We wouldn't go to fancy restaurants. We would go to like middle-class restaurants," Pavel recalled. One of those places was The Slocan, a family restaurant just up Hastings from the Atrium Inn. Gino would sometimes eat there three times a day. After a while, Bure came to like Fiasco, a swankier restaurant in Kitsilano. They'd go there too. They'd ride the gondola up Grouse Mountain and eat at the restaurant at the top. They'd visit some of Vancouver's classic restaurants, like The Cannery and Hy's Steakhouse.

But in Vancouver, there wasn't much in the way of Russian cooking. For Bure, that took getting used to. Burgers and fries and sushi replaced borscht, pickled herring, and pelmeni dumplings on his main menu. It was all an important cultural education for Bure. He was learning the North American way of life.

"You spend time with someone. You find out some things. You try to talk," Bure says. "The biggest thing for me was the language. I couldn't even order food for myself; I didn't know how to order chicken or steak or fish. Otherwise, it was happy. It was an incredible life." And so Gino would lead him around Vancouver, showing him what he'd uncovered in the year's head start he'd had on Bure in Vancouver.

When the Canucks were on a road trip, meals took on a different dynamic. "On the road, it's more easy because you can get a bunch of guys together," Bure says. There were no families for their other teammates to go home to. And when they'd hit New York, it was Bure who would take charge. "Lots of Russian people in New York," Bure notes. That meant getting something they couldn't really get in Vancouver: Russian cuisine. "I'd take Gino with me. He'd try something new there."

ON THE ICE, Odjick and Bure were paired up from the start. In Bure's sensational first game, November 5, 1991, nearly a year to the day after Gino's debut, Bure and Odjick skated on opposite wings, with veteran Ryan Walter at centre, as they had in practice. Bure had three shots on goal. He didn't score, but no one cared. His wizardry with the puck, his explosive skating talents—they were immediately obvious.

Even in that debut game, Odjick knew his time with Bure as a linemate would be short. "Oh my god, he was flying around, and I told Ryan Walter he wasn't going to stay around us too long," Odjick told Bob Marjanovich in 2022.[70] The fans at the Pacific Coliseum were constantly on their feet, roaring in approval. The long road to getting Bure to Vancouver, with all its twists and turns, was worth it.

And as Bure would come to experience, Gino's character off the ice—selfless, caring, supportive—was the same on the ice. Of course, Odjick's efforts off the ice were usually gentle. On the ice, his instincts were the complete opposite. Canucks fans who are old enough likely remember Bure's fourth game, against the Los Angeles Kings, as a massive milestone for the soon-to-be-dubbed Russian Rocket: this is the game where Bure scored for the first time. Odjick remembered the game for a different reason: it was the first time he stood up for his new friend.

Early in the game, a big, lumbering rookie defenceman for the Kings named Peter Ahola had tried to rough up Bure. The next shift out, Odjick got on Ahola's case. "I gave the guy a beating, and from that moment on, we were best friends," Odjick told Marjanovich.

His fighting talents were a revelation to Bure. At home in the Soviet Union, there was no fighting in hockey. "By the rules, we weren't allowed to fight," he said. "It just didn't exist." And if you did get into anything rough, Viktor Tikhonov, the legendary but tyrannical head coach of the Soviet national team, would staple you to the end of the bench or, worse, suspend you.

As wild as he found the enforcer role to be, Bure quickly came to understand the importance of a fighter, at least in that era of hockey in the NHL. "Especially when you get to know how tough it is," he said. Seeing enforcers break their hands because they had to punch an opponent's helmet—that was a lesson for Bure. "I saw the hands of those guys, the more I played, the more guys," he recalled. "When you see, like, how tough they are to fight, you know, obviously you appreciate what they're doing for the team."

For his part, Odjick appreciated how his friend played the game. And how he kept getting better and better. (Bure and

Odjick wouldn't last long as linemates that season, as the Russian was quickly moved up the lines while Gino remained a fourth-liner.) After winning the Calder Memorial Trophy as the NHL's rookie of the year in 1991–92, Bure scored sixty goals in 1992–93 and again in 1993–94. Odjick was in awe of Bure's talents. "The first year he thought he had to go around everybody, and it was the same thing last year," he told the *Vancouver Sun*'s Elliott Pap in March 1994. "But Pavel's been working hard on his shot, and if the defence wants to back up, then he'll shoot. When he's flying and feeling good, like he is now, you just give him the puck and go to the net."[71]

That season, Odjick had a front-row view of many of those goals, as he and Bure spent most of the first half of the season together on a line again. Odjick himself scored sixteen goals, many set up by his best friend. Odjick, Courtnall says, earned his spot on that line. "He was always working, doing extra stuff after practice," the winger recalled.

And as with Donald Audette, Odjick's teammate in junior, if you were Gino's friend and someone went after you, Gino would get them back for you—even if you didn't play on the same team. Odjick was traded to the Islanders in 1998, and Bure to the Panthers a year later, but that didn't mean Gino stopped looking after his friend. "When I played, if anyone went into Pavel's airspace, he was getting a beating," Odjick told the *Province*'s Jason Botchford in 2013. "In the last four years of my career, we didn't play together. But no one dared touch him, even still... I was on another team and if they touched him, they were going to play me sooner or later. And that's just the way it was."[72]

That loyalty meant a lot to Bure, especially his relationship with the Canucks soured. His frustrations with the front office were there almost from the moment he left Russia. He never liked how he and his brother and father had been left to languish in Los Angeles for their first two months in North America; how, in the end, he'd had to put up his own money to break the final financial impasse between the Canucks and the Soviet authorities; how, over the years, there had been endless grinding down in salary negotiations by Canucks management.

"I was down there for two weeks before [Canucks management] showed up," Bure told the *Province*'s Tony Gallagher in 1999, after he'd been traded to the Panthers, more than five years after he'd first made a trade request. "It was really hard. I thought they'd be waiting for me when I got there but there was nobody. I'd heard all this about how badly they wanted me and then I'm down there wondering what's going on. Then they finally send down Brian [Burke]. We have a quick lunch and then it's another 10 days before they have me fly to San Jose to meet the rest of the guys."[73]

One night, early in his first season, Bure had approached management post-game with a concern about his contract. They gave him a response he didn't like. Perhaps this was the time that management agreed with him that the first contract he'd signed was probably not enough for a player with his now-obvious skills. But, they said, he needed to keep showing what he could do, then they'd happily discuss a new deal. At least, this is what he told Gallagher in the same 1999 interview. When he came back down to the dressing room, he punched a wall.

"If you're gonna do it, do it right," quipped Gino, who sat nearby. The joke landed with Bure. In this gregarious new teammate of his, he found a sympathetic ear.

Bure began to open up, as well as he could in a language he barely spoke. More than once, Odjick had to ask him to repeat what he was saying. For Russians, learning English is a big challenge, not just in learning the nouns, but in understanding how verbs and basic grammatical constructions work. There are no articles in Russian, for instance—"the" or "a"—nor are there auxiliary verbs like "do" or "have" or "may," and every noun has a gender in Russian, whereas most nouns in English are neutral. And so, in the early stages, Russian speakers often just blurt out the ideas using the smattering of verbs and nouns they know, but they often come across as just a pileup of words.

Odjick, who spoke three languages, took the time to help his new friend sort through what he was trying to explain. "It calmed me down," Bure said of Gino's patience with him. Both would describe to friends that this early exchange was the pivotal moment of their friendship—Odjick showing empathy for Bure, and Bure finding someone who would try to listen. That night, Gino invited his new friend out for a post-game meal. It would be the first of hundreds of meals shared over the next three decades.

Bure's first contract ran through the 1994–95 season, but early in the 1993–94 season, the Canucks and Bure sat down to hammer out a new deal. A contract was agreed upon, but when Bure sat down to sign it, he discovered the Canucks were proposing to pay him in Canadian dollars, not American, which greatly devalued what he thought he was worth.

Frustrated, Bure held his ground. The talks went silent for months, and not just because of the discrepancy in currency. A groin strain hampered the start to Bure's season: he had "only" fourteen goals in his first twenty-eight games. Coming off the sixty goals he scored in 1992–93, that did seem slow. But it was ludicrous to suggest he didn't truly have it as an elite scorer. Then he heard someone in management had doubts he'd score sixty again. Yet another aggravation for Bure. He would request a trade for the first time: "Pay me fairly or trade me," he told Quinn and the new assistant general manager, George McPhee.

They didn't trade him, and then Bure got red-hot: he scored forty-six goals through the final forty-seven games of the season. Instead, he got a much bigger contract, which was sorted out before the 1994 Stanley Cup playoffs. He told his agent that the money may have been what he wanted, but he didn't trust management and still wanted a trade. And then, during the 1994 Stanley Cup final, a story leaked that he'd threatened to sit out during the playoffs if he didn't get a new contract. Bure and his agent said that was nonsense. The contract was signed. The Canucks just hadn't registered it with the league yet. But the rumour persisted and Bure felt Quinn could have moved faster to quash it. "By the time it was denied by Pat Quinn and everybody else, it was too late," Bure told Gallagher in 1999. "It looked like a cover-up." The idea that he'd be disloyal on the ice to the Canucks infuriated Bure: after all, he scored sixteen goals in the 1994 playoffs. Had the Canucks beaten the Rangers, he likely would have been the Conn Smythe Trophy winner as playoff MVP.

The next season was the lockout season, but there continued to be issues with Bure's contract. He said the Canucks were three months late in paying his signing bonus. He'd also secured a pay-guarantee clause in his contract, meaning he'd get paid even if there was a work stoppage. But he didn't get paid. He staged a five-day holdout to start training camp. Bure said he was owed $1.7 million.

Ahead of the 1997–98 season, Bure reiterated his trade request to Quinn. The boss had always said he didn't want to, but now he accepted. "Play your best, that will drive your value up, and I'll get a trade that I think is fair to the Canucks," Bure said his long-time boss told him. But Quinn was fired early in the season, and Mike Keenan just wasn't interested in trading the sniper. Bure had a remarkable season playing for Keenan, scoring fifty-one goals, but he still wanted out. Bure fired Salcer and hired former NHLer Mike Gillis to be his agent. Gillis told Bure not just to demand a trade, but to stay home and hold out. Giving up his salary would show how serious he was about his request, Gillis told him.

ON MANY OF those initial nights in Vancouver, before Gino found the friendly folks and good food at The Slocan, he would simply hang out at his hotel. He and Bure would frequent the bar and restaurant downstairs, having drinks with the regulars. One of the regulars was the hotel's owner: Francesco Aquilini.

Odjick and Aquilini came to know each other well. When Aquilini purchased fifty percent of the Canucks in 2004, Odjick called him up and offered to provide insight to the team if ever needed it. He also had two issues that he kept pressing Aquilini about: helping Indigenous youth, especially those who lived in poverty, and retiring Bure's number.

"I was crazy enough to believe Pavel could get into the Hall of Fame and he could get his jersey retired," Odjick told the *Province*'s Jason Botchford in 2013. "People kept saying it would never happen. I kept asking and asking. He was very skeptical at first, and didn't think it could be done... I just kept at it."[74] Bure was inducted into the Hockey Hall of Fame in 2012. A year later, he'd have his number retired, and it was mostly thanks to Gino's persistence.

Ahead of the Hall of Fame ceremony in Toronto, Gino arranged a meeting between Bure and Aquilini, where the Canucks' chairman presented his idea for a jersey retirement ceremony. Part of that plan would see Bure visit Vancouver in the spring of 2013; Aquilini invited him to be his guest at a dinner in Chinatown. Since Aquilini made the effort to visit Bure ahead of the Hall of Fame ceremony, Bure agreed. "Francesco showed me great respect," Bure said.

TO GET HIS INTERVIEW with Bure in January 1999, Tony Gallagher had flown out to New York City. Bure had returned to North America from Moscow after Brian Burke finally worked out the trade with the Florida Panthers. Bure was set to make his Panthers debut in New York, against the Islanders. Playing for the Islanders, of course, was Odjick, so it was Gino who served as driver for Gallagher, Bure, and Mike Gillis, during the visit. "He was his friend, he just wanted to be there for him," Gallagher recalls. "He ended up doing a lot of the driving to and from the hotel. To and from the rink. Gino wanted to be there to help his friend settle."

Their friendship was very "cemented," Gallagher says. Gallagher had covered the Canucks since long before Odjick or Bure joined the team. He'd seen players come and go, friendships form and then dissipate. But in getting to know Bure and Odjick, he wasn't surprised that their friendship stood the test of time.

Looking back three decades later, Bure said his friendship with Odjick had been very helpful inside the fishbowl of Vancouver. Gino would listen to Bure's frustrations, he'd make sure his friend was able to have a good time. All the things you expect from a best friend. "People feel comfortable with him, you know, because he was honest guy. He was a great man all around," Bure says.

In 1993, Odjick even flew all the way to Russia to visit his friend. As he told *The Athletic*'s Thomas Drance in 2020, he had arrived in Moscow to find that no one was there to pick him up. According to Odjick, that was on Slava Fetisov, the Russian hockey legend. Odjick had been invited by Fetisov to play in a charity game. Gino would later discover that Fetisov had hoped to make his appearance a surprise to Bure. He had no idea, though, that Moscow was so massive. He'd hopped in a cab, asked the driver to drive him to Pavel Bure's house. The cabbie looked at him incredulously. So Gino got creative. He remembered something his old friend had told him: the KGB knows everything that's going on.

"So I told the cab driver, bring me to the KGB office. He's like, 'No, no, no, you don't want to go there.' I said, 'Bring me to the KGB office!' So I knock on the door and they open the door and they have a machine gun stuck in my face, they're like 'What do you want!?' I'm like, 'I'm looking for Pavel Bure, we're playing a charity game against the Red Army!' I told them the story about Fetisov not sending anybody to pick me up."[75] Within fifteen minutes, Gino said, the KGB had him on his way to the hotel where all the players were, and sure enough, he found Bure there.

It wasn't the only time he visited Russia, either. In 2000, after Bure finished second in voting for the Lester B. Pearson Award for the league's best player as judged by members of the NHL Players' Association, Odjick travelled with him to Russia to hand out hockey gear to members of the Central Red Army hockey academy—as runner-up, Bure received $10,000 to be granted to a charity of his choice.

BURE DIDN'T SPEAK OFTEN of his problems, but when he did, he'd confide in Odjick. "We can talk about anything," Odjick told Roy MacGregor in 1994. "That is hard to find nowadays. We have a 100 per cent trust in each other."[76] After Mike Keenan traded Gino away, he was careful not to break confidence but still spoke out about his friend's situation. "If Pavel wants to leave, people have to understand a few things," he said. "He's always done his very best for the team and the organization. You have to remember we were only getting between 9,000 and 11,000 fans a game when he got here and he got the crowds back up to where they could build GM Place [now Rogers Arena]. He was basically the guy who built it." Odjick wasn't wrong.

"Who sold the luxury boxes? Whose name did they use? He gave everything he had in Vancouver all the time. Remember he played all last season with that whiplash injury and never complained," Odjick said, revealing part of the reason why Bure's 1996–97 season, in which he'd returned from the brutal torn ACL in his knee, hadn't gone so well. "If there comes a point where he definitely wants to leave, they have to understand all aspects of why he might want to go somewhere else."[77]

Gino, to no surprise, knew.

8

"THE BEST THING YOU'VE EVER SEEN"

EVEN BEFORE GINO made the leap to junior hockey, he was a father. "Native kids aren't well-informed about birth control," he told Mike Beamish for a 1992 profile in the *Vancouver Sun*, after his fourth child, Joey, was born. A fourth child, and he was only twenty-one. "You have your first kid pretty young, with your first girlfriend. When I played midget hockey, probably 10 of the 15 guys on the team had kids. Maybe it shouldn't be like that. You have to mature pretty quickly."[78]

At the age of fifteen, Gino had thought his hockey career might be over: his girlfriend June was pregnant. It was 1986. They were in high school together. Their family homes were next door to each other. Their daughter Ashley-Ann, born that year, made Gino and June parents for the first time. Patrick, their second son, was born two years later.

June was Gino's first love. "She really loved him," Gino's sister Dina says. She was always accepting of the path Gino followed. But they never really lived together. For a time, June lived with Ashley-Ann and then with Patrick in the Odjicks' basement, and later she had an apartment in Maniwaki, once Gino had gone off to chase his hockey dream. "She always let Gino see his kids anytime he wanted," Dina adds. Gino would visit, but most of the time hockey kept him away, first in Hawkesbury, then in Laval. With two kids to raise, it was hard for her to see Gino go, but in the end she encouraged him to see where hockey would take him, Dina said.

Jan "Boy Boy" Cote was a couple of years younger that Gino, but knew him well from hockey. He says Gino and June kept pretty quiet about what they were going through. "We knew he was already a dad, but the students in our class understood this reality of teenage pregnancy," he says. "Even with two kids together, they were still the stereotypical teenage couple... [but] they both seemed way more prepared for parenthood than the rest of us. There is no way that I could have handled that responsibility at that age. And it seemed that they both came to class without a worry in the world. You could never tell that these two high school students had kids."

Over the next two decades, Gino would be father to eight kids, with six different women. He was a wanderer, to put it kindly, even in high school: just a few months after Patrick was born, Gino became a dad for a third time when his son Russell was born to Doreen Decourcie, another young woman Gino knew.

The first three kids had it hardest, Gino would admit later. He was so young. Because of his hockey career, he wasn't really around; raising the kids fell to their mothers and on

Gino's parents. He sent money home, but he knew that wasn't the same. In September 1995, he opened up to the *Province*'s Jim Jamieson about the flaws in his life. Sure, he was a popular teammate and a gregarious personality off the ice, a guy who could seemingly get any girl he wanted, and who was providing for his kids as best he could, as his father had taught him to do, but he wasn't there for his kids.

"I'm 24 years old, my [oldest] daughter's nine and I don't really know her," Odjick told Jamieson. He'd had quite the role model in his father, who did everything he could for his family. Papa Joe would go away to earn money, but when the money was earned, Joe was able to come home. Being in the house, being with his kids and putting food literally on the table, was vital for Joe. Perhaps it was the memory of growing up without a father. Certainly, it was about being sent away to residential school, not being able to be with his family. Joe didn't want his kids to experience this kind of separation.

And so, as his father did, Gino went away to work and he sent money back to support his kids. And he'd visit them when he could. But he told Jamieson he just wasn't doing enough. "All I ever did when I went home in the summer was go out and party. When I'd go home in the summer, I'd have 25–30 guys at my house Thursday, Friday, Saturday," he said.[79] His conversation with Jamieson came just a few months after his terrible post-season drinking binge in May and just a few weeks after he'd finished the Journey of Healing. He'd changed his ways, he said. He'd reined in his drinking and his carousing. "I changed it this summer. I spent a lot of time with my four kids. Ashley-Ann told me: 'Dad, I'm happy you quit drinking. I see you more, and before, I was afraid of you in the morning.'"

Gino wouldn't become fully sober, but he recognized his need to dial it back around then, Peter Leech recalled. In 1999, Peter invited Gino to join him at a youth leadership workshop in Port Alberni, a small city on Vancouver Island. The two had known each other for years, but this was the first time Peter suggested Gino join him in his work with Indigenous youth. It was then that Peter revealed to Gino that he was a recovering alcoholic. He'd struggled with drinking when he was younger. He'd been sober for a few years at that point. The key, he told Gino, was to understand that if you were worried about what drinking did to you, if you were worried you were an alcoholic, then you were. Gino would continue to enjoy some beers now and then, but nothing like he did in the spring of 1995.

Being a good father was all he ever wanted. "I realized there's a lot of time with my kids that I lost over drinking. A lot of things I neglected and my relationships were one of them. I'm not single today for nothing."[80] He loved his kids and he loved the women he was with. But he struggled to stick around, even after he got his drinking under control. For better or worse, he would forever be a wandering soul.

WHEN GINO WAS playing in Laval, he met a pretty, dark-haired young woman named Elizabeth Poon. She was friends in high school with a boy named Dominic David, whose family Gino lived with while he was playing for the Titan. Gino and Elizabeth became a bit of an item.

In the fall after Gino was drafted, when he was playing in Milwaukee, he asked Elizabeth to come visit. "I went there, to stay for two weeks. But after two days, he was called up by the Canucks," she says. So she went back to Laval. A couple of months later, with Gino now firmly in the NHL, he invited her out to Vancouver. She went west and liked what she found.

Life was good on the West Coast. About a year later, in the spring of 1992, Gino's fourth child, Joey, was born to Elizabeth. Gino now had four kids, with three mothers. It wasn't until she was pregnant with Joey that she found out that Gino had already had three kids.

"He kind of knew what he was doing," she says with a laugh. "I think he changed a couple diapers. I could count them on my fingers!" But he was a supportive father. If she or Joey needed something, he figured it out. They stayed together as a couple for the first two years of Joey's life.

Not long after Joey was born, Gino invited *Vancouver Sun* reporter Mike Beamish over to his home in Port Moody. It was just about the only time in Beamish's forty-four-year career as a journalist he could recall an athlete inviting him into his home. He'd had a few meals at restaurants with his interview subjects, but never a sit-down in the living room. And certainly not with a newborn baby. It was Odjick doing what he knew: opening the door to everyone, welcoming them in. Even though he was only twenty-one and was away from his kids pretty often, he had remarkable insight into fatherhood and the experience of caring for a baby. Gino was different, Beamish realized.

"You see the pain your wife or girlfriend has to go through and then you see that pain turn to joy when the baby arrives," he told Beamish as baby Joey nodded off to sleep on his dad. "It's a beautiful thing. The best thing that can happen to you. The best thing you've ever seen."[81] But he didn't always know what to do.

For Elizabeth, life as a hockey girlfriend was hard. When she first moved to Vancouver, she spoke only French. As she started to learn English, she made a few friends, including Pavel Bure's girlfriend Elena. Elena didn't know many people either, so when the team went out on long road trips, ten, twelve days at a time, Elena would come stay with Elizabeth and Joey, or they'd go stay with Elena. She also started to learn what hockey players were like in their social lives. She didn't mind the partying, the drinking. But she didn't like the stories she heard about how there were always other girls around.

Odjick later told Jim Jamieson that Elizabeth leaving him in the summer of 1994 threw him into a spiral of despair. In the past, his drinking had at times worried some of his teammates. With the NHL lockout in October 1994—teams wouldn't return to the ice until January 1995—plus Elizabeth and Joey's departure, Gino suddenly had more free time. He filled a lot of that time with alcohol. And was now the first time he'd been truly single in Vancouver. He hit the bars and chased after women.

"That's when I started drinking lots," he told Jamieson. "I had nothing to do. It just continued right through till I was playing again. Then once I hurt my stomach muscle, I was six weeks with nothing to do. That's when I really started drinking heavy, heavy, heavy."

That changed after his Journey of Healing. He still liked to have a good time, to go out to listen to music at one of the few remaining bars in Vancouver that played country, and then go to the Roxy, the legendary Vancouver nightclub that has long been famous as the place to go for pro athletes on a night out. Or the Biltmore, a long-standing favourite hangout among Vancouver's Indigenous residents.

He also found a new and perhaps surprising girlfriend: Elizabeth's sister Genevieve. They'd been seeing each other for a few months when Elizabeth found out. She was not happy. And then she discovered Genevieve was pregnant. Elizabeth didn't speak with her sister for six years. "But I had no choice to talk to Gino, because he was Joey's father. For a while I was angry, but then I got over it," she says. "I talk to my sister now. Sometimes it's still hard, but it's been a long time."

Genevieve gave birth to a daughter, Chynna, in January 1997. Chynna and Joey are both half-siblings and cousins. "They call each other 'brosins,'" Elizabeth says with a laugh.

But Gino and Genevieve didn't last long. Gino had already made a new girlfriend from Kitigan Zibi, Jolene Commanda. He'd first met Jolene in the summer of 1994. Jolene's family lived next door to the Cotes, and Jan Cote's dad, Russell, asked Jolene if she wanted a little job working at the Gino Odjick Golf Tournament, selling beer and taking pictures. That's where they met for the first time.

That winter, with the NHL lockout in full effect, Gino travelled back to Kitigan Zibi. The reserve hockey team travelled up north to Val-d'Or to play in a tournament, and Gino went along with them. At the same time, Jolene was there to play broomball. He greeted her again. And in the summer of 1995, Gino made a quick visit back to Kitigan Zibi before he embarked on the Journey of Healing. During that visit, they had another passing encounter.

The summer of 1996 is when their relationship began in earnest. Gino was home for the summer, as always, and though she was younger than him, her friend group had started to overlap with Gino's. Her sister Lisa had become a cop, and so had Gino's old friend Itchy. They were partners for the Kitigan Zibi Police Department. So she'd come to know Itchy, Michen, and Boy Boy.

The relationship flourished, though she never lived in Vancouver with him. The couple would have a child before 1997 was out: a son, born on October 29. The date immediately stood out to Gino: the tenth month and the twenty-ninth day. It was too good to be true, he felt: those were the jersey numbers worn by his best friend Pavel (10) and by him (29). With a birthdate like that, naming his son in tribute to his best friend was a no-brainer, he said. So the little boy, Gino's fourth son and sixth kid, was named Bure. Pavel was, unsurprisingly, named as godfather.

The day Bure was born, Gino was playing for the Canucks in Chicago, on the top line with Pavel Bure and Mark Messier. After the game, he bolted north and got to spend a couple days with Jolene and Bure. But then he was back to the Canucks and his NHL life and the routine he'd long followed by that time. Six months later, that would change. After Gino was traded to the Islanders, Jolene and Bure joined him on Long Island, in Gerald Diduck's house in Cold Spring Harbor, a wealthy bedroom community about a thirty-minute drive from Nassau Coliseum.

They never married, but in news reports Gino referred to her at times as his wife. For Gino, anyway, it was a pretty idyllic time. But judging how things went for both Elizabeth before and Caroline later, it can't have always been smooth. Gino loved his life as a hockey player, and while he wanted to be a strong father, he always struggled with the day-to-day reality of that.

The couple stayed together until the fall of 2001, less than a year after their second child, Tobias, was born, and nearly a year after Gino was traded to Montreal. But it was hard; Gino was starting to show signs of mental health problems. At times, he was unpredictable. Years later, he would be diagnosed with bipolar disorder.

Gino's relationship with Jolene after they split up obviously wasn't easy, Dina recalled. "She wouldn't always let him see the boys," she says. Gino's behaviour was erratic.

As athletes, at least, the boys would clearly take after their old man. Both would pursue hockey careers: Bure eventually playing senior amateur hockey in Quebec and Ontario, and Tobias playing low-level minor pro in the southern United States. Both weren't afraid to use their fists on the ice, just like their dad.

TWO YEARS AFTER Tobias was born came Gino's eighth and final child, a girl named Rose, born to Caroline Forester. "Little did I know how he was," Caroline says, with two decades' worth of wisdom to look back on. "Now, in hindsight, there was a lot going on that I didn't understand." Caroline and Gino knew each other from Maniwaki—she had dated Gino's friend Mike Cote before—and they lived together for a time on the Musqueam reserve. Rose was the child with whom he had the longest in-home fathering relationship. Gino and Caroline were together until about 2009.

"I think he tried his best," Caroline says. "He tried, in his own way, to be a father to Rose... but he was just not a natural-born father."

Gino's experience with his own father, who worked hard but who was away from his family a lot of the time, was very different from the childhood Caroline experienced growing up in Maniwaki. Hers was much more traditional: her parents and two siblings all living together, her parents working in the community.

"I said to him, 'If we're going to have a child together, I'm not doing this alone. I want to make sure you want to do this.' Because it was the end of his career, he thought it would be different because he wouldn't be on the road for hockey." But the years that followed were fraught with difficulty, especially because of Gino's up-and-down mental health. It was very hard on Rose, Caroline says. Rose was too young to understand any of what her dad was going through. In 2009, he made his visit to the psych ward, where he was officially diagnosed with bipolar disorder. He resisted the diagnosis, and he was back in the psych ward in February 2010 (an episode that saw him miss watching an Olympic hockey game at GM Place) and again in 2012.

Caroline and Gino's relationship came to an end when he finally confessed to cheating on her. "It was probably a bit of a selfish decision to get it off his mind and his chest, because you just get caught in a web of lies," she says. "It's sad because I think at that point he had switched on to want to be a better partner, a better father. But for me, there was too much damage done. It was all very sad."

The many relationships, as tangled as they were, were of course of his own doing. But he never ran from any of it. "It was hard for Gino because all he wanted was to be able to provide for his kids," Dina says. "He never wanted for other people to provide for his kids. So Gino worked hard to be able to provide for his kids. They never missed of anything. The moms just had to call, and Gino would give. And he paid. He paid very big child support."

Joey, now thirty-two and dad to three kids of his own with his partner Dixie, just has to smile about his dad's meandering relationships. "That was just my dad," he says. Joey knew from a young age that his family was unconventional, but there was nothing to do but accept it. "If you knew my dad... there's just no other way to put it. And no, I was never embarrassed of it. I always thought it was funny and it was cool at the same time."

Obviously, Gino's children each had different experiences. The older ones have had a harder time: Patrick and Ashley-Ann lived with their mom and with Gino's parents, but never with their dad. (Although Patrick did live with Gino in Vancouver as an adult for a time.) Russell had a similar childhood. Joey lived with his dad when he was young, but Chynna never did. When he played in New York, Joey and Chynna visited him and Jolene and Bure a few times. And when Gino played for the Canadiens, they both saw their dad often, as they lived in suburban Montreal. Bure had his dad at home until he was four. Tobias was still a baby when his parents split. Rose, the youngest, had her dad living at home the longest.

KITIGAN ZIBI ISN'T that far away from Laval, and after Elizabeth and Joey moved back to the Montreal suburb, they saw a lot of Gino's parents. Elizabeth gives Papa Joe and Giselle a lot of credit for supporting all their grandchildren, no matter what. "I saw him, Papa Joe, a lot, because he used to come and get Joey halfway from Montreal to Maniwaki. He'd bring him back for a couple days, or sometimes it was a week, to see Gino, or just to see his family there," she says. "His mom, she was a lot more quiet."

Dina says her brother's understanding of child-rearing was of a more traditional type: the men worked, the women cooked, cleaned, and cared for the children. Mike Cote called Giselle "the rock of the family." She would fill the coffee cups, get the kids dressed. Giselle once admitted to Peter she'd spoiled her son rotten. "I'm getting punished now but I did it to myself," she laughed to Peter about her son needing so much attention, even as an adult.

Joey says growing up apart from his dad wasn't always easy. "Of course, it was hard to see your friends with their dads, their dads at home every day," Joey admits.

"But," he adds, getting philosophical, "it was quite a unique thing having your dad play in the NHL."

That's something he understood from an early age. His mother, Elizabeth, helped him understand. "Dad has to take the airplane all the way across Canada, or across the United States, to play hockey," she'd tell him. Joey got used to it. "At times for sure it was hard. Because I missed him. I wanted to see him. I wanted to be with him. Because it was always a fun time when I was with him. He was a great father."

Those fun times were invariably in the summer, when Gino would trek back to Kitigan Zibi and bring all his children in. "As crazy, chaotic, a funny case as it is, I'm close with all my siblings," Joey says. "As a kid I was pretty much the only one who could say 'I'm one of eight!'"

In 1994, Gino built a beautiful log house at the northern end of the reserve, on the eastern shore of a lovely little lake called Lac Pagànàkomin. (*Pagànàkomin* means "walnut" in

Algonquin.) The cabin itself has a pitched roof, two floors and a basement, big windows that look out over the lake, with a big deck that wraps around three sides. Next to the cabin, there's a wooden shack, decades old, that he lived in while the log cabin was being built.

Patrick has fond memories of the cabin. "He had a boat. We'd go tubing. We'd go water-skiing." Joey says he and his siblings would delight in their dad's company and one another's. "It was awesome. I always loved coming to Maniwaki and being with my brothers and sisters. It felt cool," he says. Joey often dreamed that he and his siblings would all live in the same house; when they'd get together, it felt a little like the dream. "They're my brothers and sisters, even if we don't have the same mom. Doesn't matter," he says flatly. "I was proud. I was happy."

Joey has come to terms with how he spent time with his dad. "When I did see him, we had an awesome father and son relationship," he says. "He taught me how to play hockey, how to skate, how to shoot, how to score—surprisingly, how to fight as well. Everybody saw him as a tough guy. But to me he was just a big old teddy bear. And very affectionate, very funny. He had a really good sense of humour and, yeah, always wore his heart on his sleeve, and that's how he was with everybody."

While Joey and Patrick have a very positive attitude toward their dad, it's not as simple for some of their other siblings. "The girls might have a different opinion," Patrick said. Peter Leech's wife Charlene agrees. The girls just didn't have the same experience, and they'd vent their frustrations to her. She'd try to share what Gino had said about them. "I'd always tell them, 'You know, your dad talks about how he's very proud of you,'" she says. "I know he didn't mention it enough, and it's hard for them to hear."

Caroline says Rose's experiences when she was young were very painful. Her parents were struggling with their relationship, Gino was struggling with how to be a father to a little girl, and he was also struggling with mental illness.

"He was great fun, very generous, very outgoing, very funny, very kind," Caroline says about dating Gino. "But him, as a father—very difficult, very painful."

Gino always showed up for his court-ordered visits with Rose, but they weren't easy. "I know in his heart he wanted to be there," Caroline explains. "But it was just too chaotic. And a child needs stability and consistency. So there was just incidents that she went through at a very young age that have marked her."

And after Caroline and Rose moved to England with Caroline's new husband, Gino's relationship with his daughter drifted. Like all of his children, Rose was not financially in need. "He would say that whatever a court says, I'll provide it," Caroline says. "But emotionally, he just didn't really know how to be there."

When Patrick was twenty-two, he moved out to BC to live with Gino and their cousin Stéphane. "I came out because I wanted to live with my dad. And my cousin was working in carpentry, so I was working with him," Patrick explains. Stéphane, who died in 2021, had moved out to Vancouver in the 1990s, and knew the scene well. They lived together for three years. Patrick said it was a blast.

Patrick has a son of his own, Sebastien. Sebastien had health issues practically from the moment he was born. He required a tracheotomy as a newborn. The stress of it all tipped

Patrick over the edge and he started abusing drugs. His life has been pretty difficult ever since, as he has battled his addiction, trying to stay clean. Sebastien now lives with Patrick's aunt Janique.

IN THE TWO SEASONS Gino played for the Montreal Canadiens, Joey got invited a few times down to the Molson Centre, the Canadiens' famed home arena now known as the Bell Centre. "The stick room. You'd get to see the new sticks that weren't even out yet," he says, smiling, the happiness of the memory raising his posture. "I got to meet all kinds of NHL players, see how it is for them. Just everything. The gym, the dressing room, the stick room, the workout facility, everything."

Joey played hockey until he was fifteen. Then, like many teens, he found himself interested in other things . . . like girls. A familiar story for many. "Maybe my dad should have pushed me harder to keep playing hockey," Joey says with a laugh. "You know, you start talking with girls, hanging around with your friends. Doing all kinds of stuff. And that seems more important than playing sports. Because, realistically, when you're playing hockey, it's every weekend. Then you practise two or three times a week and you got games on Saturday and Sunday. So, at one point, I was like, 'Mom, I want to hang out with my friends more often.'"

Now, in his thirties, there's a small regret for him. Sure, life was hockey, hockey, hockey then, but now he knows how special that time is for a young athlete. "I wasn't going to make the NHL, but maybe if my dad had pushed me a little I could have played junior?" His kids play hockey now, something he calls non-negotiable. If his kids really don't want to play, that's fine, they'll drop it. But he wants them to try. And he knows from his own experience that sometimes his kids may need a little push.

"I find in hockey, you learn a lot of things. You make new friends, you make all kinds of memories. Teaches you to be a leader, good teammate, and translates good into life as well," he says. After all, there's family history. "And, sure, people say, 'Ah, you're not making the NHL, you know, it's one in a million.' But like for me, to see my dad make the NHL, it's kind of a perspective that anything's possible."

There's that life philosophy of his dad's: you may think you're nobody, but if you put your best effort into what you're doing, you'll get somewhere—and you probably don't know where. His "just a boy from the rez" mentality.

"**IT'S BEEN HARD** on a couple of his kids," Gino's old friend Itchy says. "I grew up with his kids." Itchy knows Jolene's family, the Commandas, well. He introduced Gino to Jolene. He's Tobias's godfather. His friend meant well and did his best for his kids, Itchy says, but it was still tough at times.

"When he came, he did what he could," Itchy continues. "He was a good father. He was genuine with his kids. He wasn't hard on them. I never seen him ever be mad at them. If he raised his voice—'Hey! Listen!'—they'd listen." But Gino also had to learn to deal with the rules his exes were laying down for their kids. "It's scheduling for both parents," Itchy points out. Jolene, for instance, didn't just keep the door open for Gino to see his boys. She made it clear that there were times to come visit, that routine was important.

Genevieve and Caroline both ended up having to use the court system to sort out support payments from Gino, as well as access rules to their kids. Jolene did initially pursue a court process, and their interactions were strained for a number of years, but by about 2009, she softened her stance, abandoned the courts, and she and Gino became good friends again. In later years, she did what she could to help Gino repair the relationship with his boys.

IN PARENTING HIS OWN KIDS, Joey thinks he's borrowed some approaches from both his dad and his grandfather, like making sure his own kids have opportunities to be themselves, that they are surrounded by a supporting environment. And he sees both Gino and Papa Joe in his kids. "It's in bits and pieces of all of them, and kind of like from what I picked up, and instilled into them," he says.

Likewise, Jan Cote sees lots of Gino in his old friend's children. Bure, for example, is much like his father, not only as a hockey player ready to drop the gloves but also in the way he engages with people in their everyday lives. Gino would seek out elders when he arrived in a new community, and so does Bure. Kitigan Zibi hosted a hockey tournament in the summer of 2024 to honour the Every Child Matters movement, and at that event, Jan noticed, Bure went to sit with the elders.

Despite Gino's claim to Jim Jamieson that, during the 1990s, his personal life was off-kilter—he was partying too much, not spending enough time with his kids, not going home enough—in his later years, he obviously restored a sense of balance, and Cote saw a man who knew the importance of visiting his children before spending any time with his friends. "He was a provider... When he came back here, immediately he went to see his family. His parents, sisters, his kids. He had to do all that, it was his priority. He knew it: 'I gotta take care of my family first.'"

9

"THESE KIDS FEEL LIKE THEY'VE BEEN FORGOTTEN"

When Gino started watching NHL games on *Hockey Night in Canada* in the late 1970s, you could count the number of players with Indigenous ancestry on two hands and a foot. There was Dale McCourt, Henry Boucha, Reggie Leach, Ron Delorme, Jim Neilson, Gary Sargent, Bobby Simpson, Wayne King, Bobby Taylor, and Bryan Trottier. And then there was Stan Jonathan of the Boston Bruins, Gino's favourite player.

Growing up in Quebec, Odjick was surrounded by legions of Montreal Canadiens fans, but for him, there was no way he was cheering against his guy, Jonathan. "He was First Nations and I think he scored 27 goals one year and he was an enforcer," Odjick told Bob Marjanovich in 2022. "It was always Stan Jonathan fighting Chris Nilan," he added, referring to the Canadiens' tough guy who had a few tilts with Jonathan in the early 1980s.[82]

An Indigenous player in the NHL was still a very rare thing when Gino Odjick made his debut with the Vancouver Canucks in 1990. Odjick sure knew it. He was an outsider; his life experience wasn't much like that of anyone else's on the team. He'd experienced Canada in a very different way from his mostly white teammates. Newspaper reports at the time often cited that just six players had made the NHL "after coming off a reserve." How they arrived at that number isn't clear, but the point was obvious: even in the 1990s, not many Indigenous players made it to the NHL.

Some Indigenous players concealed their background, long-time Canucks scout and former player Ron Delorme says. Delorme is Cree, from western Saskatchewan. When he went off to play junior, fresh off the reserve, he was surprised by many things. "The first time I walked into a dressing room, I saw all these guys walking around in their underwear. I'd never taken my clothes off in front of other guys before. It was a shock. I put my gear on over my jeans, I was so shy," he says.

On the ice, many Indigenous players encountered all kinds of racism, taunts, offensive words, you name it. But Gino always said he himself didn't experience much racism when playing hockey. His theory: because he was a tough guy, no one dared to make him angry by coming at him with that garbage. A fan once lit his jersey on fire while he was sitting in the penalty box in junior, but that was about intimidation, not race, he once told Dan Russell's *Sportstalk* radio show.

His sister Dina doesn't recall much on-ice racism when she was playing either. What racism she encountered then is much different from what she sees now. Dina figures her grandson Marcus, now twelve, faces more racism now than she ever did. Marcus is a very talented player and has played high-level minor hockey in Maniwaki and in Gatineau, and he's heard all kinds of cruel taunts, she said.

Gino did face plenty of racism *off* the ice, however. "Where I grew up in the '70s, coming from the reserve," Gino told *BC Bookworld* in 2014, "I was always treated as a second-class citizen by non-Aboriginal people."[83]

Gino said his teammates only ever showed him affection. They "always called me 'Chief,' but in a good way," he'd say. They may not have truly understood him, where he came from, what growing up as an Indigenous man in Canada in the 1970s and 1980s was really like, but they sure cared about him. And yes, he was ready and willing to take some good-natured ribbing in the NHL. But even then, the ribbing could sometimes go a little too far—it became about his background. Once, he went to Pat Quinn for help, Ron Delorme said.

"He'd finally had enough. He asked Pat to do something. Gino was never a guy to complain, but this was enough," Delorme says. And so Quinn did something remarkable for the time: he recognized he didn't quite know what to do. He turned to Delorme for advice. "Pat wanted to understand a little bit more," the veteran scout recalls. "He had all these questions about Aboriginal people. So I told him it was no different from a Swede coming here. And for Gino, he dealt with it professionally. He could've dealt with it another way."

And so, armed with a better understanding of his player, Quinn went to his team and told them to tone it down.

Everyone in a dressing room gets ribbed for one reason or another, but there's a line to everything. Going too far with a Russian or a Swede wouldn't be tolerated, Delorme reasoned, so why should it be any different for an Indigenous man? And that was the message that connected with Quinn, that moved him to speak with his team.

The only time Gino noticed any real on-ice racism was when he played for the Horse Lake Thunder of the North Peace Hockey League in 2004–05, his final season of hockey. Two years after concussions had ended his NHL career, his head seemed better and he was ready for one last challenge: to try and win the Allan Cup, the Stanley Cup of amateur hockey. Until the 1960s, the Allan Cup was a big deal, with senior amateur teams in towns across the country. The winner would represent Canada at the World Championships. By the twenty-first century, weren't many true senior teams left, but the Thunder were one of them and they wanted to win it all. The Thunder snagged four ex-NHLers—Gino plus Sasha Lakovic, Theo Fleury, and Dody Wood—to help the all-Indigenous team based in Alberta's Peace River Country go after the national championship.

"It was really racist there in Alberta that year that we played there," Gino told Marjanovich. Horse Lake made it to the Allan Cup tournament, played well in their opening games, but were upset in the semifinals. That was the end of his competitive playing career. In following years, he'd suit up for beer-league games on occasion, go on hockey tours to Europe with friends like Michen, Indigenous tournaments here and there with Jan and his Kitigan Zibi friends, and he'd help coach a few youth teams here and there, but his regular connection with the top tiers of hockey ended with that year's Allan Cup tournament, played with the Thunder.

IN HIS YOUTH back in Kitigan Zibi, Gino had been a polite, quiet boy, doted on by his parents. Dina remembers her brother, the only boy in the family, being spoiled rotten. "Gino got everything he always wanted," she laughs. "He'd yell, 'Mom! I want a peanut butter sandwich. Get the girls to make me a peanut butter sandwich!' Or 'Mom! I want the TV!' And, of course, Mom and Dad would give it to him."

At school, even if his real interests lay outside the classroom, he took to reading. "I had a teacher in grade one who introduced me to reading," Odjick told *BC Bookworld*. "And I've had a love affair with books ever since. When I was playing hockey, I would read about 150 books a year while I was on the road. I still read a lot, mostly self-improvement books but history too, biography—anything, really, so long as it's good."[84]

Reading, learning new ideas—these helped him deal with life's challenges. "A good book allows you to just disappear inside it and forget everything else that's going on around you. I love that about my books," he said.

FROM VERY EARLY ON in his NHL career, Gino was aware of the power and influence of his position as a professional athlete. He became even more aware of this after his bout with alcohol abuse in the spring of 1995. He felt an impulse, a sense of duty to help Indigenous communities and especially Indigenous young people who might be struggling with alcohol themselves. Once he'd made the NHL, he'd almost always said yes to invitations to help out at Indigenous hockey schools, no matter where they were in Canada. He'd meet with kids too, telling them, here he was, just a boy from the rez, but he'd made it. He'd made it because he'd worked hard, he'd taken direction from his elders, and he'd made sure he was always learning.

"The young kids have to know that they're not dumb stupid Indians like they're often told," Gino told *The Globe and Mail*'s Gary Mason in 2014. "They have to know that education is the key to their lives. Education will unlock freedom for them. That's how I want them to succeed, not by fighting all their life like me."[85]

The summer of 1995's Journey of Healing, which he organized in the weeks after his drinking binge, was an effort to create something wholly his own. And it would prove to be a pivotal moment in his life, making this trek from Calgary to Vancouver, meeting Indigenous youth and leaders along the way. Over the three decades of his life that followed, he would meet with young people across Canada, spreading a message of personal empowerment and the importance of education, using his own story to show them that the answer to their troubles lay within.

For help in organizing the journey Gino turned to then head of the British Columbia Assembly of First Nations Wendy Grant-John. He knew Grant-John from all the time he'd been spending on the Musqueam reserve in Vancouver. Grant-John was well known there; her dad Willard Sparrow had been chief years before, and she would serve three terms as chief herself. The importance of Gino's proposal to meet with young people, to seek to inspire them and point them toward a positive life, to lend his celebrity to community-minded causes, was clear to her, so she turned to a couple of younger women she knew, Jen Thomas and Trudi Guerin, to help Gino. Today, Thomas is chief of the Tsleil-Waututh Nation, on the north shore of Burrard Inlet. Her face is familiar to Canucks fans: she's among the Indigenous leaders who appear on the video board pre-game at Rogers Arena, welcoming fans to the traditional territories of the Tsleil-Waututh, Musqueam, and Squamish peoples.

Plans for the Journey of Healing had to come together quickly, Thomas remembers. It was May when Gino started asking for help with organizing his run; three months isn't much lead time. But lead time never was a Gino thing. He had the idea, and he'd figure out how to get it done. Thomas approached an artist from her community, Damien George, to design the T-shirt. "And I remember having the big poster, and the trailer came to my parents' front yard, and we got to design the poster, the big flag that went on his trailer," she recalls.

Her main job was to contact all the communities in BC and Alberta Odjick was hoping to visit, to see if they wanted the NHLer to visit. Invariably, the answer was yes. "His goal was just to reach out to as many youth as he could along the way," she says. "I didn't have one negative response or anything like that. He was just excited to go into these communities and meet the young people."

Nearly thirty years later, Sandy McCarthy remembers the journey fondly. The two first encountered each other during the Hawkesbury Hawks' 1988 training camp. That was the fall after Gino's first and only season with Hawkesbury, in which he'd won the favour of head coach Bob Hartley. In the off-season, Hartley suggested Odjick's name to the Morrissettes, the brothers who owned the Laval Titan. But before heading off to Laval, Odjick came down to Hawkesbury to do some pre-season workouts.

Happenstance had brought McCarthy to Hawkesbury. A reasonably skilled big man, he'd been playing junior C hockey for the Midland Centennials, not far from his home in Barrie, Ontario, when he attended a power-skating camp run by none other than Bob Hartley. Hartley saw his size and didn't take long to sign him to the Hawks.

Over the next few seasons, he'd follow in Odjick's footsteps. After a hard-fought (sometimes literally) season in Hawkesbury, Hartley put his name to the Laval organization. McCarthy's first season in with the Titan, 1989–90, was Odjick's second. Laval had three tough guys on the roster that season: Odjick, McCarthy, and Michel Gingras, the team's captain. Odjick and McCarthy were linemates that season, on one of the best depth lines in the Quebec league.

The two became fast friends. "We had similar upbringings," says McCarthy, who is part Indigenous. "He grew up on a rez. I didn't grow up on the rez, but it was similar, I grew up on the outskirts of town. We didn't have a ton of stuff, we had enough to get by. I think he was unsure about who I was until I showed him a few times. Then I remember I went after one of the tougher guys in the league and did really good with him. And then on the bus ride after he says to me, straight, 'Well, I wasn't sure about you, but now I know.'"

Gino's team played in the famous Quebec International Pee-Wee Tournament; they got their picture with Jean Béliveau. Gino's in the back, showing off his tongue. (Courtesy Michel Branchaud)

Gino last played for the Maniwaki Braves in bantam; he's in the middle of the back row. (Courtesy Michel Branchaud)

Gino and Sandy McCarthy arriving at Musqueam on August 20, 1995, at the end of the Journey of Healing. (Ian Smith/*Vancouver Sun*)

Gino and Sandy McCarthy began the Journey of Healing with a ceremony at Tsuut'ina Nation outside Calgary. (Ian Smith/*Vancouver Sun*)

Gino met many people on his Journey of Healing. Here he is greeting Tom Harris of Seabird Island First Nation. (Ian Smith/*Vancouver Sun*)

Pat Quinn met Gino and Sandy McCarthy in Vancouver, as they made their way to Musqueam at the end of the Journey of Healing. (Ian Smith/*Vancouver Sun*)

Gino and his Canucks teammates took the Tokyo subway to practice during the Japan Series to launch the 1997–98 NHL season. (Jeff Vinnick/*Vancouver Sun*)

Gino's run in the first half of 1993–94 was epic: he scored fourteen goals before Christmas. Here he is celebrating an early-season goal against the Edmonton Oilers with Greg Adams. (Nick Didlick/*Vancouver Sun*)

Gino met many people on his Journey of Healing. Here he is greeting Tom Harris of Seabird Island First Nation. (Ian Smith/*Vancouver Sun*)

Pat Quinn met Gino and Sandy McCarthy in Vancouver, as they made their way to Musqueam at the end of the Journey of Healing. (Ian Smith/*Vancouver Sun*)

Gino and his Canucks teammates took the Tokyo subway to practice during the Japan Series to launch the 1997–98 NHL season. (Jeff Vinnick/*Vancouver Sun*)

Gino's run in the first half of 1993–94 was epic: he scored fourteen goals before Christmas. Here he is celebrating an early-season goal against the Edmonton Oilers with Greg Adams. (Nick Didlick/*Vancouver Sun*)

No doubt about focus here. Gino scored his tenth goal of the 1993–94 season on December 19 against the Dallas Stars. (Colin Price/*Vancouver Province*)

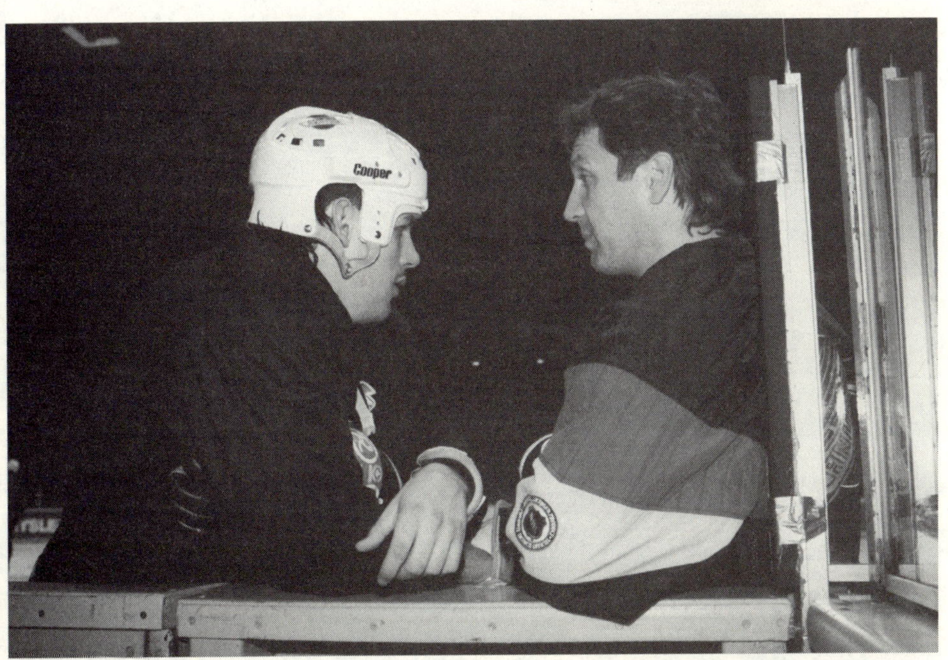

Stan Smyl was one of Gino's first linemates, then became a trusted voice when Smyl retired as a player and became an assistant coach in 1991. (Colin Price/ *Vancouver Province*)

Gino battling future teammate Tim Hunter on October 19, 1991—the same night Gino scored his epic penalty shot goal against the Calgary Flames. (Gerry Kahrmann/*Vancouver Province*)

Pavel Bure and Gino at a player-organized skate at Kensington Arena in Burnaby in October 1994, early in the 1994–95 owners' lockout of the players. (Les Bazso/*Vancouver Province*)

Gino gets after the Los Angeles Kings' Peter Ahola after the big defenceman had taken liberties on Pavel Bure; it was just the fourth career game for the Russian Rocket. (Peter Battistoni/*Vancouver Sun*)

Pavel Bure kept the list of dignitaries who joined him on-ice at Rogers Arena for his 2013 jersey retirement ceremony short: Gino, Pat Quinn, and Pavel's wife Alina and mom Tatyana were among them. (Steve Bosch/Pacific Newspaper Group)

Gino and Shawn Antoski (right), horsing around at practice with Cliff Ronning (centre), on November 28, 1991. Gino had just been suspended for six games and Antoski was called up to fill in. (Colin Price/*Vancouver Province*)

Gino and his oldest pals at the 2003 Gino Odjick Golf Tournament in Kitigan Zibi. Left to right: Andy "Itchy" Dewache, Randy McDougall, Mike "Michen" Cote, Gino, and Jan "Boy Boy" Cote. (Courtesy Mike Cote)

Four of Gino's kids: Chynna, Bure, Tobias, and Joey. (Courtesy Joey Odjick)

Gino with Ashley-Ann (left) and Patrick (right), his oldest kids, at the Ottawa Civic Centre for a Canucks versus Ottawa Senators game in January 1994. (*Ottawa Citizen*)

Gino and Mike Cote at the 2007 Kitigan Zibi Gino Odjick Golf Tournament. (Courtesy Mike Cote)

Joe Odjick and Gino during the 1994 Gino Odjick Golf Tournament. (Courtesy Roy MacGregor)

Gino and Trevor Linden on the Canucks' bench on February 7, 1996. (Colin Price/*Vancouver Province*)

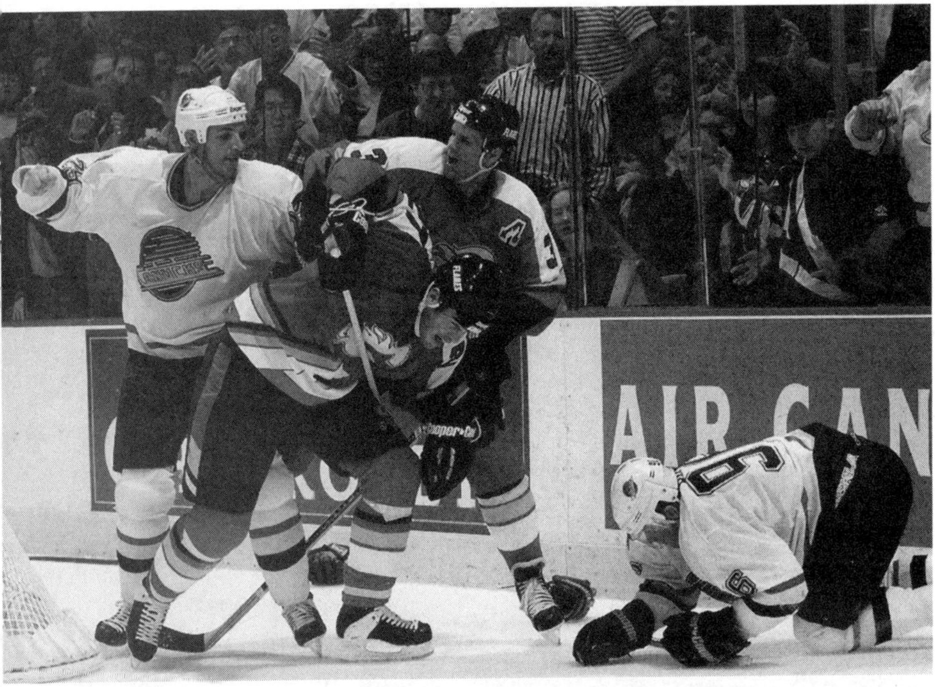

Gino going after the Calgary Flames' Todd Simpson (front), after the Flames' defenceman cross-checked Pavel Bure to the ice. This was the first game of the 1996–97 season; it was Bure's first game since his right knee ACL tear in November 1995. (Ward Perrin/*Vancouver Sun*)

Gino showing off his basketball skills to Squamish Nation youth in November 1997 at an event to launch a new youth empowerment initiative called the Seventh Generation Club, which is still active today. (Arlen Redekop/*Vancouver Province*)

The first game after his March 1998 trade to the New York Islanders was against the Canucks, and Gino fought the guy he was traded for: Jason Strudwick. (Colin Price/*Vancouver Province*)

Gino in new colours for the first time since 1990, practising with the New York Islanders at GM Place, on March 24, 1998. (Ian Lindsay/*Vancouver Sun*)

After moving back to Vancouver in 2003, Gino was a regular with the Canucks' alumni team until his battle with AL amyloidosis began in late 2013. (Ric Ernst/*Vancouver Province*)

The face of AL amyloidosis. Gino greets fans outside Vancouver General Hospital on June 29, 2014. (Arlen Redekop/Pacific Newspaper Group)

Peter Leech and Gino, brothers-in-arms, at Peter's home in February 2015. Gino was on the comeback trail from chemo. (Ric Ernst/Pacific Newspaper Group)

Gino and Elizabeth Poon at home, in November 1991, getting ready for the arrival of their son Joey in early 1992. (Mark van Manen/*Vancouver Sun*)

Gino and Pavel Bure at Canucks training camp in Whistler in September 1996. (Bonny Makarewicz/*Vancouver Province*)

Gino and Pavel Bure sitting together, of course, with rookie Mattias Öhlund behind, on the bus to Whistler for training camp in September 1997. (Mark van Manen/*Vancouver Sun*)

Gino and Pavel Bure mugging it up with twelve-year-old Aaron Kumar at BC Children's Hospital in November 1997. (Ward Perrin/*Vancouver Sun*)

The debut. Gino in front of the net being checked by the Chicago Blackhawks' František Kučera, after Ed Belfour was pulled for backup goalie Jacques Cloutier. This is the only time he'd wear No. 66. (Steve Bosch/*Vancouver Sun*)

That season, McCarthy was on the radar of many scouts—Canucks' included—but he wasn't drafted for another year, by the Calgary Flames. He wasn't the greatest skater, but he could clearly play: he scored twenty-one goals in his second season with Laval. With Gino already playing for the Canucks, McCarthy knew that if he made the NHL with the Flames, a confrontation between the two would be inevitable.

McCarthy played another year in Laval—scoring thirty-nine goals as a nineteen-year-old, to go with a career-high 326 penalty minutes—followed by one season in the AHL with Calgary's farm team (eighteen goals, 220 penalty minutes). Then the NHL door opened for him in 1993, at training camp with the Flames.

And in a late pre-season contest between the Canucks and Flames in Calgary, the two old friends finally did what they knew they would one day have to do: they had a fight. "I'm sure he wanted to give me a chance to show my stuff," McCarthy remembers fondly. Afterward, they went out for dinner.

"We never butted heads about anything. We were always on the same page, even when we fought," he says. "After the fight, I was laughing bad. We just thought we're good friends; I was trying to make the team, and he'd already made the team, and I wanted to be where he was."

When Gino called up his friend in the late spring of 1995 and told him of his plan for the Journey of Healing, meeting Indigenous youth and leaders along the way, McCarthy didn't hesitate. "When do we start?" he asked. "In my mind, all I was thinking is, my friend needs help, and I helped."

It was a cause that he identified with closely. "It was spreading a positive word and showing people that have different heritages in their backgrounds, like Indigenous people," he says. "I'm part Indigenous, part Black. I cover a bunch of grounds. For me, it was about spreading awareness to people, and then showing people also, like, 'Look, we did it, you guys can do it too.'"

On their winding path from Calgary to Vancouver, they visited a couple dozen communities. In many places, the young people would run out to meet them well outside the community, then run in alongside Odjick, McCarthy, and their entourage.

"The devastating stories that have come with addictions through some of those communities—each one was different, but there were still similarities," McCarthy recalls. "A lot of people say, 'Well, you help one person, you did your job.' But, you know what, in our lives, we helped a lot more than one person, right? So we were trying to spread the word as much as possible that 'Live a clean life and good things can happen.' Doesn't mean they're gonna, but they can."

By the end of the trek, the party travelling with them had grown to about thirty people. Some were there for just a short time, others were in it for the long haul. Often, local leaders would suggest that certain kids from their community, maybe needing a break from the day-to-day challenges of their lives, join up and run for a while. "We picked up five teens at Merritt [in BC]. Some elders [from the Lillooet band] thought they could use a little guidance since they were getting in trouble with alcohol," Gino told reporters who'd gone out to the city of Mission—several hours east of Vancouver by foot—to witness Odjick and his group on the final leg of their journey. "[The youth] were in pretty bad shape the first day with us. They were puking their guts out after about two miles."

But after a few days, they were now doing just fine, he said. "They have no trouble keeping up now. And they're helping around the campsite every night, setting up tents and helping prepare the food."[86]

Odjick learned something important from those teens. They felt disconnected from the people around them. But here he was, arriving in their community as an outsider, a familiar outsider, but an outsider nonetheless. Often, it's the outsider who brings the most clarity to a situation. So he called on Indigenous leaders to do their part. "The elders have to realize what they owe to our youth," said Odjick. "These kids feel like they've been forgotten. It's up to the bands to provide programs and keep them occupied so they don't turn to alcohol and drugs."[87]

He knew how important it had been for his own upbringing to keep busy. His dad knew it too. "Idle hands" and so forth. That's why Joe got Gino playing hockey and encouraged him in school. But even before the Journey of Healing, he was getting an inkling of what he needed to become.

"Whether as a dentist or hockey player, a Native kid who leaves the reservation will always feel lonely, like an outsider looking in," Gino told *Sports Illustrated* in 1994. "I tell kids to ignore prejudice. If you work hard, you can make it."[88] That's a message he would come back to repeatedly as he spoke with youngsters.

GINO'S WORK WITH Indigenous people would extend far beyond his Journey of Healing. In 1997, he backed Wendy Grant-John when she ran for national chief of the Assembly of First Nations. She didn't win, finishing second to Phil Fontaine. But her loss didn't mean he stopped being interested in Indigenous issues. And, indeed, Fontaine recognized that Gino—because of his prominence as a hockey player, as well as because of his smarts—would be useful.

"Gino took his fame and used it for the benefit of his people," Grant-John told *The Globe and Mail* in 2023. "He said: 'This is who I am, and I want you to understand there is more to us than stereotypes.'"[89]

Fontaine served three terms as national chief; Gino supported him because Fontaine also saw how important it was to work with Indigenous youth. In 2005, Gino was present for the signing of the Kelowna Accord, an agreement reached between multiple levels of government and several national Indigenous groups to improve education, employment, and living conditions for Indigenous people across Canada. Prime Minister Paul Martin endorsed it, but then lost an election to Stephen Harper, who didn't support the agreement.

In 2009, Fontaine led a delegation to the Vatican, seeking an apology from the Catholic Church for its role in the foundation and operation of Canada's residential school system. "We suffered needlessly and tragically. So much was lost for no good reason," Fontaine wrote in a letter he delivered to church authorities. There was some hope that Pope Benedict XVI would deliver an apology. Included in the delegation were Gino and Caroline. But rather than meeting with the whole group, the pope would meet only with Fontaine and four others, and rather than offering a full apology, Benedict merely expressed regret for the abuse that had taken place at residential schools. And while Fontaine said at the time he was satisfied, the broader feeling was the pope's comments had come up short.

"We were expecting an apology. But it was such a joke," Caroline says. "There was supposed to be fifteen people to meet the pope, Gino and I being two of them. But at the last minute, they changed it, knocked it down to five people. So the pope, he sits on that little stage, and then people sit on either side of them. We were then directed to sit. We were front row, but they then made us move back to accommodate other people that were 'more important.' It was an absolute joke."

More than a decade later, Benedict's successor, Francis, would come to Canada to "humbly beg forgiveness for the evil committed by so many Christians against the Indigenous Peoples."

"Phil Fontaine tried, he really tried," Caroline continues. "But you could tell even then [in 2009] we were, like, second-class citizens. And I remember thinking, 'What is this joke?' I even said, 'How are they so disrespectful?' But being Native, like, you don't talk loud, you kind of just respect it. I thought not that long ago, when the other pope finally did apologize, I was like, 'That only took about another fifteen years!'"

AFTER RETIRING FROM pro hockey, Gino went into business. He'd always saved his money. When he signed his first big contract in 1992, $875,000 over three years, his agent urged him to put most of it in the bank, which he did. In retirement, he continued to be smart with his money. He invested in housing developments and advised Indigenous communities, like the Musqueam, Squamish, and Tsleil-Waututh, on development opportunities in front of them. Gino's longest-standing West Coast Indigenous relationship was with the Musqueam people. He'd lived on the Musqueam reserve off and on, especially in the later years of his time with the Canucks. He became an investor in the Musqueam golf course in 2004. Once they assumed control of the course from the previous owners, Gino and Caroline spent a lot of time refining the course's operations, building it into one of the more popular courses in the local golf scene.

When Gino travelled home to Quebec in the summer, he and his friends would spend a lot of time at the local courses near Kitigan Zibi, and they were fond of how laid-back things were. The key, he would say, was who he'd hired to run the place. "At Musqueam, we have a woman general manager, she hired an assistant general manager, and we also have a woman head pro," he told news outlet *Vancouver Is Awesome* in 2011. "Having these women around has been the secret of my success. Women not only give life, but they've brought life into this business. I've learned to just stay out of the way and let them do their thing."[90]

In 2008, they hired Kumi Kimura, a long-time manager of a popular Vancouver restaurant, The Cannery, to manage the course. "He just said he would like golf to be more friendly, and he's like, 'Can you do what you did at The Cannery?'" Kumi remembers Gino asking her.

As a well-regarded business consultant, Gino helped the Tsawwassen First Nation. Their small oceanside reserve sits at the southwestern edge of Metro Vancouver. It's a beautiful setting. To the west, there are views of the Salish Sea stretching thirty kilometres or more across to the Gulf Islands, with the mountains of Vancouver Island rising behind. After years of talks, they won a fruitful land-claims settlement in 2007. They were ready to build.

Kim Baird was chief of the Tsawwassen First Nation from 1999 to 2012 and got to know Gino well. They first became connected through Tsawwassen's efforts to build a waste energy facility in partnership with the Aquilini family, owners of the Canucks. Gino had often advised the Aquilinis on how to pursue opportunities with other Indigenous groups. The project didn't come to pass in the end, but Gino's wisdom was helpful to Baird in many areas, she said. He "always had a different angle about any opportunity we were looking at, whether it was business, political, or otherwise," she says, looking back almost twenty years. "He was good at understanding the First Nation side of the opportunity, and the Aquilini side of the opportunity, and would be able to provide some analysis that would just provide a new light on how it might benefit."

That was a thing Gino would commonly do, Caroline explains. "We just realized that in a lot of the business deals they had, they were being taken advantage of," she says. "So we tried to promote business development on First Nations land because they were land-rich but cash-poor."

The relationship with the Aquilinis wasn't always easy; at times there were disagreements over contracts. But in the end, after Gino died, his daughter Rose told the crowd at a memorial service at Musqueam that her dad was proud of the business relationship he'd forged with the Aquilinis. They'd taken him seriously as a partner, helping him in the second chapter of his life. They'd recognized he wasn't just a dumb jock. "He was thankful for the second opportunity and the many benefits it brought his people," she said.

TO INDIGENOUS YOUTH across Canada, hockey players or otherwise, Gino became a figure to emulate. He was proud of his heritage, proud of where he'd come from. And he knew what he'd achieved gave him a voice. Younger professional hockey players like Wacey Rabbit, Micheal Ferland, and Ethan Bear have spoken often about how important Odjick was to them as young Indigenous athletes—how Odjick's presence inspired so many young people.

Rabbit calls Gino a hero. Rabbit is from the Kainai Nation in southern Alberta, so you might have thought that would've made him a Calgary Flames fan. But for Rabbit, it was all about the former Canucks pugilist. Rabbit was a star in junior for the Saskatoon Blades and Vancouver Giants and then had a fantastic career as a pro: he didn't make the NHL, but he played all over the world.

Rabbit first met Gino when he was six, at a Ted Nolan hockey school. (A former NHLer, Nolan was the second Indigenous person to coach in the NHL.) Odjick was one of the instructors. Then, later that year, Rabbit was at the pre-season game in Calgary where McCarthy and Odjick went toe-to-toe. After the game, he was able to meet both players and take photos with them.

The third meeting came when the Journey of Healing passed through his community. "I got to run in with them. I was blown away when they came through," he recalls, fondly.

He doesn't know how he wound up running alongside his hero, but he's sure his dad, Marvin Yellowhorn, had something to do with it. "My dad knew Gino. We'd have just shown up and he'd have said, 'Run.'" Marvin told Wacey how Odjick had left his community to find his way to success. At the age of ten, Rabbit and his family moved to Lethbridge so he could play better hockey. Lethbridge is all of forty minutes away from Kainai, but it may as well have been across the continent in his mind. It felt big-league to him. Big-league scary.

But to chase his hockey dream, moving to the bigger place was necessary. He realized this pretty young. That visit on the Journey of Healing stuck with Rabbit. "They had to leave, and it was scary, but these guys did it, right? So that gave me confidence that, if these guys can do it, maybe there's a chance for me," he said. And meeting Gino in the flesh taught him a lot. He quickly saw the authenticity in Odjick. "He was like me. It stuck in my head. I was going to cheer for him," Rabbit told the *Province*'s Steve Ewen in February 2023. "He was a very humble person. He was one of the boys, a big kid. He wanted to play hockey, meet people and make them smile."[91]

WHEN ODJICK WAS YOUNG, NHLer John Chabot, who was also from Kitigan Zibi, came home to put on a hockey camp. It meant a lot to young Gino to see another Indigenous player make it as a professional and then give back to his people. "It was a big thrill for our community to see someone play in the NHL," Odjick once told the CBC, while he was working at a Manitoba hockey camp in 2001. "Hopefully it's the same for these kids here."[92]

In the summer of 1993, Canucks scout Ron Delorme invited Gino, along with other Indigenous pro players like McCarthy, Rich Pilon, Jamie Leach, and Blair Atcheynum, to help run a hockey camp for young Indigenous kids in Lloydminster, on the Saskatchewan-Alberta border. Delorme felt it would be good for young Indigenous players to encounter and be inspired by Indigenous athletes who had made it. Delorme would run the camp for nine years, with loads of corporate support to help keep costs down and make it possible for Indigenous youth from across Canada to take part. Gino's instincts to engage with new people, no matter their age or background, shone in these scenarios. He made the kids feel at ease.

Delorme says Gino was essential to growing the camp. Not only did he quickly take to working with kids and deploying his quirky sense of humour to connect with them, but he also helped Delorme fill out the coaching staff. And it was Gino who brought in his friends Sandy McCarthy and Chris Simon.

Delorme asked Gino to pay attention to everyone he interacted with. "I told him to always give a little something of himself, to never walk by kids that were standing outside the rink, hoping for his autograph. Talk to them. Gino was very, very good at that," Delorme says. Delorme knew very well the experience of being a young Indigenous man in the NHL. "I was never a star, but I made sure everybody standing outside would get my autograph."

This principle took hold of Gino. In September 1993, weeks after Gino had appeared at Delorme's hockey camp, and while the Canucks were holding training camp in Kamloops, BC, Delorme connected him with Fred Sasakamoose, one of the first Indigenous players to make the NHL. He played eleven games for the Chicago Black Hawks in 1953–54. Originally from Saskatchewan, Sasakamoose's brother Peter had settled on the Tk'emlúps te Secwépemc reserve just outside Kamloops after he and Fred moved west to play hockey for a team in Kamloops. Fred would visit there often.

Even if his stint in the NHL was short, it still carried great significance, his sister-in-law told the *Province* after Fred died of complications from Covid in 2020. "The thing of it is in the '50s there was no First Nations people recognized in any major sport. He was the first one. He was a trailblazer. He was an icon," she said.[93] Sasakamoose was an important mentor to Delorme. He taught his young protege the importance of giving young people hope, of showing them there was a way forward, a way out of poverty.

After retiring, Sasakamoose would often visit Indigenous communities in northern Saskatchewan, especially ones where mental health issues, alcoholism, and suicide were rampant. He'd speak with young people, telling them how he'd struggled in his youth with alcoholism and depression, and how he'd rediscovered his spirit after engaging with his Plains Cree culture: he hailed from the Ahtahkakoop reserve outside of Saskatoon. At that 1993 meeting, he took Gino, Pavel Bure, and a couple other of their teammates out fishing. There's little doubt that encounter left a lasting impression on Odjick. During that Canucks training camp, Gino visited the Tk'emlúps te Secwépemc reserve, as well as the former residential school on the reserve—the same school where, years later, evidence of burial sites would be found, the news of which pushed Gino to tears.

THE JOURNEY OF HEALING also prompted Gino to talk more about his foster brother Clarence Jacko. Jacko had joined the Odjick family when he was eight, after his mother, who'd struggled with alcohol and substance abuse, hanged herself. But the difficulties his mother had faced obviously haunted her son as well, and when Gino and Clarence were only twenty, Clarence also hanged himself. Odjick told Jim Jamieson in 1995 that he'd long struggled to talk about Clarence, but his experience with the Journey of Healing had helped him open up.

"He hung himself... killed himself with drugs and alcohol," Gino said, adding that the two had started drinking at age twelve, an age most people know is too young but was common in those days on the reserve. "Everybody drank, it was a part of growing up for us. When I was a kid I'd drink for four or five days at a time."

In the summer of the Journey of Healing, Gino went home, as he'd always done. But this time, things were different. He was looking to push himself forward, to make himself better. To be a better father. "In the summer I went back to the way I grew up. I learned our ways again. A long time ago we didn't drink and didn't do drugs. We had respect for everybody and we worked together," he said. "That's got to come back and it's got to come from the leadership on down. There's a lot of people working hard to better ourselves as First Nations."[94]

ODJICK'S SELFLESSNESS became legendary. If someone needed help, no matter who they were, he was ready. "He'd buy kids lunch," Jan "Boy Boy" Cote says. He recalled a time they were at the Maniwaki arena together and Gino bought poutine for a random kid he saw there. Another time, Gino and Boy Boy were playing a round at the Algonquin Golf Club, just south of Kitigan Zibi. Gino talked up a young kid he didn't know, found out he knew the kid's father, and then bought the kid a cheeseburger.

And then there was the time in the early 1990s when Geoff Courtnall found himself helping the Canucks' ticket office figure out who had left tickets for an unnamed Indigenous kid who had long hair and would be wearing a track suit. "Gotta be Gino," Courtnall thought. "So I go over to Gino and I go, 'Hey, did you leave tickets for a guy in a track suit?' He goes, 'Yeah, it's my track suit. I don't know his name. I just met him,'" Courtnall says, laughing. The kid obviously got the tickets and came to the game, because the next day, Gino was skating around in the track suit he'd lent to the kid.

GINO COUNSELLED Micheal Ferland, a Cree professional hockey player from Manitoba, over the years. Ferland first made it to the NHL—the Calgary Flames—in 2014–15, but his path to the league was far from direct. While Ferland was in junior, he struggled with alcohol abuse. The Flames heard the stories about their prospect, a big, strong winger who scored goals and threw heavy hits. Gino's old junior coach Bob Hartley, who was now coaching the Flames, thought about an old player of his who might be able to help.

So he gave Gino a ring. Hartley "was really high on him," Odjick recalled on the *VANcast* podcast in 2020. "But Micheal at that time was young. He showed up a bit out of shape, a little heavy, and he was drinking a lot. So management was really mad at Mike. So Bob says, 'Come and talk to him.'

"So I had a good talk with him. I told him, 'This is a once in a lifetime opportunity. It's not going to come up often where you have a chance to make an NHL team.'"[95]

Then Gino harked back to that 1993 lesson, when he was a healthy scratch during the playoffs even though he'd seen a lot of playing time in the regular season and was seen by many as the toughest player in the NHL. He'd learned that none of that regular season bravado mattered in the playoffs, he told Ferland. In the crunch time of the playoffs, it was all about whether he could keep up. "I told him to make sure, y'know, that when I played I wasn't the most talented guy, but I made sure I was one of the fittest guys on the team—to give myself a chance to get some ice time and to play," he said. "You need to be in shape, you need to be the most fit player on the team. You need to take this opportunity that you have and make a life for yourself, for yourself and your family. You can set yourself and your family up for life if you take this opportunity."[96]

Whether it was Odjick's message that sealed the deal or not, it was in the mix. Ferland first found his way to sobriety. Then he got fit—really, really fit. "To his credit, Mike quit drinking and he started working out. I think he lost thirty-five pounds or something," Odjick noted on the *VANcast*. A second-half call-up for the Flames in 2014–15, he became a playoff phenomenon—against Gino's old team, the Canucks. His rambunctious play kept the Canucks on their heels and helped turn the first-round playoff series between the two teams Calgary's way. He became an NHL regular because of his playoff performances: scoring goals and throwing big hits.

When the Canucks signed Ferland in the summer of 2019, Odjick was excited to see what his young friend could do for his old team. "He made a career out of it and he's doing pretty well. He was hurt this year, but he's a guy that can get you twenty goals and can protect your stars and finish his checks. I don't think the Canucks want him fighting, just want him finishing his checks and protecting [Elias] Pettersson and these types of players."[97]

Sadly, things didn't go well for Ferland. His aggressive style of play led to a series of concussions. He came to Vancouver with questions hanging over him about whether he would be able to continue as the physical player he'd always been. He lasted just fourteen games for Vancouver before he suffered a concussion in a fight against the Los Angeles Kings' Kyle Clifford. That head injury essentially ended his career. For months, he suffered from vertigo and other post-concussion symptoms, including difficulty with his coordination. He'd say he felt drunk, an especially disturbing feeling given his efforts to stay sober. Ferland badly wanted to keep playing. Undaunted, he put in plenty of work, keeping himself in shape and meeting with specialists, hoping to find a solution to these effects he was experiencing.

Twice he seemed to recover and tried to return to play—in February 2020 with the Canucks' Utica farm team, and again in July 2020, during the NHL's pandemic re-start season. But both times his symptoms eventually recurred. At that point, it seemed pretty clear that hockey for him was over; it had become unsustainable. He shifted his attention to just getting back to a normal life, to being a dad.

Early in the summer of 2021, Odjick said Ferland told him he'd overcome his symptoms. He'd sat out all of the 2020–21 season, but there was still a year left on his contract. He was thinking about trying to play again.

"I told him no," Gino relayed on the *Donnie and Dhali* TV show, about a year after the call from Ferland. "You should worry about your quality of life." Gino recalled his own experience. As much as he wished he could have returned to the NHL, it was better that he hadn't. Ferland would never play in the NHL again.[98]

ETHAN BEAR, a defenceman who played for several NHL teams, including the Edmonton Oilers and Vancouver Canucks, cited Gino as an inspiration during his youth. Later, when was Bear grown up and at a crossroads in his own NHL career, Gino became more than just an inspiration—he became an actual advisor, helping Bear find a way forward as a professional hockey player. Bear wasn't struggling with concussions; he was just struggling with getting another chance in the NHL.

Bear grew up in Ochapowace Nation near Whitewood, Saskatchewan, far from Vancouver, far from Odjick's home in Kitigan Zibi. But that didn't matter. Even though he was only five when Odjick's career came to an end, the big Algonquin man's influence was well known to Bear. "Everybody knew Gino Odjick growing up, coming up. And he was definitely one of the first Indigenous players to kind of make a trail for the rest of us," Bear said on January 15, 2023, the day Gino died.[99]

For Bear, that day was a dramatic one. He scored a goal for the Canucks in a game in Raleigh, North Carolina, against the

Carolina Hurricanes, a thrilling and highly emotional moment for him. He had played for the Hurricanes the previous season, but they had moved on from him after a brutal bout of Covid knocked him from the lineup.

He began the 2022–23 season with Carolina as a surplus part. The Hurricanes said they'd see if they could find him another team. Eventually, it was the Canucks who came calling. On that emotional Sunday afternoon, when Bear scored a goal not long after Odjick died thousands of kilometres away, the Canucks won the game in a shootout. Shortly after the players came off the ice, Canucks assistant equipment manager Brian "Red" Hamilton told Bear the tragic news.

In the dressing room after the game, Bear's eyes welled with tears. It was a lot to take in. But he was also more than ready to pay tribute to a man who'd been first a hero to him, then a mentor. He then stepped in front of a handful of reporters, who knew a little bit about the connection between Bear and Odjick.

"He is a legend, someone who's obviously a big influence in the Native community. It's tough," Bear said.[100] He was struck by the fact he'd scored a goal on the day of his hero's passing. "It's like, you can't make this up, you know what I mean?"

Bear had gotten to know Odjick through Ferland. Five years older than Bear, Ferland was a player that the young defenceman looked to for guidance. Plus, they shared the same agent. As he'd been for Ferland, Gino became a trusted voice for Bear. "He'd always message me and stuff like that, if I was playing well. If I need to step it up. He was always there to give some little advice," Bear said about his relationship with Odjick. "That's all you can ask for. This league's as hard as it is. And every day you try to get better, but some days are harder than others. It's always nice to have someone who you can look up to and who's been through it as well and to support you. Definitely gonna miss him."[101]

Earlier that season, when Bear had come through Vancouver with the Hurricanes, he was a healthy scratch. The Hurricanes had said they weren't going to play him and were ready to trade him. Bear and Odjick spoke about his situation. The Canucks were interested, but it was Odjick who convinced Bear to speak to his agent to urge Carolina to work out a trade with Vancouver.

"I talked with Gino before, and he said he was rooting for me to come here," Bear recalled. "I just got to sit with him and chat. It was pretty cool. And then he's pretty much one of the guys who kind of pushed me to come here."

SO MUCH OF Gino's wisdom came from own life experience, as the guy who, as he used to say, "came off the rez," and had to figure the world out mostly on his own. As he worked more and more with young people, he learned more and more about himself. As so many do in life, even after they've achieved big things, Gino suffered somewhat from imposter syndrome, despite having had a successful NHL career, which had delivered a comfortable life to him. People looked up to him, and it was hard for him to understand why. "I'm just a guy," his instincts would tell him.

In the workshops he would lead alongside his good friend Peter Leech, he'd speak openly of his own self-doubts. "I want to be as smart as Peter," he would say, despite the mountains of books he'd consumed. He looked back at himself and didn't think, "Here's a brilliant, successful guy"—just thought of himself as a guy.

Nonetheless, he recognized that his success playing professional hockey also meant something bigger: he was an Indigenous hockey player. Indigenous people across the country looked up to him. His mere presence meant something. He'd always hoped that his words might matter as well. The guy who was able to advise Ferland and Bear so well was built over the preceding two decades, leading youth leadership workshops alongside Peter. The workshops worked as medicine for him, he'd say—Peter would say the say same—because he came to realize just how much his words did matter. Gino would hear what Peter was saying in the seminars about fatherhood or relationships and it would give him more things to ponder. It was also medicine because he realized his ability to influence young people was good for his soul.

For Gino, the Journey of Healing was a beginning. A powerful beginning. In 1999 he first joined Peter to lead workshops with youth, usually with Indigenous young people but also in public schools with non-Indigenous students. Peter, who'd played hockey and soccer at a high level as well as being a boxer and a former protege of famed BC Indigenous leader George Manuel, had been working with young people for several years at that point. He was confident in front of a crowd. But Gino, despite having played hockey in front of thousands of fans, and having done plenty of interviews on TV, was intimidated by the idea of helping lead a full-day workshop. He would say he couldn't imagine speaking for a whole day. "How are we going to do this?" he pondered to Peter.

The key, Peter told him, like any public speaker or teacher would suggest, is to say only as much as you need to: to make a lesson work, you need to get the participants talking. Your priority is to listen. To become part of the group. You make your point, show you care, then see what comes back at you. And as Gino did this more and more, he found a confidence that allowed him to connect with his audiences even more. If they connected with one person per day, they'd succeeded, they felt.

One time, a fifteen-year-old girl stood up in a workshop and said, "Y'know, my brothers play hockey, my uncles played hockey. And I thought you were going to be kind of like a dummy. Just a hockey player. But you come across pretty confident."

Gino, who had often asked Peter how he could show confidence, snuck a look at his friend and found Peter was smiling at him. Confidence was something to project, Gino learned. His self-assurance grew, of course, as he came to understand more and more the message he and Peter were working with: that everyone has the power within themselves to find the way forward, to overcome their own fears. And then he'd find his own words to explain the concepts.

When the kids were talking, Gino and Peter knew the kids were engaged. They were responding, reacting to the prompts being put to them, like what their goals in life were. Usually, this was because Gino and Peter had showed they cared about what they were talking about; they found that by showing they cared about a topic, there was a good chance the kids would care too.

Peter and Gino tried to avoid delivering lectures because that wasn't interesting for the kids—it wasn't interesting for Peter or Gino either. The stories would get more personal for Gino and for the kids when they could engage on a more personal level. Big group or small, they still had to be focused on how they were presenting. It was the quality of the work, not the quantity, that mattered to them. This would become especially true after Gino's health started to fail in 2014. The first fifteen years, they'd often run two workshops a month in the summer. By the end of his life, they were doing just two per year.

GINO DIDN'T FIND his voice right away. "You know how to communicate with them. You know how to get the message across to them. I want to know how to do that," he would say to Peter. Even though Gino was a jovial, chatty conversationalist with his teammates and with the local media, speaking with kids in a group setting, as a leader, intimidated him at first.

But to Peter, Gino already knew how to speak to kids: he just needed to find confidence in himself. And Peter told him that. "You do know what to say. Be confident in what you know. Don't be so judgmental of yourself. Don't be so hard on yourself."

It was an appeal to the personal strength Odjick had learned from his dad, about showing he was worthy, especially to the people who dismissed him out of simple racism. "I always wanted to prove those people were wrong, that we weren't second-class citizens," he told *BC Bookworld* in 2014. "My dad approved of that, but he never allowed me to feel sorry for myself. If I was in a situation where someone else was getting the upper hand, he would tease me or joke around with me until I dealt with it. It made me stronger and wiser, able to deal with that kind of situation."[102]

The confidence that he showed on the ice, in his personal life, finally transferred to speaking in front of young people. Gino found the energy that Peter had long felt when working with youth, helping them make breakthroughs with themselves. They'd get the kids to write down their emotions, their fears. Sometimes the kids would produce pages and pages of material. The idea was to help them understand themselves, to help them see what was in front of them and figure out how to overcome these mental obstacles. This simple act of writing things down was often enough for the kids to begin figuring out a path toward their goals.

As a public speaker, Gino quickly crushed any notions he was just another dumb hockey player: here was a guy who took the time to understand, took the time to learn. "I always do it with Peter because he can do a whole workshop for the entire day. As for me, I can speak for an hour," Gino joked to a reporter in Kamloops in 2022.[103]

HELPING YOUTH FIND a path forward, showing them that they needn't despair about their future, was a huge motivator. "I've lost lots of relatives to suicide," Odjick said in Kamloops in 2022. "I'm happy that I asked for help and I try to share that with the kids to ask for help if they aren't feeling well. I always tell the kids, no matter how great an athlete you are to make sure you stay in school and get an education. Because education is freedom and gives you the opportunity to have a career."[104]

That path could be difficult, he'd tell kids. Don't be afraid of difficulty. Gino would tell workshop attendees how, when he was in his teens, his dad took him to a spot in the bush not far from home. A trail was there, over a mountain. Father and son hiked the five-kilometre trail together.

"We walked up and over it together that first time. It was no big deal," Gino told *BC Bookworld*. "But then around the time of the next full moon, he drove me to the base of the mountain after dark and this time he said, you walk across by yourself and I'll pick you up on the other side.

"He just said, 'Do what I tell you.' So off I went. It may have been full moon time, but the path was in the forest and it was pretty dark. I was nervous about what might be out there, but I made it over OK. When I got to the other side, he was waiting to pick me up. In the truck he turned to me and said, now you keep doing that until you feel comfortable doing it. You just keep doing it until it becomes second nature."[105]

The visits with young people would often go so well that Gino and Peter would be invited back, sometimes years after they'd made a visit to the community. "We want to bring you back, because this is a different generation of kids," they'd be told. Clearly, elders believed Gino and Peter had made a difference with their original visit, and now they hoped a new group of kids would benefit.

Stephanie Johnson was one of the young people who felt the impact of their words. She first met Gino and Peter as a teen when they gave a workshop in Esquimalt on Vancouver Island. Later, she'd attend the University of Victoria and earn a law degree.

A few years later, Johnson was doing some work with the First Nations Summit, and she wanted to thank Gino and Peter. Gino, who had many connections with Indigenous leaders, was also involved with the summit, which was set up mainly to further treaty negotiations between the BC provincial government and the province's First Nations.

Stephanie told Gino and Peter she'd become a lawyer. The messages they'd shared with her and her peers in the workshop had resonated with her—even at thirteen. They changed her thinking, helped her realize what was important: basically, education, education, education.

It was that saying they used to share with the kids, and it had stuck with her. Peter and Gino used to say, "We're two little Indian boys who grew up on the rez. We can do it. So can you. What's stopping you? That's what we're here to talk about: What's stopping you from accomplishing the things that you need to accomplish?" It was a mantra the guys repeated everywhere. It started with Peter, but it carried forward to Gino.

EVERYWHERE THEY VISITED in BC, they would see poverty. On most visits, they'd end up spending one-on-one time with one or two of the kids, learning about them, seeing what their lives were like. Seeing if there was a wise word or two they could share with them. On a visit to Bella Coola in 2007, they connected with a young boy named Adrian. It was August, a sunny and warm time of year on the central coast of BC.

Bella Coola is an idyllic spot, nestled at the end of a wide fjord beneath towering mountains, next to the mouth of the Bella Coola River. Eons ago, the river cut a long, winding valley inland, with plenty of fertile land along its shores. The Nuxalk people have lived here for thousands of years. The fishing is good, especially for salmon—a vital food source—and eulachon, a fish that gets so fatty when it's spawning, it can be dried out and then used as food, as well as a fire starter, preservative, medicine, and lubricant.

But a century and a half of encroachment by European settlers had damaged the society the Nuxalk had developed here. Between the long-term influences of disease and residential schools, the Indigenous people of contemporary Bella Coola were facing many of the same social issues that Indigenous communities across the country face. The community in which young Adrian was growing up was struggling with poverty and alcoholism. Adrian's home life was difficult. There wasn't a lot of food in the house. His dad wasn't in the picture.

When Gino and Peter sat down to have a meal with him, they realized he was slipping some of the food from the table into his pocket. "Why are you doing that?" they asked. "I'm gonna save it for later," he said. They kept talking. Seated with them was an older sister, but she kept quiet. He also had a younger sister, he told Gino and Peter, but she was at home with their mom.

Adrian mentioned he'd seen commercials on TV about the Pacific National Exhibition, the PNE, the big annual fair held in Vancouver during the last two weeks of August. He'd never been to Vancouver, let alone the PNE, but he said he dreamed of going. The farthest from home he'd ever ventured was Williams Lake, a city in the Interior about five and a half hours away by car.

He'd never flown before. "What's it like being on a plane?" he asked. Gino and Peter talked it over. "Let's take these kids to the PNE," they decided. And so they did. They arranged for the kids to fly down to Vancouver.

The PNE takes place on the grounds of Hastings Park, also home to the Pacific Coliseum, where the Canucks played for Gino's first five NHL seasons before moving downtown to GM Place. Across the street from the PNE's main entrance is the Atrium Inn, the hotel where Gino lived when he first moved to Vancouver. Fittingly, perhaps, that's where Adrian and his sisters stayed. The night before the big day at the PNE, Gino and Peter went to check on things. The kids were in a metaphorical candy store. They were so excited. They wept joyful tears for the excitement of the adventure.

They hadn't even gone to the PNE yet, but the moment overwhelmed Gino. He had to step away and collect himself. "You've done a good thing," Peter told him. "We've done what we could. We've showed these kids what's possible."

"I really did the best I could do there, to create opportunity and to let people know there were opportunities. I'm really proud of that part," Gino told the *Province* sports columnist Ed Willes years later.[106]

IN 2002, Gino travelled to Kashechewan, Ontario, a small, isolated Cree community on the shores of James Bay. It's a tough place to grow up. Poverty is rampant. The townsite, on the Albany River delta, has long-standing problems with flooding. There's no direct road to the rest of Ontario. To get in and out, you have to fly, and flights aren't cheap. The rest of the world feels very, very far away.

Having an NHL legend like Gino Odjick and two other Indigenous hockey stars—former NHLer John Chabot and then-rising star Jonathan Cheechoo—come to the community was a very big deal for the people of Kashechewan. Famous people didn't visit their community.

One of the kids there was Stephane Friday.

"He was the talk of the weekend," recalls Friday, who has grown up to lead Hockey Indigenous, a non-profit that promotes and celebrates Indigenous people and athletes. The organization addresses systemic challenges Indigenous hockey players face, such as access to equipment and coaching, as well as promoting a more general understanding of these issues among the Canadian populace.

For Stephane, a boy of eight at the time of Gino's visit, hockey was a thing from far away, something he'd watch on TV with his grandfather. But playing the actual game wasn't an option in Kashechewan, Friday said.

Even so, young Stephane never thought getting himself to a big NHL arena as a fan one day was an impossible dream. "I always believed it. I knew it. It can happen," he recalls. That was his attitude toward life in general. And it's no surprise that he connected with the message Odjick was sharing. During the 2002 visit, Friday got a photo with Odjick, an image he cherishes to this day. Odjick's visit and message resonated with Friday's natural view of the world: that community is important, that life can get better through working together.

"I've always seen things beyond me," Friday says. "I think this is part of the community spirit, whether you're Cree, Algonquin, Ojibwe, Gitxsan, we all have this just instilled in our hearts. We want to motivate each other. We want each other to have the best."

A few years later, he saw Odjick again, this time playing in a hockey tournament in Cheechoo's hometown of Moose Factory, Ontario. Odjick hadn't played in the NHL for about five years at that point, but he still loved to mix it up on the ice. When opponents wound up to take a slapshot, for instance, Odjick tapped the opponent's stick at the top of their wind-up so they couldn't complete their shooting motion. "My community's players were frustrated by him," Friday says between laughs.

Friday credits his encounters with Odjick and Cheechoo as essential moments in his own journey. "I met Cheechoo, he pretty much grew up like two communities away from me. I met Gino. I've seen Gino play... and I was like, 'Okay, he's an Algonquin legend, and he's always helping other communities, giving back to Indigenous communities,'" he says. He took inspiration and built his first website in 2016 to document professional hockey players with Indigenous roots. "I was like, 'Okay, if he's doing this, if there's other people doing this in their own way, I can do this. We have the freedom and the aspirations to do things.'"

When Friday was in high school, he moved with his mom, Stephanie, south to Timmins, to pursue a bigger life than they could achieve at home in Kashechewan. Heading south was a long-standing dream for both of them. Of course, none of it would have happened without his mom's initiative, without her efforts to move to a new city, where there was work and a chance to live in their own home. Back in Kashechewan, housing was cramped. Stephane and his mom usually had to share accommodations with others. "She had a job, she did food sales, she did a lot of things to save money," he said.

Friday's great-grandparents had been sent to residential schools, but his grandparents and his mom had managed to avoid being sent away. Still, the trauma has spread across generations. "I went through a lot as a kid myself because of that," he said. "But I'm breaking that cycle for my kids."

In his teens, Friday got involved with youth leadership programs. In 2016, he was part of the Nishnawbe Aski Nation Youth Delegation that met with Prime Minister Justin Trudeau about the issues facing Indigenous people in Northern Ontario, such as access to health care, education, and clean drinking water. (As of September 2024, there were still thirteen long-term drinking water advisories affecting twelve Nishnawbe Aski communities; that's forty percent of the long-term drinking water advisories in place across Canada.)

After finishing high school in 2016, Friday moved back to Kashechewan and helped run youth sports programs in the community. He then served as a band councillor and headed up the band's search for a new townsite, one less prone to flooding. The federal government has pledged more than once to help the community move upriver. He also led a group of schoolchildren to Ottawa in 2018 to call out the federal government for the unhealthy conditions of the community's school building.

Amid all these frustrations about the state of things in his community, he sees forward momentum at the grassroots level with organizations like Hockey Indigenous. "I often think back to my reality and how I'm trying to create this reality for Indigenous youth. I can see the trends. You can see the upsurge from years ago to now: there's a lot more kids playing in mainstream hockey," he says.

Friday's story is exactly what Odjick hoped to help create. Friday thinks of Odjick as a trailblazer. He wouldn't be running Hockey Indigenous without Odjick having planted the seed in his mind, simply by showing up, by showing him what could be.

DURING THEIR WORKSHOPS, Peter and Gino would focus on a teaching device called the Wheel of Fear. You need a tool to fix your house, a tool to fix your car. A counsellor can offer you tools to fix yourself, but the best tool is yourself, they'd tell the kids. The wheel's purpose is to teach workshop participants that in the end, the only way forward is to find a way for you to fix yourself. The process of using the wheel helps identify your fears. Every emotion you're feeling. Peter and Gino would give some examples: fear of shame, fear of abandonment.

In one session in Alberta, a girl wrote out all her fears. She wrote down so many that they took up page after page. She went over and over them. Then she thanked Gino and Peter for getting the words out of her, and they reinforced in her that the only way to understand what we're thinking is by hearing it. It forces you to think about it. It's like looking into a mirror.

When Gino was getting ready for a session, Peter would ask him about what Gino saw in the mirror. "Talk to that person," Peter would say. "Ask him why he's grooming himself. Why are you making yourself look good? Can you relate to that person? Can you talk to that person? That's you. There's two people, one on each side of the fence. There's you today and who you want to be going forward."

DID GINO EVER get in touch with that person in the mirror, the one he wanted to be? Hard to say. He'd always say, "I've got to get to know myself." But there were things about himself he didn't like. He was always thinking about himself, about who he was presenting to the world. He wanted to be a better person, that natural instinct that most of us have. He felt he could be doing a lot more emotionally for his children, that he could be a better father. But rather than talk openly about his doubts about himself, he would often deflect the conversation away from himself, then tell himself that things were going well. Gino didn't like to think he was using emotional crutches. He didn't like the term. He felt it was labelling him, saying that he was no good, that he wasn't bright. He thought if he admitted that he might be using crutches for his emotions, this would make him look less confident.

Still, he was always trying to be a better person. He was helping people not just for their sake, but for his own. Helping people engage with their emotions helped him do the same.

In the early days of the workshops, Gino only talked about playing hockey. It was what he knew. But toward the end of his life, he was talking about himself, the wheel, education, fear, and shame. He'd talk about the fear of losing control, of being judged. He'd always had a brave face when he read something about himself that wasn't appealing or flattering. But he was always bothered by how people judged him.

At one workshop, Peter and Gino were speaking with kids about abuse, both physical and sexual. They knew that when talking about difficult topics, they had to gauge what the audience was ready for. In this particular session, they were ready for some pretty heavy stuff. Peter asked a kid about whether he'd been abused. The boy started fidgeting and got uncomfortable. Peter said to him, "It's okay, you don't have to say it, your body has told me." Peter's dad, Walter Leech, who was a substance-use counsellor, always said that when you cut somebody open, they're bleeding, so you've got to make sure you close the wound. Don't put a band-aid on it. You tell the kid they have a lot of strength; don't run from the uncomfortable truths you hold, don't hang your head about them. With this boy, they acknowledged his discomfort but also helped him recognize that he wasn't being judged for his discomfort; rather, he was being accepted—it was understood he was carrying a burden.

Gino got to be good at reading his audience. He and Peter would walk into the day with a rough schedule in mind, but they didn't necessarily stick to it. The young people might want to talk about something else. One time, while driving back from Merritt, Gino looked at Peter and said, "I was gauging the audience, and then I saw that the giggling had stopped, that they were engaged. What we were talking about connected with what they were dealing with in their own lives."

10

"WHAT'S WRONG WITH GINO?"

GINO WAS RIDING in an elevator at Vancouver General Hospital with some of his old Canucks teammates in May 2014 when he had a moment of clarity. He looked around the elevator at these faces he'd known for two decades, guys who had meant so much to him in life. Gino was frail, terribly ill, but his spirit remained strong. "I don't want to die," he declared.

He was in a fight again, but this time for his life. Until even six months before, he'd been the same giant, fit man he'd been since his teens. But now his face was gaunt, his arms and shoulders mere bone racks. He looked like a ghost, not a big, tough hockey player. Aged forty-three, he could barely walk. He used a wheelchair to get around. He could barely walk three metres. He had an oxygen tank to help him breathe.

Doctors had diagnosed him with AL amyloidosis, a serious and extremely rare heart condition that was depositing proteins on his heart muscle. The proteins constricted the muscle, reducing his heart's function and keeping it from pumping properly. Unlike the elastic band that your heart is supposed to be, Odjick's heart was turning into old, dried-out leather. With his heart working at just twenty-five percent, his doctors had told him that he had a year to live. Maybe.

"You don't think when you're 43 years old they're going to tell you you have one year to live," Gino told the *Province*'s Ed Willes at the time. "It was the last thing on my mind. There's been a lot of soul searching."[107]

Gino had long thought of himself as invincible. "If there's an airplane crash, everybody will die but I'll survive," he would say.[108] He'd been one of the toughest guys in the NHL. Sure, he'd had some ups and downs with his mental health, but physically he'd always been in top shape. In retirement, he'd work out three times a week. He skated with the Canucks alumni once a week—the former pros had been playing a mid-day game at Rogers Arena for years—and he would golf just about any other day.

At Pavel Bure's retirement ceremony the previous November, Bure was escorted all over the arena, visiting many people in many suites around the building. Gino accompanied him everywhere, but struggled to get around. Just as Pavel had done the day before at the card signing event, Pat Quinn asked Peter: "What's wrong with Gino?"

The next day, at Peter and Pavel's urging, Gino finally relented and said he'd go to Vancouver General Hospital after they dropped Bure off at the airport. Once he was finally at VGH, cardiologist Dr. Amir Ahmadi concluded within a matter of hours Gino was suffering from amyloidosis. Ahmadi scheduled Gino to meet with a number of specialists, hoping to find a way to stave off the otherwise inevitable deterioration of his heart. Gino would stay in the cardiac ward, but then, three weeks after the Bure ceremony, Gino's father died, and he travelled home. Sorting out his heart would have to wait. And, as it turned out, he would need to get his head sorted out first.

PAPA JOE WAS seventy-four when he died from cancer. He had kept his poor health from everyone. Gino and his family were devastated. Gino travelled home to be with his mom and his sisters and his kids. But the stress of Papa Joe's death triggered a new bout of psychosis. After visiting home, he went down to Montreal to visit friends. He made a TV appearance on a sports panel show called *L'Antichambre*, in which he was practically incoherent. He struggled to explain himself. Those on the panel with him—like former NHL enforcer Georges Laraque and journalist François Gagnon—were visibly concerned during the segment. Those watching at home were similarly concerned.

Away from the TV studio, he started accusing his sister Janique as well as Peter of being devils, of conspiring against him. Paramedics were called, who recommended he be taken back into psychiatric care. He spent two days in a Laval hospital, then was released despite the pleadings of his friends and family.

Gino headed back up to Kitigan Zibi, but within days he was back in hospital, this time at the Centre hospitalier Pierre-Janet in Gatineau, across the river from Ottawa, about ninety minutes south of Kitigan Zibi. His brain was a turbulent swirl of thoughts and emotions. While in hospital, he spoke with Marc de Foy from *Le Journal de Montréal*.

Gino told him about all his stints in psychiatric care. Then he made an audacious claim: that he'd spoken with Montreal Canadiens GM Marc Bergevin and coach Michel Therrien—Gino's old coach had been rehired in 2012—and that they said they'd arrange for the team's top doctor, Dr. Vincent Lacroix, to meet him. But when de Foy approached Therrien and Lacroix about Odjick's claims, they had no idea what he was talking about. Gino was in a bad way, de Foy wrote.[109] He needed everyone's help.

By December, Gino was back in Vancouver. In a column that month for the *Province*, Ed Willes reported Gino was still resisting his friends' help. "I just want to heal. I don't want to be in pain. I don't want to be angry," Gino admitted to Willes. "I'm not going to function as a normal human being," he added. "There will be times when I have to go and rest. But I'll focus, eat healthy, live healthy and stay in shape."[110]

A few days later, on a sunny but cold day back in Vancouver, Gino was sitting with Peter on the patio of a Starbucks when he looked at his friend and said, "I need help." Peter asked him to take off his sunglasses and Gino did, revealing deep emotion. There were tears in his eyes. Peter realized that Gino was at the lowest point in his life. Peter told him the only way to get better from there was to commit to accepting help and following a plan. That meant listening to his doctors, listening to his friends. From then on, Gino did.

He went back to Dr. Edwin Tam, who finally sorted out which drugs had been causing huge problems for Gino. It was the prednisone that was prompting him to make gregarious requests, to have a false sense of self, to hide his true personality. The Prozac was making him too hyper, sometimes even angry—as in the incident two months before, when he locked

Kumi in the truck and the police had to be called. Instead, Tam prescribed a trio of drugs that Gino would take for the rest of his life: Xylac (an antipsychotic), Lamotrigine (a mood stabilizer), and Jamp-Quetiapine (an antipsychotic). They worked. "His brain straightened out," Kumi said. His mind would be settled for the rest of his life.

WHEN HE RETURNED to Vancouver, he began to see the specialists Dr. Ahmadi connected him with as an outpatient. He met with Dr. Kevin Song, a veteran hematologist, and Dr. Margot Davis, a cardiologist with a special focus on amyloidosis. He was trying, the doctors were trying, but he was only getting worse.

In March, while hanging out with friends, his heart went into real crisis. His shortness of breath was accompanied by chest pain. An ambulance rushed him to VGH. The doctors determined he was having a heart attack. He spent the next couple of weeks in the cardiac intensive care ward at VGH. The news prompted Gino's son Joey and Joey's mom Elizabeth to travel out to Vancouver. Sister Dina and niece Roxane also spent hours and hours with him in hospital. But after a time, Gino's heart stabilized again, and he was sent back up to the cardiac ward on the sixth floor.

That April, Pat Quinn was added to the Ring of Honour at Rogers Arena. Gino badly wanted to be there for his old coach, but he was too ill. The visits from his teammates increased. Caroline and Rose went to visit Gino too. They weren't living with him anymore as a family, but their care for him never ceased. "We did think that was going to be the last time," Caroline said.

Mid-month, he had another heart attack. He survived, barely. Next to Pavel Bure, Geoff Courtnall and Cliff Ronning had been Gino's favourite teammates in Vancouver. After hearing about the heart attack, the two rushed to the hospital and saw their old friend. Ronning recalls thinking, "Is this really it?"

In a late-April visit Courtnall made with Quinn, Gino's condition was so poor, it seemed impossible he would recover. "He was really non-responsive most of the time. I really thought that was going to be the last time I saw him," a stoic Courtnall recalled. (Quinn himself was struggling with his health, but he insisted that no one tell his old enforcer that he had cancer. He knew how much Odjick cared for him, and he feared what the bad news might do to Gino.)

The idea that, two months later, Gino would walk outside and greet a mob of fans, then fly back home, let alone be on the road to recovery, would have seemed impossible. And yet he did.

WHEN DR. AHMADI first sorted out that Gino was suffering from AL amyloidosis, the tests used to confirm the condition had only recently been developed. Amyloidosis was a well-known health concern, but Gino's particular form was rarely seen: according to Dr. Song, in the decade since his diagnosis, about twenty British Columbians per year are diagnosed with cardiac amyloidosis.

Amyloidosis has been generally understood as a condition for more than a century, but research started to ramp up in the 1960s. The disease can affect many different organs, but the form that Gino had, which deposits proteins solely in the heart, had been nearly impossible to detect in living people until only a few years before.

At the time, there were no proven treatments. Amyloidosis is not a cancer, but there were some chemotherapy drugs being tried on a preliminary basis as a treatment for Gino's particular form. Given Gino's dire condition and the near-certain terminal realities of his disease, Drs. Davis and Song looked at chemotherapy as a Hail Mary option: maybe they could buy him some time, the doctors told him.

"Amyloid is very closely related to a cancer called multiple myeloma," Song explains—a cancer he regularly treats in his work. Like amyloidosis, multiple myeloma involves malfunctioning bone marrow that produces abnormal proteins, known as amyloids, that cause damage elsewhere in the body. Song treats the handful of amyloidosis patients that come through the hospital.

A common chemotherapy drug called bortezomib offered a possible solution, Dr. Song said. Bortezomib is what's known as a proteasome inhibitor: it halts the function of a cell's proteasome, which is essentially a garburator that disposes of the cell's waste. Blocking this metaphorical garburator from working means the diseased cell's waste piles up and the cell dies. At the cellular level, it's a beautifully simple process, but chemotherapy isn't a beautiful process: these drugs are toxic to just about everything in your body; it's just that they're more toxic to cancer cells. Common side effects of bortezomib include blood platelet loss, fatigue, fever, digestive-tract issues—both constipation and diarrhea—nausea, joint and nerve pain, and lung issues, like coughing and even pneumonia. It's a brutal but effective treatment.

When bortezomib works in treating amyloidosis, it stops malfunctioning bone marrow from producing the protein that damages organs like the heart and other soft tissue. In theory, then, if bortezomib does its job, no amyloid will be produced, and the heart, at the very least, will cease to further degrade. It was worth a shot, Dr. Song told his patient, though there were no guarantees. They could try the Hail Mary, or they could send him to hospice care.

Bortezomib would only pause production of the proteins, they cautioned, so in the long term, it was unlikely Gino would be a candidate for a heart transplant. And since the drug doesn't rewire the bone marrow, there remained a chance the malfunction could recur. The underlying problem would remain. Furthermore, the damage that had already been done to Gino's heart was extensive and couldn't be reversed. Nothing Gino had done in life had caused his heart to slowly turn into leather: this was a genetic issue, not a lifestyle issue. Bad luck of the draw.

By late June, after two cycles of bortezomib treatment, the medicine did seem to be working some. Gino was able to stay awake a lot more, was more responsive to his visitors. It had bought him some time, but AL amyloidosis is a fatal, life-limiting condition. How long another cycle or two of bortezomib would cool the malfunctioning bone marrow wasn't known, nor was it clear if Gino's prognosis had improved beyond having only a year to live. He knew it was time to start making plans.

Being from Vancouver, Song was well aware of the fierce on-ice reputation of his patient, but he only found Gino to be calm and considerate. "He was always very kind and very gentle and very respectful, and whenever we talked, he'd listen to what I had to say and went with the suggestions that I made. He was a very easy person to take care of," he says. "He asked the right questions."

Meanwhile, the public surge of support was direct and overwhelming. On June 29, the day Odjick revealed his illness to the public through an interview with the *Province*'s Ed Willes, an impromptu celebration was organized by fans, who assembled outside the hospital to lend their support. "*Gi-no! Gi-no! Gi-no!*" they chanted, just as they had two decades before.

As the rally was assembling, Gino was actually away from the hospital. He'd been told he could pay a visit to Peter's house in Burnaby, about thirty minutes away, to get a break from his hospital life. It wasn't until Peter flipped on the TV and saw news reports that they realized fans were congregating outside the hospital for their hockey hero. After some urging, Gino let Peter drive him back to VGH, where hospital security arranged for Gino to re-enter the hospital through a back entrance. They went up to the tenth floor of the Centennial Pavilion to get a look at the crowd below; Gino was reluctant to go down. But then the fans spotted him at the window, waving in recognition of the chanting fans below. A few minutes later, after a wheelchair had been secured for him, he appeared in front of them, with his walker and his oxygen tank. The fans repeated their *Gi-no! Gi-no! Gi-no!* chant. Others shouted "We love you!"

Gino stood up, the crowd calmed for a moment, and he thanked them for coming. Approached by the *Province*'s Ian Austin, Gino said the crowd's energy was buoying him. "It was amazing and inspiring," he responded. "It'll give me everything I need to win this battle."[111]

Davis and Song offered Gino a proposition: because the first two courses of bortezomib had stabilized him somewhat—certainly an improvement over where he'd been in late April, even though they still thought he had only months to live—would he like to continue his treatments in Ottawa, so he could be closer to his family in Kitigan Zibi? Then Gino was connected with Dr. Sam Haddad, one of Canada's top cardiologists, at the University of Ottawa Heart Institute. The bortezomib had made Gino well enough to travel, the doctors said, though given his grave condition the rigours of a four-hour flight would be taxing. It wasn't even guaranteed that he'd survive the flight. Gino wanted to try. The Canucks arranged and paid for him to fly on a private medical charter flight. Gino's sister Debbie accompanied him and the medics on the flight; no other passengers were allowed on the small aircraft. Gino made it to Ottawa, but he still had a long road ahead.

ORIGINALLY FROM SYRIA, Dr. Haddad had met a Canadian woman and moved to Canada in the 1980s. He had trained at medical school in Syria and, after arriving in Nova Scotia, spent many years getting his Canadian certifications as a cardiologist. By the time Haddad found himself sitting across from a man he would learn had once been one of hockey's toughest players, he'd been running the Heart Institute for more than a decade.

"We are going to do our best," Haddad said to Gino in their first encounter. "I am here to try to save your life." There are no guarantees in medicine, but the veteran cardiologist knew there are good chances. And he told Gino he wasn't there just to make him comfortable; he was going to do all he could to give Gino a chance to live.

Haddad's words meant everything to Gino. He was scared. He knew he was in trouble. He didn't want to die. "This guy cares, this guy is going to save me," Gino thought. His words pushed Gino to tears. Here was the kind of doctor he'd been looking for.

"I couldn't believe he'd survived the trip," Haddad recalls of their first meeting. "He'd lost all his muscle mass. He was on oxygen, breathing quickly." Two cycles of chemotherapy had gotten him this far, but between the disease itself and the intense treatment, his body was in awful shape. Time was still running short.

Gino's son Joey said his regular visits with his dad—both in Vancouver and again in Ottawa—were brutally difficult. "My whole childhood, he was like Superman," he says. "I remember being a kid. He surprised me at school sometimes; we're all so small and short, you know? And he was, like, the size of the door."

Haddad didn't know of Gino's hockey-playing past, of how Gino had forever been this fit, powerful man. A man who stood out, even in his early forties. All he saw was a desperately ill patient. If Gino was going to live, there was a lot of work to be done.

Of course, Haddad also had to prepare his patient for all outcomes. The truth about cardiac amyloidosis is that the diagnosis is almost always fatal. With that reality in front of them, Haddad asked Gino a simple question: What would you like us to do if there's a cardiac crisis?

"I'd like you to do everything you can," Gino told his new doctor. A note was added to Gino's file so that the night staff would know just how much this patient wanted to live. And with that, Haddad and his colleagues set to work. The first task: to simply stabilize their patient. For his chemotherapy to continue making a difference, Gino had to able to physically withstand it. In Haddad's estimation, his body needed to be shored up before further treatments could be administered.

Gino's physiology was poor. His belly was swollen and tense, Haddad noted. "That tells me his stomach is congested, his bowel is congested," he says. When you become backed up like that internally, your appetite diminishes. And when your health is as poor as Gino's was, not eating only exacerbates your problems.

Gino couldn't even stand up when Haddad first met him. Not eating wasn't going to improve that. His muscles were simply wasting away. What little nutrition was coming into his body wasn't going anywhere: blood tests confirmed that his albumin was very low. Albumin is a blood protein that helps vitamins, enzymes, and hormones circulate around your body. Low albumin is a sign of a poor diet or liver failure.

On top of this, Gino's body was swelling up, a condition known as edema. Amyloidosis can cause edema, as fluid leaks from small blood vessels into the surrounding tissues. So, along with finding a way to improve Gino's nutrition, Haddad and his team essentially needed to dry his body out using diuretics.

"We had to dry him out very slowly," Haddad said. Going too fast could cause the amyloidosis to trigger tachycardia, an abnormally rapid heartbeat, something that Gino might not have been able to survive in his depleted condition. But if they could dry him out and get some nutrients into him, they could start to restore some of his strength. And at that point, the chemotherapy might have a chance to work.

The X factor in Gino's recovery was good vibes. Count Haddad in the camp of physicians who say that the most important influence on patient outcomes is attitude. A positive outlook gives you a chance to live. As for his own positivity, Gino was a model patient. "His spirit was very high. He was one of the nicest patients I've ever had," Haddad said. "And the family support was second to none." There was always someone visiting him, there to support him while he was meeting with Haddad and his colleagues.

Gino's body took to the treatment quickly. After three days of treatment, Gino finally stood for the first time in front of his new cardiologist. Once he got on his feet, Gino made rapid progress. He regained his strength. He'd call friends on the phone and declare: "It's working!"

It seemed like a minor miracle. With his heart and body stabilized and the chemo working, Gino was able to return to Maniwaki and Kitigan Zibi to complete his course of treatment. He needed the medication injected into his belly once a week; it was Dina who had the honour. She was more than happy to oblige and was thankful for Haddad's efforts. "I loved Dr. Haddad," she says. "He really gave Gino those nine years."

Gino spent the summer and much of the fall in Kitigan Zibi. The bortezomib took control of his amyloidosis and his body started to recover. He wasn't his old physical self, but he was alive and he was happy. That was what mattered. By November, he wanted to go back to BC, back to where he was most comfortable. He moved in with Peter and Charlene and would live most of the rest of his life in a room in their house.

He'd still travel back to Kitigan Zibi often, but the West Coast remained his home.

Trevor Linden wasn't surprised his old teammate rebounded as well as he did. Linden was among the group of ex-Canucks who made those regular visits to VGH in the late winter and spring of 2014, when Gino's health was rapidly declining. Linden knew the prognosis. But if there was a guy who was going to make an unexpected comeback, it was always going to be Gino. "Gino always defied the odds," he says. "Looking at his career, where he came from, it's pretty amazing. So why would you be surprised that he battled through something that was supposed to take his life?"

Bortezomib stopped the amyloids and Gino got nine more years. But his health wouldn't be the same. He had to continue taking medications and they caused his body to retain water. He was a shadow of the physical specimen he used to be. His body swelled. He had to watch what he ate, but wasn't always careful to so, Dina remembers with a chuckle. "He loved Pepsi, but he wasn't supposed to drink it," she says. "I'd ask him, 'Did you have a Pepsi?' and he'd say, 'No,' so I'd say, 'Show me your tongue,' and he'd have to show me his tongue and there would be that brown stain. He'd laugh about it."

The drugs took their toll on Gino's body. Between heart pills and painkillers and brain medications, he was taking thirty-two pills a day after he got out of the hospital in 2014. By the end of his life, he was taking fewer, but still seventeen a day.

ONE THING GINO and his dad had in common was pure stubbornness. Like his dad, Gino never wanted to talk about his own health, much preferring to talk about what everyone else was doing. Both were proud men and wanted to present a strong image. Giselle would talk to Peter about her son—about both what he could be like in the moment and what she believed was brewing deep down inside him. He'd do what he wanted—and would resist if he felt like he was simply being bossed around. He was always happy to help, always happy to chip in when asked, but if he felt like he was being told what to do, more likely than not he'd dig his heels in.

One example: on January 4, 2020, during the Canucks' fiftieth anniversary season, the organization hosted a celebration of the team of the 1990s. Gino was invited to be involved. They had a uniform and equipment for him to wear. But it had been years since he'd suited up to skate, let alone play hockey. He was bigger than he used to be. He didn't want to embarrass himself. And so, at the last moment, when he and his old teammates were in the dressing room they'd been assigned, he hesitated to put on his old Canucks gear. "I don't want to do it," he told Peter, who accompanied him to the rink, as he almost always did. "It's not about you, Gino," Peter replied, digging into his friend's sensibilities. "You want people to think well of you." Gino had to concede on that. But he didn't want to be embarrassed. His body wasn't what it once was. Nonetheless, he put on the gear. He got his skates on, with the help of Cliff Ronning. Then he stepped onto the ice and skated gingerly to centre. He went out for the fans.

The roof blew off. People went crazy. It was like he'd scored a penalty shot goal again, and then some. It was a special moment for all: here was their old hero, who had been at death's door six years before, returning in triumph. It didn't matter that he wasn't playing, or that he looked jittery on his skates. His presence was enough, it sparked a thrill deep inside the fans in the stands. "*Gi-no! Gi-no! Gi-no!*" they chanted, not knowing it would be the last time they'd do so for him in life.

HIS AMYLOIDOSIS RECURRED in 2020. Another course of chemotherapy stopped the amyloid production. But his body took another pounding and started to retain water again. Dr. Song and Dr. Davis tried all kinds of tests. They couldn't figure out the source. No matter what, his body was struggling. And Gino ate a lot. He gained a lot of weight. He didn't have the same spark for working out, even a little bit, let alone getting up and walking, like he used to. Add it all up and his weakened heart was working overtime because of water retention and increased body weight. His teeth were also in terrible condition: years of taking Percocet had worn them down.

In November 2022, Gino developed blood poisoning. The extra water his body was retaining caused his legs to swell and he developed small sores on his legs. He'd scratch the sores. Sometimes, they'd get infected. This time, it was a very bad infection. And it caused new heart issues. So the doctors suggested defibrillation, a procedure in which the heart is stopped briefly by an electric shock, then re-started. Gino agreed to try it out. After the procedure—Gino needed two shocks to re-start his heart—he was disappointed: he hadn't seen "the light." Rather, he told Peter, he hadn't felt anything at all.

His fifty-two-year-old heart finally gave out January 15, 2023. He was at a wound care clinic in Kerrisdale, a leafy, affluent neighbourhood in Vancouver, to get some sores on his legs checked. He went into cardiac arrest in the waiting room. Peter had dropped Gino off for the Sunday appointment and was outside with his truck when he was called in by the staff at the clinic, who said Gino had slumped out of the chair he'd been sitting in. Most of his body was on the floor, but his head and shoulders were propped up awkwardly on the base of the wall. Peter rushed in and Gino looked over at him, awkwardly. He was having a hard time breathing. He was panting, trying to draw air in. "Slow your breathing," Peter and the nurses told him. A vein was protruding in Gino's neck, a warning sign Peter had learned to watch for from Gino's doctors over the years. The nurses weren't big enough to move Gino, but with Peter's help they were able to pull him away from the wall so he could lie flat on the floor.

"I think he's having a heart attack," Peter said. "Oh, he definitely is," one of the nurses replied. They tried to strike him in the chest, to stimulate his heart, but Gino pushed back.

That's when the paramedics arrived. Shortly thereafter, his eyes started to glaze over. He could still see the people around him, but it was obvious things was getting foggier and foggier for him. He reached out, hoping to draw Peter close. His old friend grasped his hand, but quickly Gino went limp. Peter urged him to fight on as the paramedics started CPR and tried a defibrillator for the first time. Not long after, firefighters arrived to help. More paramedics too. There were now fifteen or twenty people in the room, all hoping to help.

The medics had been working on Gino for about fifteen minutes when he revived. The paramedics said they could hear that his heart was pumping hard. Peter stood for a moment in relief. But Gino's eyes remained closed. And then Gino's heart stopped again, for what would be the final time. They tried to revive him for another half hour; at one point, the firefighters proposed trying to lift Gino onto a gurney so they could transport him by ambulance to hospital. Peter spoke with the fire captain, who was on the phone with an emergency room doctor at VGH.

It was time to make the call for Gino, the captain told Peter. He put Peter on the phone with the doctor, who told him it had been too long. "This is Gino Odjick we're talking about, correct?" the doctor asked Peter. "Yes, I'm his friend," Peter replied. The doctor then explained they'd pulled up Gino's chart and were well aware of the heart troubles he'd been living with, and also noted that Gino's brain and heart would have sustained serious damage in the previous forty-five minutes, even if they revived him again somehow.

In the end, Gino's heart finally broke. Maybe it had just been too big.

11

"HE PAVED THE WAY... BUT THERE'S STILL A WAY TO GO"

AFTER GINO DIED, a couple of things struck Kumi Kimura. The first was seeing all his kids look over items—jerseys, sticks, photos, posters—in a display about their dad at the celebration of life organized on the Musqueam reserve in February 2023. For the kids who hadn't spent much time on the West Coast, it was a revelation. They were seeing up close how widely popular he had been with hockey fans in the Lower Mainland. Chynna, Gino's daughter with Genevieve, asked Kumi if she could have one of the jerseys. And that's when it hit Kumi: when you were in Vancouver, you would see Gino Odjick memorabilia everywhere. It was easy to find. But for the kids growing up back in Quebec, seeing a Gino Odjick jersey or poster was a rarity. "And I could just get something signed anytime," Kumi explains. "Now I can't. And they didn't really have the opportunity."

The second thing that resonated with Kumi was what the City of Vancouver did for its fallen hero: flags were flown at half-staff at City Hall. That doesn't happen often. "That's him and who he was for Vancouver," she says. "He'd made Vancouver his home. He's one of ours."

At the celebration of life, Jen Thomas, who had helped organize the Journey of Healing and was now chief of the Tsleil-Waututh Nation in North Vancouver, was struck by how much he meant to all people, no matter what their background was. Of course, there was his family and an array of Indigenous people whose lives he had touched. But there was a swath of non-Indigenous people too. And, of course, his teammates. When the Canucks honoured his memory at Rogers Arena on January 18, three days after he died, the roar of the crowd caught her too. They chanted *Gi-no! Gi-no! Gi-no!* one more time. "Gino gave back more than he received," she said. "It really moved me to hear that cheer, but also to be at his celebration of life, to hear the stories that his former teammates talked about—I was just even more in awe of the person he was."

GINO WAS BURIED wearing a shirt that had special significance. It was a traditional Indigenous-style ribbon shirt that was given to Ron Delorme back home in Saskatchewan. It was white, with a Canucks logo sewn on the front, with vibrant blue and green ribbons adorning it, in the style of the jersey the Canucks started wearing again in 2008. "It was made for me, for a Canucks Indigenous night," Delorme says. He offered it to Gino's family, to dress him for the funeral home visitation. They said accepted. "That was a real pleasure, I know he would have been proud," Delorme added.

Gino had learned well from his mentor, taking on the lessons that Delorme taught him about speaking to every kid you could, no matter who they were. Talking to people, of course, came naturally to Gino. But creating an impact—that was harder. Gino showed young Indigenous hockey players they could be proud of who they were, that they could be themselves in a way Delorme never felt comfortable doing when he was playing. Gino spoke up for himself. "He paved the way," Delorme says. "But there's still a way to go. We've come a long way. Look at all cultural celebrations teams host now. It's not just Indigenous night. They've changed for the better. But we still need progress."

Delorme brought up a youth hockey tournament that took place in recent times in Onion Lake, a small Indigenous community in Saskatchewan, just off the Alberta border, a half-hour north of Lloydminster. There were a bunch of young players that scouts would have been wise to have a look at. "But they were afraid to go there," Delorme said, incredulously. "They were afraid their cars would get stolen, they said. 'Are you serious?' I said. That's the perception people still have."

THE RINK IN Maniwaki is now called Centre sportif Gino-Odjick. In July 2014, when the end seemed near for Gino, the town announced they were renaming their community arena after their local hero. Mike "Michen" Cote had been pushing for the move for years, repeatedly rallying the local business community for support. But the city council only hemmed and hawed. The mayor had reservations about what he'd heard about Gino's lifestyle. "I can tell you wherever he goes, people know he's from Maniwaki. He represents us well, they think positively about us. People wouldn't know about this place without him," Michen replied to the mayor. But it wasn't until Gino was near death that Maniwaki's council finally agreed to make the change. At a quickly arranged ceremony days later, Gino made a surprise appearance. Some thought there might be a recorded video message from their guy. No one thought they'd see him in person.

He'd flown to Ottawa just a few days before, to continue his bortezomib treatments under the care of Dr. Haddad. It was a total shock to see Gino. But it was a statement of the confidence and self-assurance Gino still carried, one that Haddad immediately saw he could lean on when working to save his patient. He was still weak and frail, but his mere presence in Maniwaki raised the spirits of the crowd, and the crowd's energy raised his spirits in return. Just to be there was a blessing.

He'd arrived in a wheelchair, but when the time came, Gino stood up and found some energy deep inside, walked gingerly to the front of the stage, took the mic, and thanked everyone in attendance. "This is a special day. Obviously, having an arena named after you is not something that happens every day, so I'm really happy, and I'd like to thank everybody," Odjick told the thousand-strong throng of fans in French. Many people in the crowd were sporting "Gino

Strong" T-shirts, which Michen had had printed up. Gino himself wore one of the red shirts, along with a red "Gino Strong" ballcap.

To have the rink where he'd played youth hockey named for him, a testament to all he'd done in his life, touched him. "We played a lot of good hockey and a lot of good tournaments and had all sorts of fun. It's so special to be here," he said.

His old friend Jan "Boy Boy" Cote came forward to present him with a Kitigan Zibi Bulls jersey, the team that represents the reserve in Indigenous tournaments across Canada. "Gino had played with our men's team in a few tournaments—Maniwaki, Val-d'Or, Ottawa—with those jerseys, but I feel that it was more of a symbolic gesture letting him know that he was still forever one of us and would always remain in our hearts," Boy Boy explains.

There was also a drum circle; everyone paused a moment to listen to the rhythm of the drums, paying tribute to the moment. It was smiles all around, everyone's heart filled with happiness by the sight of their recovering hometown hero. A decade later, Gino's name is still emblazoned across the front of the arena. Inside, you find a classic old Canadian hockey barn, with bleachers all around. Hanging high above centre ice, a trio of photos of Gino in his playing days, two of him in the black-yellow-red uniform of the Canucks, one in the *bleu-blanc-rouge* of Le Canadien.

Despite it being the reminder of a tragic loss, having Gino's name on the rink means a lot, Itchy says. "We're proud of his success. He did well. He was somebody. It's just sad he passed on, even though he took care of himself. One day, you could be the healthiest person. Next, you're diagnosed with something like cancer. Our road we travel on in life, we never know when it can take a left turn or a right. That's just part of life sometimes, and it's not stuff that we always want to accept."

SANDY MCCARTHY took a break from hockey after he retired. There were many reasons why, but more than anything he needed to try something else. At first, he ran a marina on Georgian Bay in Ontario. Later, he coached hockey in New Brunswick, where his dad was from. He directed the Grand Falls Rapids and then the Campbellton Tigers in the Maritime Junior Hockey League. He was pretty good at it too. But he stepped aside for health reasons in September 2021.

Not sure what to do next, he got in his car and just drove. "I'd had enough of the Maritimes," he told his daughter Charlotte, whom he brought along with him. They saw the country. Then he got a call from Danny Gaudet in Délı̨nę, Northwest Territories. Gaudet is a businessman from this small community on the southwestern shore of Great Bear Lake, who toiled for years as the chief negotiator for his community, dealing with the federal government—in 2016 he helped win self-governance for his people, who are Sahtu Dene. In 2022, he was elected chief.

McCarthy first met Gaudet at the 2015 edition of the Gino Odjick Golf Tournament in Maniwaki. Their first conversation may not have actually been twenty hours long, but that's how long it feels in McCarthy's memory. During their conversations, Gaudet suggested McCarthy come visit Délı̨nę.

"We sat there all day long, back and forth. The conversation never got boring and never got tiring. It was just like we were meant to talk to each other," he says. In 2016, McCarthy took up Gaudet's invitation and flew north for a visit. The eight days he spent in the community stuck with him.

"I told Danny, 'One day I'm gonna come back here, live here, live this lifestyle,'" he says. And so there he was in September 2021, driving across the country to see what he could find. Gaudet would end up finding him.

"He was like, 'Are we ready to do this?' I'm like, 'Wow. It's just, the timing is perfect,'" he said. So McCarthy moved north to help run the hockey programs based at the Déline community's ice rink, a job that would allow him to follow his instincts to inspire and guide youth.

Déline is where Sir John Franklin's party overwintered in 1825–26, on their way up the Mackenzie River. Franklin is famous for his third visit to the Arctic, beginning in 1845, in which he and his crew searched for the Northwest Passage, the elusive route through the Canadian North. The voyage ended in disaster as the expedition's two ships, *Erebus* and *Terror*, became locked in ice and the entire party succumbed to the winter conditions. Franklin's trip up the Mackenzie was his second visit to the Arctic, but unlike his visit two decades later, it was overland, not in ships. According to Franklin's journal from their time on the shores of Great Bear Lake, his men would skate on the lake ice. He describes his men playing a game using field hockey sticks that sounds remarkably similar to modern ice hockey. Because of this account, Déline now often claims to be the true birthplace of ice hockey in Canada.

This is where he is meant to be, McCarthy said. And in a way, it's Gino who first put him on this path that led north.

"We were two straight-up people," McCarthy said, explaining his affinity for Gino. "We never butted heads about anything. We were always on same page. And even when we fought, after the fight, I would feel bad!"

GINO'S DEATH WAS devastating for all of his kids. For Patrick, his father's passing came just a couple of months after the death of his mom, June. "I go home now, and I see my brothers and sisters, but my mom's not there. It's hard." His dad was a tower of strength. Losing his dad not long after his mother spun him off into another bout of despair and back into drugs.

But Patrick is managing better now. The demon is still there. He's found supportive housing in Vancouver, and he'd got Kumi supporting him too, taking him to get groceries when he needs them. Gino left a mountain of savings for his kids; the amount differs from child to child, based on academic and work accomplishments. In a couple of cases, he put in a condition that they not be abusing drugs and alcohol.

NO DOUBT, fighting exacted a toll. Scientists have found that blows to the head cause all kinds of neurological damage, with serious effects on cognition, mood, and memory. Chronic traumatic encephalopathy is understood to cause problems with thinking, behaviour, and mood, and eventually leads to dementia. It has been found in the brains of many former athletes who played contact sports like football, hockey, and rugby. CTE can only be confirmed by direct posthumous examination of the brain.

In the months before he died, tests taken on Gino's brain showed signs he was going to develop Alzheimer's disease, maybe within three years. Other medical assessments had suggested he was at risk of developing Parkinson's. When he heard researchers had found evidence of CTE in NHL enforcer Derek Boogaard's brain after his death, Gino was scared. Gino's brain was never examined, though he'd joked about being ready to donate it while he was still alive—"Do I really need it?" he would say with a laugh to friends. But there were signs he had CTE, such as emerging memory issues, dizziness, and headaches.

The *Sun*'s Mike Beamish was at the 2014 symposium where Odjick admitted to his addiction to fighting. "That was typical Gino," Beamish recalls of the guy he'd covered for many years as a player. "He was very forthcoming." It was Odjick speaking the truth, as he always had. Not afraid of the consequences. Just sharing what he knew.

THERE WERE TIMES when the oppositional takes Tony Gallagher expressed in his columns for the *Province* frustrated Gino, but there's little doubt Gino paid attention to what the combative columnist had to say about Vancouver's leading sports team. Gallagher had no qualms with Gino: he remembers a complex character who meant a lot of things to a lot of people. He witnessed many of Odjick's on-ice triumphs. He saw first-hand how he connected with fans, not just in Vancouver but across North America. He came to learn a bit about his friendships, about the people he influenced away from the rink. But it was an intimate few moments in particular that stand out for Gallagher.

"The times I cherished with him were these quiet times. Like the four of us in the van," he recalls, mentioning the van ride around New York alongside Pavel Bure and Mike Gillis, with Gino at the wheel. Another time, years later, Gallagher found himself on the same flight as Gino and Peter Leech. He spotted them from a distance. Normally, he'd have gone up to his old acquaintance, said hello. But it was late. Everyone was pretty busted from travelling, Gallagher says. So he didn't bother Gino.

Now he wishes he'd done so. "I just didn't stop and talk. And I regret that moment," he says. Never again would he have a chance to speak to one of the great characters from during his long career as a sportswriter.

GINO'S BOND WITH those who knew him will go on forever. Itchy keeps a screenshot in his phone of a very special message. It's the final one he ever received from Odjick—on January 15, 2023, the day Gino died. "He told me his blood pressure was down. That was our last discussion. We always connected. We always talked to each other all the time."

Elizabeth Poon, Joey's mom, who was Gino's partner for many of his early years in Vancouver, will still send messages to his old social media accounts from time to time. She thinks of their grandchildren, what he's missing. "I hope you can hear me," she'll write. "I'll wish him the best, and like, happy birthday and stuff like that. I'll wish he would still be here to see the kids, Joey's kids."

At the memorial service in Gino's memory at Musqueam in February 2023, Gino's youngest, Rose, spoke proudly of her dad. "The old saying goes, you should never meet your heroes. In the case of Gino, this couldn't be further from the truth," she said. "If Gino was not your hero before you met him, he certainly was afterward."

Her father's legacy went far beyond his time as a player, or as a father.

"Gino's [legacy] will be the many lives he touched and inspired," she said. "My dad visited countless First Nations communities, even after he was sick. His message was always one of encouragement and about the importance of education. He did not want the youth to have to fight for a living the way he had."

"EDUCATION IS FREEDOM," Dina remembers her brother always saying to his kids and the other young people he'd meet in his travels. The power is within. He just wanted to help people find their way forward. "Education is what he wanted for everyone."

Boy Boy lingers on how his old friend handled himself in groups, in times like when he'd return to the reserve in the summer. "He was so needed by everybody," Boy Boy says. "Like us, his friends. His family. The elderly people. The kids, the men, the women. His presence. He was such a good guy. He was genuine. Authentic. What you'd see? He's not trying to hide anything. You got him. And he was so good. It's like a bright light walked into a room. People would turn around and be like 'Gino!' The feelings were so good when he'd come. He'd make people feel really good."

ACKNOWLEDGEMENTS

BEING ASKED TO write 75,000 words is a huge task when you're used to each story being a hundredth of that length, as is normally the case in my day job, which is mostly covering the Canucks. But as you have read, Gino was a remarkable person with a mountain of stories in his life. I'm so thankful to all the people who spared the time to be interviewed, especially Gino's sons Joey and Patrick; his sister Dina, who drove me around Maniwaki and Kitigan Zibi on a brilliant November day; and his former partners Elizabeth and Caroline.

Obviously I'm indebted to my co-author Peter Leech, who first approached me about this project in late 2023. The reason we found ourselves working together to assemble this story is sad, but the process proved to be joyful for me. Peter's wife, Charlene, provided very helpful reflections on Gino's last decade.

Thanks to our editors, Brian Lynch and Derek Fairbridge, whose feedback was essential, and to Greystone's Jennifer Croll and Rob Sanders for their support. Also to my dear friend Asher Mullard, whose science-journalism knowledge proved invaluable and who was an excellent Ottawa host to boot. His car got me to Maniwaki and back. Jeff Cullis's story on flying with the Canucks always stuck with me; thanks to him for sharing it again. Many thanks to Ed Willes and Roy MacGregor for their insights into how to actually write a book, as well as the man himself. Tony Gallagher, Iain MacIntyre, Mike Beamish, and Jim Jamieson, who all covered Gino as a player, also provided tremendous insight. This book doesn't happen without the many stories from Gino's teammates, Pavel Bure, Stan Smyl, Geoff Courtnall, Cliff Ronning, Corey Hirsch, Donald Audette, Robin Bawa, Sandy McCarthy, and Trevor Linden, and his oldest friends, Mike and Jan Cote, Andy Dewache, and Michel Branchaud. Thanks also to Stu Grimson, Ron Delorme, Mike Penny, Marty McSorley, Bill Faminoff, Wacey Rabbit, Louie DeBrusk, and Paulin Bordeleau, who all knew the man in their own way. Here in Vancouver, Kumi Kimura's help was invaluable, and I really enjoyed reminiscing about youthful fandom with my pal Randip Janda. I'm grateful to Gino's doctors, Drs. Sam Haddad and Kevin Song, for the information they were able to provide. Dr. Kevin Valettas provided further background information on amyloidosis.

I am also indebted to the archives of my real job at the *Province* and *Vancouver Sun*, the source of so much of the historical interviews in this book, as well as the support of my boss, Paul Chapman, and our librarian Carolyn Soltau. Also to Bob Marjanovich for his additional insights beyond what he recorded in his interview with Gino.

Finally, I'd be nowhere without my family. My mum, Kathryn, taught me to love stories and my dad, Richard, to love data. My brother, Rory, and my sister, Ellen, have always been there for me and are filled with endless encouragement. The tireless support of my in-laws, Jim and Sylvia, especially in looking after my girls, Molly and Alice, was and is remarkable. Molly and Alice, I love you two turkeys very much, as much as I love your mom, Candice, the love of my life, who encouraged me to take on this project and was my most essential sounding board all the way through.

PATRICK JOHNSTON, Burnaby, BC, April 2025

WOW. It has taken many years to get to this point. Gino and I started talking about doing a book more than a decade ago, when he and I did a youth workshop in a small Indigenous community called Bella Bella (Heiltsuk Nation), BC. We were in one of the local restaurants when a gentleman came up to Gino and asked him when his book was going to be coming out. Gino told the man: "I think you will be waiting for a long time, because I don't think one will be coming out anytime soon."

But over the coming days and months, I started talking about it with him. Gino was reluctant at first, because he said the book would be boring and he thought no would read it. Then I came home one day and Gino was sitting where he normally sat throughout the day. He was reading *All the Way*, Jordin Tootoo's book. He told me I should read it; it was not a bad read. I asked Gino if a book about him could be just as good. He said, "yes, lots of similarities." Then he asked, "if I do a book, will you write it for me?" I told him I was an okay writer, but far from an *author*—we would need a good professional for it. I told him, "If you're ready to do the book, I will help you find a good writer and a good publisher." We made a few inquiries and spoke to a few people, and thanks to the suggestion of Ed Willes, Gino's attention was turned to Patrick Johnston. After a few months of reading Patrick's writings for the *Province* newspaper, Gino asked me, "Do you think we should go with Patrick?" I said, "He's young, fresh, and gung-ho." Just perfect for his book.

I would like to thank Patrick, for Gino and I were right—he was passionate, articulate, sensitive, and forthright in his writing. Gino would be very pleased. Before Gino passed on to the Spirit World, I did find out from him what his fears really were about doing a book: He truly feared judgment—that people would judge him for his imperfections and his struggles with fatherhood, intimate relationships, and his health and mental well-being. I told him, "You're scared of people judging you for being a human being." He laughed and said that was probably the best way of defining it. So, thank you Patrick for articulating Gino's imperfections as a human being. Big thank you to the publishers and editors from Greystone: Rob Sanders, Jennifer Croll, Jen Gauthier, Bryan Lynch, and Derek Fairbridge. If I forgot anyone from Greystone, my apologies in advance. A huge thank you to all of Gino's teammates—Stan Smyl, Pavel Bure, Donald Audette, Geoff Courtnall, Cliff Ronning, and Trevor Linden, just to name a few—for their funny stories and personal reflections, which provided insight into Gino the player and the person.

I would especially like to thank the Odjick family and Gino's children. I am sure it was not easy for his sons Joey and Patrick. And more so, thanks to Gino's sister Dina Odjick, for coordinating the interviews in Quebec and Gino's hometown of Maniwaki. Gino had many friends, especially his long-time and childhood friends, like Ron Delorme, Mike and Jan Cote, and Andy Dewache, just to name a few. They probably felt the same way I did with the writing of this book: some sadness over Gino not being there with us to share in the funny stories and laughs.

Finally, a big thank you to my family, for all their help and support over the years, especially when Gino was still with us. My wife Charlene, son Christophe, and daughter Keanu were honoured to call Gino family. I helped Gino these past number of years, but I could not have done it without the help and support of my family. There are many people to acknowledge, and I apologize that I can't list them all, but a big thank you to all of you. I personally would like to thank my late brother Gino. He believed in me, he called me his friend, and he called me his brother. He would be very happy today that I am co-author of his book, and I am extremely honoured to be a part of it. A book like this immortalizes my brother. No matter whether he's in the Canucks' Ring of Honour or not, he will be remembered for years to come. To all the young people, remember: "Education is freedom." If the little old Indian boy who grew up on the rez can do it, so can you.

PETER LEECH, Vancouver, BC, April 2025

SOURCES

INTERVIEWS

All quotes not cited in the notes below are from interviews conducted by the authors with the following individuals:

Donald Audette (October 9, 2024)
Kim Baird (February 7, 2025)
Mike Beamish (June 25, 2024)
Paulin Bordeleau (October 7, 2024)
Michel Branchaud (January 28, 2024)
Pavel Bure (August 9, 2024)
Jan "Boy Boy" Cote (November 12, 2024)
Mike "Michen" Cote (January 15, 2025)
Geoff Courtnall (July 9, 2024 & February 18, 2025)
Jeff Cullis (November 17, 2024)
Ron Delorme (December 23, 2024 & January 12, 2024)
Andy "Itchy" Dewache (November 12, 2024 & February 24, 2024)
Caroline Forester-Smith (January 14, 2025)
Stephane Friday (October 29, 2024)
Tony Gallagher (December 5, 2024)

Stu Grimson (December 17, 2024)
Corey Hirsch (January 11, 2024)
Sam Haddad (November 21, 2024)
Randip Janda (November 18, 2024)
Kumi Kimura (December 2, 2024 & February 19, 2024)
Charlene Leech (November 26, 2024)
Trevor Linden (January 20, 2025)
Roy MacGregor (October 13, 2024)
Sandy McCarthy (November 22, 2024)
Marty McSorley (October 10, 2024)
Dina Odjick (September 24, 2024, November 12, 2024 & December 27, 2024)
Joey Odjick (November 12, 2024)
Patrick Odjick (January 6, 2024)
Mike Penny (October 16, 2024)
Elizabeth Poon (January 8, 2025)
Wacey Rabbit (November 25, 2024)
Cliff Ronning (October 15, 2024 & February 18, 2025)
Stan Smyl (July 11, 2024)
Kevin Song (December 3, 2024)
Jen Thomas (December 12, 2024)
Ed Willes (February 19, 2025)

NOTES

1 Scott Morrison, "Horror! The Kid Hits the Big Three-Oh," *Toronto Sun*, January 27, 1991.

2 Mike Beamish, "Hope Just About Ends," *Vancouver Sun*, January 15, 1987.

3 David Banks, "The Odjick of Fans' Desire," *Province*, November 28, 1990.

4 David Banks, "New Canucks Fight for Spots," *Province*, November 21, 1990.

5 "Gino Odjick and Meghan Agosta—Canucks in Cars," Canucks, YouTube, April 13, 2022, youtube.com/watch?v=aOUCEGb_Adw.

6 Elliott Pap, "Groggy Gamble Dazzles 'Hawks Before Departing," *Vancouver Sun*, November 22, 1990.

7 Patrick Johnston, "From Brawl to the Hall: Canucks Legend Gino Odjick Set for BC Sports Hall of Fame Honours," *Province*, June 2, 2021.

8 Jim Jamieson, "Bullpen Insurance," *Province*, April 8, 1991.

9 Tony Gallagher, "Quinn Focuses On Future," *Province*, June 17, 1990.

10 Brian Burke, "Offers Not Enough to Give Up Nedved," *Province*, June 18, 1990.

11 "*Trajectoires*—Gino Odjick selon Pat Quinn," RDS, YouTube, May 14, 2014, youtube.com/watch?v=5XpTWndEnQw.

12 Johnston, "From Brawl to the Hall."

13 Bob Marjanovich, "Gino Odjick," *MOJ on Sports* (podcast), episode 12, March 17, 2022.

14 Iain MacIntyre, "Gino Odjick: Real Tough Guy," *Vancouver Sun*, November 30, 1991.

15 Roy MacGregor, *The Home Team: Fathers, Sons & Hockey* (Viking, 1995), 232.

16 Marjanovich, "Gino Odjick."

17 MacIntyre, "Gino Odjick."

18 Marjanovich, "Gino Odjick."

19 Ibid.

20 "Gino Odjick se remémore ses belles années avec l'équipe de Vancouver," *L'info de la Vallée*, March 20, 2020.

21 Rod Mickleburgh, "Vancouver Canucks Fan Favourite Gino Odjick Was a Role Model for Other Indigenous Players," *The Globe and Mail*, January 17, 2023.

22 MacIntyre, "Gino Odjick."

23 Johnston, "From Brawl to the Hall."

24 "*Trajectoires*—Gino Odjick selon Pat Quinn."

25 Tony Gallagher, "Gino's Magic Wand Makes Flames Disappear," *Province*, October 20, 1991.

26 Archie McDonald, "Odjick Uses Playoff Snub as Motivation to Become More Complete Player," *Vancouver Sun*, November 12, 1993.

27 Jim Jamieson, "Linden Will Be Front and Centre," *Province*, February 17, 1994.

28 *Ice Guardians*, directed by Brett Harvey (Sophia Entertainment, Score G Films, Super Channel, 2016).

29 Frank Luba, "Odjick Toughs It Out," *Province*, June 7, 1994.

30 Marjanovich, "Gino Odjick."

31 Ibid.

32 Elliott Pap, "Ley Suspended Five Games Despite Plea for Leniency," *Vancouver Sun*, September 28, 1994.

33 Jack Keating, "Gino's Pumped for Return," *Province*, February 5, 1995.

34 Jack Keating, "Gino Lays Down the Law: Facing Suspension for Wild Melee," *Province*, May 19, 1995.

35 Ibid.

36 Roberta Staley, "Gino's Vision of Healing," *Province*, July 28, 1995.

37 Jim Jamieson, "Sobering Prospects: What Else Does Gino Odjick Have Up His Sleeve?" *Province*, September 10, 1995.

38 Terry Bell, "They Said It," *Province*, November 5, 1997.

39 Marjanovich, "Gino Odjick."

40 Tony Gallagher, "I Blame Messier: With the Canucks Captain in His Sights, Gino Odjick Hits His Mark," *Province*, April 2, 1998.

41 Iain MacIntyre, "Messier Isn't in Agreement With Odjick's Comments," *Vancouver Sun*, April 3, 1998.

42 Marjanovich, "Gino Odjick."

43 Mike Keenan with Scott Morrison, *Iron Mike: My Life Behind the Bench* (Random House Canada, 2024), 255.

44 Ibid., 256.

45 Anthony McCarron, "Odjick Gets Eight Games for Penguin Sucker-Punch," *Hockey News* 53, no. 19, January 21, 2000.

46 Associated Press, "Flyers Acquire Odjick From Isles," February 17, 2000.

47 Lance Hornby, "Berard Exempt From Draft," *Toronto Sun*, May 27, 2000.

48 Mike Beamish, "Ex-Canucks 'Algonquin Enforcer' Gino Odjick Opens Up About Post-Career, Concussion-Related Struggles," *Vancouver Sun*, January 28, 2014.

49 Marjanovich, "Gino Odjick."

50 Red Fisher, "Odjick's Headache Could Turn to Heartache: Concussion Has Enforcer Worried," *Montreal Gazette*, November 17, 2002.

51 Bill Beacon, "Odjick Case a Mystery: No Longer With Habs, Injured Player, Team Are Sworn to Secrecy," *Montreal Gazette*, March 15, 2003.

52 Ibid.

53 Marjanovich, "Gino Odjick."

54 Beamish, "Ex-Canucks 'Algonquin Enforcer' Gino Odjick Opens Up About Post-Career, Concussion-Related Struggles."

55 Ed Willes, "Gino Still Fighting, but This Time for His Life," *Province*, June 29, 2014.

56 MacGregor, *The Home Team*, 225.

57 Ibid., 225.

58 Johnston, "From Brawl to the Hall."

59 Ibid.

60 MacGregor, *The Home Team*, 226.

61 Katharine Gordon, "The Literate Side of Gino," *BC Bookworld*, July 8, 2014.

62 "*Trajectoires*—Gino Odjick selon Gilles Lupien," RDS, June 26, 2014, YouTube, youtube.com/watch?v=Dt41WoNnpTg.

63 MacGregor, *The Home Team*, 231.

64 Ibid., 234.

65 Iain MacIntyre, "Odjick: Hero to Kids in Maniwaki," *Vancouver Sun*, November 30, 1991.

66 Mathias Brunet, "Odjick sans réserve," *La Presse*, March 16, 2002.

67 Jef Choy, "Vancouver's Most Awesome: Gino Odjick!" *Vancouver Is Awesome*, March 13, 2011.

68 Brad Ziemer, "Friends Worry as Odjick Admitted to Psychiatric Wing in Quebec," *Vancouver Sun*, December 4, 2013.

69 Lisa Fitterman, "Reflections of a Superstar: What Canuck Ace Pavel Bure Is Really Like, Out of Uniform," *Vancouver Sun*, February 6, 1993.

70 Marjanovich, "Gino Odjick."

71 Elliott Pap, "Contract Slowed Bure, but He's on Track Now," *Vancouver Sun*, March 25, 1994.

72 Jason Botchford, "'I Was Crazy Enough to Believe'; Gino Odjick Was the Key Player in the Saga to Retire Bure's Jersey," *Province*, November 3, 2013.

73 Tony Gallagher, "Why I Wanted Out: Bure Finally Lists Reasons Why He Demanded Trade From Vancouver," *Province*, January 20, 1999.

74 Botchford, "'I Was Crazy Enough to Believe.'"

75 Thomas Drance, "Gino Odjick Talks His Health, Micheal Ferland and Finding Pavel Bure in Moscow," *The Athletic*, May 8, 2020.

76 MacGregor, *The Home Team*, 242.

77 Gallagher, "I Blame Messier."

78 Mike Beamish, "Joey's Dad: Goals of Life, Goals on Ice Receive Equal Billing for Man Called Assassin," *Vancouver Sun*, March 21, 1992.

79 Jamieson, "Sobering Prospects."

80 Ibid.

81 Beamish, "Joey's Dad."

82 Marjanovich, "Gino Odjick."

83 Gordon, "The Literate Side of Gino."

84 Ibid.

85 Gary Mason, "A Phone Call From Gino Odjick That I'll Never Forget," *The Globe and Mail*, June 27, 2014.

86 Andy Ivens, "Odjick Plays Pied Piper," *Province*, August 17, 1995.

87 Ibid.

88 Tim Crothers, "Gino Odjick," *Sports Illustrated*, January 17, 1994.

89 Mickleburgh, "Vancouver Canucks Fan Favourite Gino Odjick Was a Role Model for Other Indigenous Players."

90 Choy, "Vancouver's Most Awesome."

91 Steve Ewen, "Gino Odjick's Example Made Deep Impression on Ex-Vancouver Giant Wacey Rabbit," *Province*, February 15, 2023.

92 "Throwback to Jordin Tootoo and Gino Odjick Teaching Kids Hockey [2001, Winnipeg]," CBC Indigenous, YouTube, March 19, 2024, youtube.com/watch?v=5TFjBKUU-EU.

93 Patrick Johnston, "Hockey 'Hero' Fred Sasakamoose Left a Lasting Impression in Kamloops," *Province*, November 25, 2020.

94 Jamieson, "Sobering Prospects."

95 Thomas Drance and Jeff Paterson, "Catching Up With Gino," *VANcast* (podcast), episode 50, May 7, 2020.

96 Ibid.

97 Ibid.

98 Don Taylor and Rick Dhaliwal, "June 1st 2022," *Donnie and Dhali*, CHEK-TV, June 1, 2022.

99 Patrick Johnston, "Canucks 4, Hurricanes 3 (SO): Ethan Bear Pays the Ultimate Tribute to Gino Odjick," *Province*, January 15, 2023.

100 Ibid.

101 Ibid.

102 Gordon, "The Literate Side of Gino."

103 Michael Reeve, "Former Canuck Gino Odjick Speaks With Indigenous Students About Mental Health," *CFJC Today Kamloops*, June 22, 2022.

104 Ibid.

105 Gordon, "The Literate Side of Gino."

106 Willes, "Gino Still Fighting, but This Time for His Life."

107 Ibid.

108 Ibid.

109 Marc de Foy, "Gino Odjick a besoin d'aide," *Le Journal de Montréal*, December 2, 2013.

110 Ed Willes, "Odjick Vows to Beat Mental Illness," *Province*, December 22, 2013.

111 Ian Austin, "Gino Odjick Says Fans Chanting Outside Hospital Room Was 'Everything I Need to Win This Battle,'" *Province*, June 29, 2014.

INDEX

Note: "plate" followed by a number refers to the photo pages.